Road Biking
Wisconsin

A Guide to Wisconsin's Greatest Bicycle Rides

M. Russ Lowthian

FALCONGUIDES ®

GUILFORD, CONNECTICUT

Contents

Preface...viii
Introduction 1
Road and Traffic Conditions 4
Safety and Comfort on the Road...5
How to Use This Book 6

Northern Wisconsin 9
1 Cornucopia Challenge 10
2 Moonshine Alley Cruise..15
3 Firehouse Classic 20
4 Greg's Packer Ramble 25
5 Tranquil County Cruise...29
6 Pleasant Place Cruise 33
7 Musky Cruise...38
8 Hodag Cruise...44
9 Rib Falls Challenge 49

Western Wisconsin 54
10 Mound Builders Challenge...55
11 Step Back in Time Challenge 60
12 Stardig's Co-Motion Cruise..67
13 Leinenkugel Classic 72
14 Red Cedar Challenge...80
15 Pepin County Challenge 86
16 Trempealeau County Classic...92
17 Cranberry Cruise 100
18 Sparta/Elroy Classic 105
19 Coulee Country Challenge 111
20 Hustler Ridge Challenge 116
21 Round the River Cruise 121

Southern Wisconsin...127
22 Beetown Challenge 128
23 Pearl of Pecatonica Cruise 132
24 Mineral Challenge 136
25 Devil's Head Challenge 143
26 Commuters Cruise 149
27 Sugar River Ramble...154
28 Five Arch Cruise 158
29 Round the Rock Cruise 163
30 Lance's Wisconsin Challenge..168

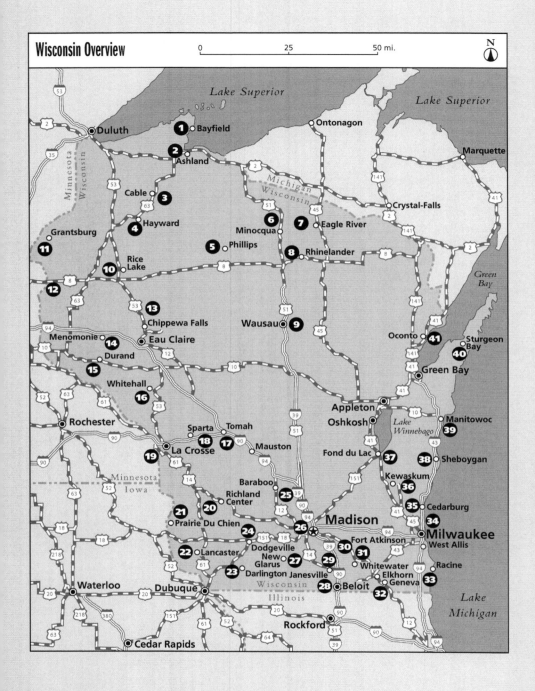

Wisconsin Overview

0   25   50 mi.

N

Lake Superior

Lake Superior

1 Bayfield

Duluth

Ontonagon

Marquette

2 Ashland

Michigan
Wisconsin

Minnesota
Wisconsin

Cable **3**

Crystal-Falls

6

7 Eagle River

Minocqua

Hayward **4**

5 Phillips

8 Rhinelander

Grantsburg

11

Rice
Lake

10

Green
Bay

12

13

Chippewa Falls

Wausau **9**

Oconto **41**

Sturgeon
Bay

Menomonie **14**

Eau Claire

40

Durand

Green Bay

15

Whitehall

Appleton

16

Rochester

Sparta

Tomah

Oshkosh

Lake
Winnebago

Manitowoc

18

17

Mauston

39

19

La Crosse

Fond du Lac

Sheboygan

37

38

Minnesota
Iowa

Baraboo

Kewaskum

Richland
Center

25

36

21

20

Madison

35

Cedarburg

Prairie Du Chien

24

26

34

Milwaukee

22 Lancaster

Dodgeville

Fort Atkinson

West Allis

30

New
Glarus

31

Racine

23

27

29

Whitewater

33

Darlington

Janesville

Elkhorn

Waterloo

Dubuque

28 Beloit

Geneva

Wisconsin

32

Illinois

Lake
Michigan

Rockford

Cedar Rapids

31 Southern Kettle Challenge 174
32 Chocolate Lovers Ramble 179

Eastern Wisconsin 183
33 Pickerel Cruise 184
34 Beer Barrel Ramble...190
35 Covered Bridge Ramble...195
36 Northern Kettle Challenge...200
37 Wanikamiu Cruise 206
38 Two Lakes Cruise 212
39 Manitowoc Challenge 218
40 Door County Classic 224
41 Three Rivers Classic 231

Appendix...237
Ride Index...240
About the Author...241

Preface

It wasn't easy choosing just forty-one rides that best represent Wisconsin. With so many paved secondary roads in the state, the choices were endless in selecting the rides that best represent the state's great road-biking opportunities. However, I've included additional options for shorter routes with most rides, so the actual number of potential rides in this book is far more than forty-one.

Are you curious as to how or why a town you ride through received its name? What really makes this guidebook stand apart from other touring books on cycling in Wisconsin is the brief overview of historic information on each community you explore. After Wisconsin became a territory in 1836, and then gained statehood in 1848, many towns were settled and took names influenced by the local Indian tribes or the railroads. As you review the chapters in the southern half of the state, you will learn how the lead-mining rush of the 1820s, the Black Hawk War of 1832, and the Civil War affected the towns and villages along the described routes. In the northern half of Wisconsin, logging was the settlements' major influence. I hope you will find the additional historic information of interest as you ride the routes in this book.

The starting locations for all rides included in this book had to offer free and adequate parking, along with proximity to provisions and to visitor centers. Rides were designed to strike a fine balance of secondary road riding with scenic and historic highlights along the safest routes. Of course, terrain, traffic volume, and road conditions played a significant role. Most, but not all, of the rides in this book are very rural. Except for Milwaukee, I intentionally avoided major population areas and found suitable routes through smaller towns. Most rides have at least one shortcut option, so you can adjust the mileages to your comfort level.

I would like to thank the Wisconsin Department of Transportation, the Wisconsin Historical Society and its county and local chapters, the Wisconsin Office of Tourism, the Wisconsin Department of Natural Resources, and all the local tourism bureaus that helped to make my research easier by supplying me with historic facts and route suggestions used in this book. In addition, my thanks to the fine ladies and gentlemen of practically every visitor center and chamber of commerce in the state that I visited; the many establishments that supplied information and tours; and all the bike shops and clubs that offered help and recommendations. My deep gratitude goes to Michael Fredericks of *Minnesota Cyclist Magazine;* Gerald Bauer from Hudson; Lisa Austin from Twin Cities Bicycling Club; Dan and Carolyn Robinson, Ian Lindridge, Marcy Kelash, and Carol Wahl from Hiawatha Bike Club; and Dick and Denise Stardig, Sharon (Scott) Johnson, Greg and Marion Headland, Gunnard Lanners, and John Driscoll from Northstar Ski Club. Finally, I would like to thank Sandy Johnson and Marcy Kelash for their help with editing, my mother for her encouragement, and The Globe Pequot Press for allowing me the opportunity create this book.

Introduction

Every place, it seems, has something about it that you can sense, that you can feel. Sometimes you like what you touch, sometimes you don't! For the most part, people like Wisconsin. As any proud native of the state will tell you, "We live in the land of cheese, beer, and the Packers." But more impressively, between the state's glaciated hills and ridges are thousands of lakes and hundreds of streams flowing across its rolling terrain. From open prairies to rolling hardwoods to thick pine and aspen forests, you will find a favorite place to ride when cycling in Wisconsin. And, by and large, you will find the people you meet while visiting the towns in this book friendly and helpful.

That calming aspect is also noticeable along most of the lakes and waterways you'll see as you ride your bike through the countryside. Unlike western rivers that violently cascade down steep mountain slopes, most of Wisconsin's waterways rise from massive marshes or from one of the countless prairie or forest lakes and gently flow where geology dictates. Of course, if you visit the south shore of Lake Superior and watch rivers such as the Brule tumbling wildly through the rocks, you'll see a behavior that doesn't fit most streams in the state.

You will notice that most of the rides in this guide have something to do with water. Most routes circle lakes, follow rivers, and/or roll through the countryside with creeks that flow through the valley floor. Whether you're enjoying the scenic beauty of Door County while riding along the jagged edges of the peninsula, or dancing on your pedals up an imposing bluff along the Mississippi River, or touring past the wildlife areas on the Step Back in Time Challenge where migrating birds, deer, and turtles are plentiful, you'll find it's the waterways that continue to shape Wisconsin.

In addition to having incredible amounts of water inland, the state of Wisconsin is bordered by Lake Superior to the northwest and Lake Michigan to the east. The 820 miles of combined shoreline make up a complex arrangement of nature containing a rich variety of natural features. Wetlands near the coasts of both lakes provide rich habitat for plants and animals that greatly influence the larger ecosystem processes of the Great Lakes region. The coastal wetlands that cut across the state between land and water are often rich in species diversity and provide critical habitat for migratory and nesting birds, spawning fish, and rare plants along the routes.

Wisconsin occupies three transition zones and sits in a region where weather systems from the north, south, and east collide. Although the state doesn't experience as many violent storms as the southern plains, there are weather quirks. Without the benefit of large elevation differences, it may be 80 degrees in southern Wisconsin but 50 degrees 150 miles to the north along Lake Superior. Even in an area far removed from the big lake, the weather can change dramatically. Fortunately for cyclists, the weather in Wisconsin doesn't change as quickly as it can in the mountains. While it

1

Riders enjoy some shade between rollers along a scenic Wisconsin backroad.

Whitetail deer are a common Wisconsin roadside attraction.

may snow after a 70-degree afternoon in the spring or fall, you will usually experience slower changes in temperature.

When the trees and bushes change from their summer wardrobe of green to the vibrant crimsons, yellows, and oranges of fall, every ride described takes on a new personality. The lush display of summer gives way to the colorful showings of plant life, bidding farewell till next spring. And with the heat of summer gone, the crisp air of fall awakens the senses as you ride the roads of Wisconsin.

No matter what time of the year—spring, summer, or fall—plan to make each ride in this book a two-day outing. Spend the night in a cozy inn and enjoy conversation with the local residents. Review your options: hike up to that overlook; have your picture taken next to that gristmill or round barn; walk over one of the battlefields from the Black Hawk War; see some of the grotto art displayed throughout the countryside; cycle through the Chequamegon National Forest or one of the many state parks; bike over one of the last remaining covered bridges in the state; ride on one of Wisconsin's prized bike trails; or learn more about the local history in each town you pass through. Now, page through the selected routes and start discovering what the state really has to offer.

Road and Traffic Conditions

Wisconsin is indeed a fabulous state in which to cycle. An extraordinary network of county and secondary roads offsets the lack of bike lanes and wide shoulders on many of the state's main arteries. Several of the larger communities are striving for bike lanes and wider shoulders on the main roads, but don't expect much after leaving their city limits.

You will naturally encounter heavier summer and weekend traffic on routes located in tourist areas. Also, take into consideration the extra traffic in forested areas caused by logging trucks and tourists looking at fall colors. The colorful forest canopy sometimes preoccupies motorists, who may not pay attention to cyclists on the road.

In the southern and western regions of Wisconsin, most routes involve climbing a bluff or ridge. Remember that what goes up must come down, so enjoy! Keep your speed under control and make sure your brakes are working properly before your ride. Pay particular attention to each chapter's "Terrain" and "Traffic and hazards" sections for more detailed safety instructions.

Safety and Comfort on the Road

Wisconsin laws governing bicycles are similar to those in most states. Bicyclists must ride with traffic on the right side of the road and as close as practical to the right edge of the roadway, unless making a left turn. Cyclists may ride on the shoulder, and in most cases this is highly advised if the pavement is in good condition. It is unlawful to ride on interstate highways and other controlled access roadways in Wisconsin.

Every bicycle ridden between sunset and sunrise must have proper lighting. Bicyclists riding on roadways must use continuous arm signals during the last 100 feet of a turn (unless needed to control the bike) and while stopped waiting to turn. Cyclists may ride two abreast in Wisconsin, if it doesn't impede the normal and reasonable movement of traffic. When riding on a two-lane roadway with medium to heavy traffic, riders should be single-file. Bicyclists must yield to pedestrians on sidewalks and crosswalks, and give an audible signal when approaching.

Most of all, cyclists should ride defensively. Stop at all stop signs and red lights, and keep an eye out for motorists making an illegal turn into your path. Use a rearview mirror or listen for vehicles approaching you from behind. Anticipate cars continuing their progress as though no cyclist is present.

Play it safe and wear a helmet. Wearing headgear that is properly fitted has saved many cyclists from severe head injuries. Doctors can easily mend a broken bone, but a brain injury can affect you and your family for the rest of your life. Also wear padded gloves when biking. They help buffer road shock that can lead to the hand numbness commonly experienced by bicyclists.

Always carry a few tools, a spare tube, a patch kit, and a tire pump. Before leaving on your ride, make sure your bike tires are inflated to the recommended pressure. The amount is usually printed on the sidewall of the tire.

Finally, always carry with you at least one water bottle and a snack bar in case the rest stops are farther apart than you expected. A good rule of thumb is to drink one bottle of water for every 10 miles you travel. Be prepared and bike smart.

Map Legend

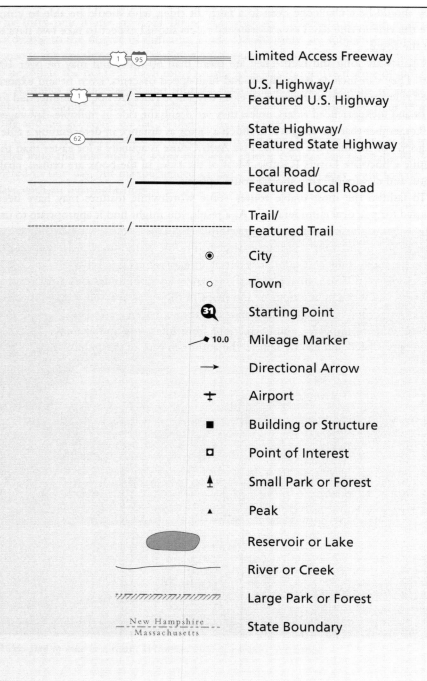

Limited Access Freeway

U.S. Highway/
Featured U.S. Highway

State Highway/
Featured State Highway

Local Road/
Featured Local Road

Trail/
Featured Trail

City

Town

Starting Point

Mileage Marker

Directional Arrow

Airport

Building or Structure

Point of Interest

Small Park or Forest

Peak

Reservoir or Lake

River or Creek

Large Park or Forest

State Boundary

Northern Wisconsin

1 Cornucopia Challenge

Famous for its fish boils and berry farms, this section of Lake Superior's rugged shoreline juts out into the lake to create the Apostle Islands. This adventurous ride leaves from Bayfield, a community named for a British Royal Navy surveyor, then meanders south along the bay's shore to Washburn, a community named after one of Wisconsin's earliest governors and a great place to stop for breakfast. From there you climb up from the bay enjoying the rolling forest floor as you travel inland. At the geographic high point of this challenge, shift into your high gear and revel in the long descent to a fishing village named for the horn of plenty. Then circle back through the northeast section of Chequamegon Bay, enjoying the flora and fauna as you make your way up to the point near Big Sand Bay Road. Soon you will pass through an Indian village named for its precipitous red cliffs, and then it's an easy scenic ramble back down to Bayfield.

Start: Bayfield fishing pier.
Length: 58 miles.
Terrain: Rolling with some major hills to climb; island option is flat.

Traffic and hazards: On Highway 13, after County Road K, there is no paved shoulder, and between Bayfield and Washburn, the traffic on the 4-foot paved shoulder can be heavy at times.

Getting there: From Highway 2 take Highway 13 north into Bayfield. At Manypenny Avenue take a right and go 5 blocks, then take a right on Second Street (there's a parking lot on the left). At Wilson Avenue turn left and travel 1 block to the fishing pier and city park.

When you arrive in Bayfield, a small village on Chequamegon Bay known as the "Berry Capital of Wisconsin," you'll discover why this destination is such a gem. The settlement was originally named La Pointe by Father Allouez, who established a Jesuit mission here. In 1856 the town was renamed for Henry W. Bayfield of the British Royal Navy, who had surveyed Lake Superior for the English government twenty years earlier. Today the Red Cliff band of Ojibwa Indians and residents of Madeline Island enjoy a community proud of its fish boils and berry farms.

You will pass several shops and restaurants as you ride out of town from the village's fishing pier. After turning south on Highway 13's paved shoulder, you will be offered many scenic vistas. As you pass Pike's Bay, notice the Bayfield State Fish Hatchery. A little farther along, find a roadside historic marker for Madeline Island. This island, to the east out in the bay, was first known as *Moningwanekaning,* an Indian name that means "a place where there are many lapwings" (woodpeckers). It is the largest of the Apostle Islands and was settled by the Chippewa Indians around AD 1500. After completing this challenge ride, you can take the ferry over to Madeline Island for a ramble loop.

A pair of bikers pedal a tandem out of Bayfield.

At the 11-mile mark you are in the town of Washburn. This village was named for C. C. Washburn, an early governor of Wisconsin. Now that you have had a taste of the terrain, you may want to consider a couple options for breakfast while here.

Climb out of town on County Road C (a 7 to 9 percent grade), then ride over several Wisconsin rollers for the next 15 miles. After crossing the Sioux River, you'll need to adjust your cadence to the rolling terrain as eagles soar above. You will find the scenery especially spectacular along Four Mile Creek. Then after passing Perch Lake, enjoy a smooth ride over the next 4 miles as you coast into Cornucopia.

This friendly fishing village, located on Highway 13 in the west end of the Apostle Islands National Lakeshore, was named by F. J. Stevenson around 1900. He chose the "horn of plenty" title because of the abundance of fruit being grown here. As you take a right on Highway 13, consider stopping at the Village Inn for lunch or coming back for dinner. Their house specialties include broiled whitefish almondine and trout cakes. If you are adventurous, try the whitefish liver appetizer, a local delicacy. The inn also has four special rooms, named for each season, if you prefer to start your ride in this quaint fishing village.

Before leaving town, take time to visit the picturesque harbor with its sandy beaches. The community continues to reflect on its fishing heritage, with a museum and old fishing boats displayed along the harbor. The city park on the edge of town is a great place to fill your water bottles from the refreshing artesian well.

1 Cornucopia Challenge

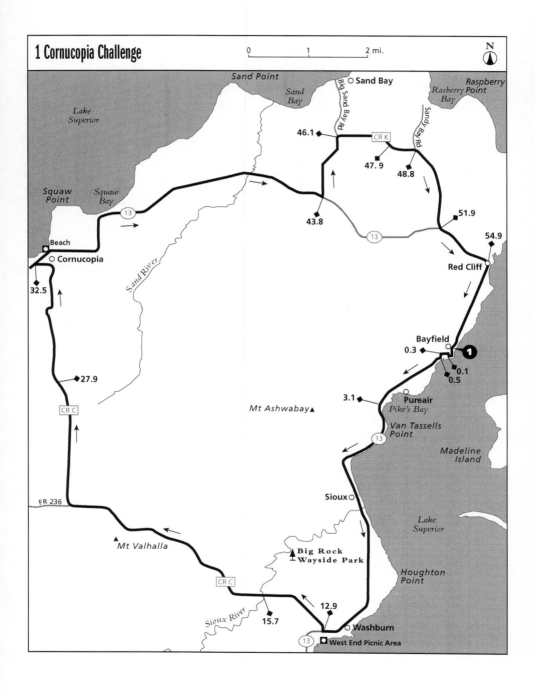

After riding east out of town on Highway 13, turn north on County Road K at 43.8 miles. As the challenge circles up to the north on this quiet rural road, your adrenaline will rise as you go over a few enormous rollers. Notice the new-growth forests along the way, with patches of meadow where deer are frequently seen grazing. Turn east and continue on the rollers; soon you will pass the original site of the Raspberry School, between Big Sand Bay Road and Sandy Bay Road.

Built by local Scandinavian families, the log cabin schoolhouse stood next to the Raspberry River and served the area from 1896 to 1914. The schoolhouse has been moved and is now part of the Norwegian cluster in Old World Wisconsin (see the Southern Kettle Challenge). Those who prefer to shorten the ride can continue east on Highway 13 and deduct 3.6 miles.

Returning back to the paved shoulder of Highway 13, you will soon pass through the village of Red Cliff, home to the Red Cliff band of Lake Superior Chippewa Indians. This village was originally called *Passa-bikang,* meaning "steep cliff." Nearby you will pass the powwow grounds where singers, drummers, dancers, and craftspeople from all around Lake Superior come together for the annual Woodland Indian Cultural Event.

Now cruise along the bluffs and enjoy the vistas from the Apostle Islands National Lakeshore. On your descent back into Bayfield, you will pass the Bayfield Pavilion. Here is where the ferry departs to Madeline Island, if you want to add a few more miles to your ride or check it out another day. Back in town enjoy the rest of the day exploring Bayfield.

Miles and Directions

0.0 From the fishing pier on the corner of First Street, head west on Wilson Avenue.

0.1 Take a right on Broad Street.

0.3 Turn left on Manypenny Avenue.

0.5 Turn left on South Sixth Street/Highway 13.

3.1 Pass Bayfield State Fish Hatchery.

3.5 Pass Salmo.

6.4 Pass Bayview Campground.

8.3 Pass history marker for Madeline Island.

11.0 Enter Washburn.

12.9 Take a right on County Road C.

15.7 Cross the Sioux River.

27.9 Pass Perch Lake.

32.1 Ride into the town of Cornucopia.

32.5 Take a right on Highway 13.

32.9 Enjoy the city park and beach.

43.8 Turn left on County Road K. **Option:** You can deduct 3.6 miles from the ride by continuing on Highway 13.

46.1 Pass Big Sand Bay Road.

47.9 Pass site of the Raspberry School.

48.8 Pass Sandy Bay Road.

51.9 Turn left on the paved shoulder of Highway 13.

54.9 Pass through Red Cliff.

56.7 Ride back into Bayfield.

57.2 Turn onto First Street. **Side-trip:** Take the ferry to Madeline Island for a 33-mile ramble.

58.0 Return to fishing pier.

Local Information

Bayfield Chamber of Commerce; (715) 779-3335 or (800) 447-4094; www.bayfield.org.

Bayfield County Tourism and Recreation; (715) 373-6125 or (800) 472-6338; www.travel bayfieldcounty.com.

Washburn Chamber of Commerce; (715) 372-8558 or (800) 533-7454; www.washburn chamber.com.

Local Events/Attractions

Madeline Island Ferry, Bayfield Pavilion, Bayfield; (715) 747-2051; www.madferry.com.

Firehouse 50, Grandview; first Saturday in August; (715) 763-3333; www.firehouse50.org.

CAMBA Fat Tire Festival, Cable; mid-September; (715) 798-3599; www.cambatrails.org.

Restaurants

The Egg Toss Bakery Cafe, 41 Manypenny Avenue, Bayfield; (715) 779-5181.

Pies of Bayfield, 124 Rittenhouse Avenue, Bayfield; (715) 779-5702.

The Village Inn, Highway 13 and County Road C, Cornucopia; 715-742-3941; www.village inncornucopia.com.

Accommodations

Apostle Islands Area Campground, 85150 Trailer Road, Bayfield; (715) 779-5524.

The Village Inn, Highway 13 and County Road C, Cornucopia; (715) 742-3941; www.village inncornucopia.com.

Bike Shops

Bayfield Bike Route, 27240 South Pratt Avenue, Bayfield; (715) 779-3132.

Restrooms

Start/finish: Public restroom at the corner of First Street and Wilson Avenue.

6.4: Bayview Campground.

12.9: West End Picnic Area.

32.9: Cornucopia Park and Beach.

Maps

DeLorme: Wisconsin Atlas and Gazetteer: Page 103 B6.

Ashland and Bayfield County Bicycle Map. Wisconsin State Bicycle Map (Northern Section).

2 Moonshine Alley Cruise

This ride starts in a well-known town on the south shore of Lake Superior. You will leave from a park with not only great wildlife viewing, but also an artesian well to fill your water bottles. The cruise travels counterclockwise, first along the sandy beaches of Lake Gitche Gumee as the seagulls frolic in the breeze and then west past the Northern Great Lakes Visitors Center. You then head south on a tour past several small towns that contributed to the area's history. Along the way, stop at a cheese shop in a town named after a French settler, then roll down Moonshine Alley to a village named for the Freemasons. After riding past a field of sunflowers, travel through a community with a large sawmill operation before returning back through the historic district of Ashland.

Start: Prentice Park in Ashland.
Length: 42 miles with 14-mile and 29-mile options.
Terrain: Rolling with a couple medium hills to climb.

Traffic and hazards: Use caution when riding on Highway 2, especially when passing the intersections on Highway 13 and Highway 63.

Getting there: From Highway 2 on the west side of Ashland, turn south onto Turner Road. Take a right at Park Road and follow it west to the parking lot.

This cruise leaves from the town of Ashland, offering many traces of the town's logging and railroad past. Ashland was originally called *Zham-a-wa-mik,* Ojibwa for "the long-stretched beaver." In 1854 it was platted by the Milwaukee, Lakeshore & Western Railroad and renamed Ashland by one of its earliest settlers, Martin Beaser, in honor of the Kentucky homestead of statesman Henry Clay, who Beaser greatly admired. The ride starts on the western edge of the city at Prentice Park, where you will find many of the necessary amenities, plus an artesian well to fill your water bottles.

The counterclockwise route heads west on the paved shoulder of the Blue Star Memorial Highway/Highway 2. Along this stretch you will pass Maslowski Park, which has restrooms. At the intersection of Highway 13, use caution and veer to the left side of the lane to allowing vehicles heading north toward Bayfield room to get around you on your right. In another mile you will pass County Road G and the entrance to the Northern Great Lakes Visitors Center. This nine-county historical research center provides area information, interactive exhibits, and special nature programs. Just before reaching the University of Wisconsin Experiment Station, you will pass Ashland Junction, which was built as a railroad town and had two rail lines, the Omaha and the Northern Pacific. As you pass Highway 137, those who prefer the 14-mile ramble option will turn left here, while the cruise continues southwest.

The historic Depot Museum in Mason makes a great rest stop.

After passing Highway 63, start watching for County Road F and make a left onto it. You are now cruising south and will find the road winding back and forth as it gradually climbs up to the town of Benoit. This small community was originally named Thirty Mile Siding because of an extra set of railroad tracks that ran through there at the time of the logging boom. After the timber era, the name was changed to Benoitville in honor of John Benoit, a French settler who was the first postmaster, and was later shortened to Benoit. If you need to stop in the town, look for the G & M General Store or the NFO Cheese Company.

The cruise then takes a right on Moonshine Alley Road and continues south. Those who prefer the 29-mile option will continue east on Highway 118. For the next 5 miles, the cruise route offers views of gentle rolling meadows with a few old farmsteads along the way. At the 16.8-mile mark you enter the village of Mason, established in 1882 by John Allen Humbird, who hired an enthusiastic civil engineer to plat the town and named it for the Freemasons. In the village you will find the historic Depot Museum and the White River Saloon across the street if you need to stop.

After leaving Mason, turn south on Highway 63. Jog on the paved shoulder down to County Road E and turn left. You will encounter your first hill at the 19-mile mark, with a 7 percent grade climb. At the top you will find open meadows with patches of jack pine forest, and soon you will be rolling through a sunflower field. After passing Four Corners Store Road, the ride turns to the left at County

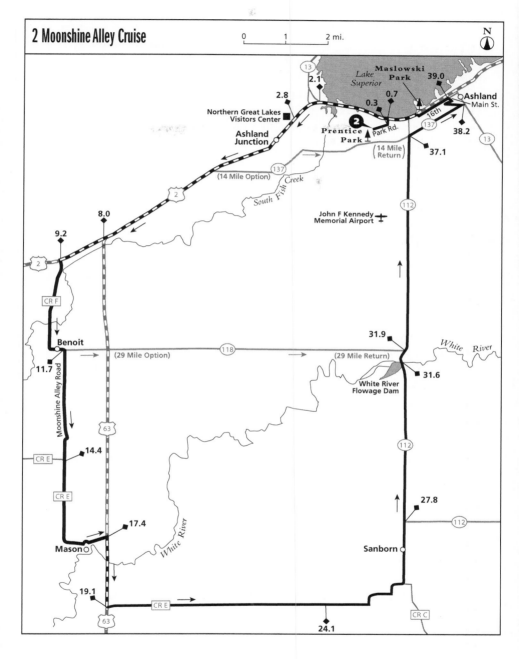

2 Moonshine Alley Cruise

0   1   2 mi.

N

Lake Superior

Maslowski Park 39.0

13 2.1

2.8

0.7
0.3

Ashland
Main St.

Northern Great Lakes
Visitors Center

2

16th

137

38.2

**Ashland
Junction**

**Prentice
Park** Park Rd.

(14 Mile
Return)

37.1

13

137

(14 Mile Option)

South Fish Creek

112

John F Kennedy
Memorial Airport

2

8.0

9.2

2

CR F

Benoit

(29 Mile Option)

118

(29 Mile Return)

31.9

White   River

31.6

11.7

White River
Flowage Dam

Moonshine Alley Road

63

14.4

CR E

112

CR E

27.8

17.4

White River

Mason

Sanborn

19.1

24.1

63

CR E

CR C

Line Road then jogs northeast a couple times before reaching the village of San-born, which was named for Senator A. W. A. Sanborn, who owned a large tract of land here. Today, due in no small part to a large sawmill, the town is still very active. You will find a couple taverns with grills if you need to stop.

Leaving town you will pass Sanborn Memorial Park as you travel north, and then merge onto Highway 112. For the next several miles the terrain is flat until you cross over the hydro dam powered by the White River Flowage. As you pass Highway 118, the 29-mile option returns for the ride back to Ashland.

In Ashland, turn east on 6th Street and tour through the downtown historic dis-trict. Here you will enjoy the beautifully restored nineteen-century brownstone buildings with shops that can be visited after the ride. If you are a railroad buff, swing by the Soo Line Depot at 400 Third Avenue and see the 950 Locomotive, built in 1900, which in its time was the world's largest decapod (ten-wheel-drive) locomo-tive. Back across town in Prentice Park, stretch your legs by taking a stroll on the boardwalk that offers some great wildlife viewing.

Miles and Directions

0.0   From Prentice Park, head east on Park Road.

0.3   Turn left on Turner Road.

0.5   Turn left on the paved, rumble-strip-protected shoulder of Highway 2.

0.7   Pass Maslowski Park.

2.1   Pass Highway 13, using caution.

2.8   Pass County Road G and Northern Great Lakes Visitors Center.

4.1   Pass Ashland Junction.

5.1   Pass Highway 137. **Option:** Turn left on Highway 137 for the 14-mile option.

8.0   Pass Highway 63.

9.2   Turn left on County Road F.

11.5   Ride through Benoit.

11.7   Take a right on Moonshine Alley Road. **Option:** Turn left on Highway 118 for the 29-mile option.

14.4   Continue south on County Road E as it merges in from the west.

16.8   Ride through Mason.

17.4   Take a right on Highway 63.

19.1   Turn left on County Road E and head east.

22.2   Pass through sunflower fields.

24.1   Pass Four Corners Store Road.

25.1   Turn left on County Road E at County Line Road, then jog northwest a couple times.

27.1   Pass through Sanborn.

27.8   Merge onto Highway 112 as it curves to the north.

31.6   Cross over the hydro dam on the White River Flowage.

31.9   Pass Highway 118. (Note: The 29-mile option returns here.)

37.0 Pass Highway 137. (Note: The 14-mile option returns here.)

37.1 Take a right on Highway 137/6th Street into downtown Ashland.

38.2 Turn left on Highway 13/Ellis Avenue.

39.0 Turn left on Main Street.

40.2 Take a right on 16th Street.

40.3 Turn left on Highway 2 (bike trail runs parallel with highway).

41.0 Turn left on Turner Road.

41.3 Take a right on Park Road.

42.0 Return to park.

Local Information

Ashland Area Chamber of Commerce; (800) 284-9484; www.visitashland.com.

Bayfield County Tourism and Recreation; (715) 373-6125 or (800) 472-6338; www.travel bayfieldcounty.com.

Northern Great Lakes Visitors Center; (515) 685-9983; www.northerngreatlakescenter.org.

Local Events/Attractions

Superior Vistas Bike Tour Ride, Ashland; third weekend in June; (715) 373-2114; www.superiorvistas.org.

Firehouse 50, Grandview; first Saturday in August; (715) 763-3333; www.firehouse50.org.

CAMBA Fat Tire Festival, Cable; mid-September; (715) 798-3599; www.cambatrails.org.

Restaurants

B's Lakeshore Cafe, 2806 Lakeshore Drive, Ashland; (715) 682-9344.

Breakwater Cafe, 1808 Lakeshore Drive, Ashland; (715) 682-8388.

Molly Cooper's, 101 Lakeshore Drive, Ashland; (715) 682-9095.

Accommodations

Hotel Chequamegon, 101 Lakeshore Drive, Ashland; (800) 946-5555; www.hotelc.com.

Kreher Park and Campground, between Ashland Marina and oredocks, Ashland; (715) 682-7071.

Bike Shops

Bay City Bicycles, 412 West Main Street, Ashland; (715) 682-2091.

Bodin's on the Lake, 2521 Lake Shore Drive West, Ashland; (715) 682-6441.

Restrooms

Start/finish: Prentice Park.

0.7: Maslowski Park.

2.8 Northern Great Lakes Visitors Center.

11.5 G & M General Store in Benoit.

17.7 Depot Museum in Mason and White River Saloon.

27.1 Sanborn Tavern.

Maps

DeLorme: Wisconsin Atlas and Gazetteer: Page 103 D6.

Wisconsin State Bicycle Map (Northern Section).

Ashland and Bayfield County Bicycle Map.

3 Firehouse Classic

This ride shares some of the same roller coaster excitement that the Grandview Firehouse 50, a citizen bike race and recreational ride, enjoys each August here in the northwoods. The classic leaves from a community named in honor of the first locomotive engineer to pull a train into town. The route then heads northwest over rolling wooded lanes and meanders around forested glacial potholes, then over the Ice Age Trail. Soon you are rolling into a town named for the vice president of the lumber company that platted it. You then continue north through the Chequamegon-Nicolet National Forest to discover an old village that has been reincarnated into a great rest stop, with a transformed railroad diner car that allows you to enjoy lunch while learning more about the town's past. Now turning east through farm meadows and stands of new timber growth, the route swings south over the Continental Divide (called Great Divide on the sign.) As you cruise down the slope, you follow the shoreline of a lake named after an Indian chief who legend says has a lost silver mine. You then leave the lake and head west, following the winding river named after the same chief, and soon return to Cable.

Start: Corner of First Street and County Road M in Cable.
Length: 75 miles with 37-mile and 50-mile options.
Terrain: Very rolling with a few major climbs.

Traffic and hazards: Most roads are low traffic; county roads may have extra traffic on summer weekends but are designated bike routes. Take care when riding on the paved shoulder of Highway 63 from Mason to Grand View. When the moon is full, deer have been know to bolt into the road.

Getting there: From Highway 63 turn east onto County Road M in Cable. Street parking is available on First Street by the visitor center.

Located in the heart of the 844,000-acre Chequamegon-Nicolet National Forest, this ride starts in Cable, a village surrounded by a pristine environment with an abundance of wildlife, clean air, and an unhurried pace of life. In 1878 this was the end of the line for the Chicago, St. Paul, Minneapolis & Omaha Railroad, and the village was named for the first locomotive engineer who pulled into the train stop. You will find several options here as you prepare for your ride.

From the town's visitor center, the route heads north up along Lake Owen; for the first 15 miles, watch for deer as you cruise along this rolling forest road. Also use caution if a black bear is spotted along the way. Don't be alarmed—they are more frightened of you, so give them plenty of space and they will disappear into the forest in a blink of an eye. Turning onto Lake Owen Road, the route jogs to the northeast. Those who prefer the 37-mile option will turn onto Pioneer Road and head east. The classic continues north and follows the lake up to Two Lakes Campground.

GREAT DIVIDE
OF
NORTHERN WISCONSIN

PRECIPITATION FALLING HERE FLOWS INTO THE CHIPPEWA AND NAMEKAGON RIVERS THEN WESTERLY TO THE MISSISSIPPI RIVER AND SOUTH TO THE GULF OF MEXICO.

PRECIPITATION FALLING HERE FLOWS INTO LAKE SUPERIOR THEN EAST THRU THE GREAT LAKES INTO THE ST. LAWRENCE RIVER AND ULTIMATELY THE ATLANTIC OCEAN.

CHEQUAMEGON
National Forest

After a 4-mile climb to the Continental Divide, riders will be rewarded with a long down-hill cruise.

For another 5 miles of winding forested road, you roll around glacial pockets and past the National Ice Age Scenic Trail. In another mile you reach Drummond.

A true company town, the village was platted by Frank H. Drummond of the Rust-Owen Lumber Company, which in 1882 sent a crew of men here to cut timber, set up a mill, and lay out a town. Within a year the company had a boardinghouse, store, and blocks of look-alike houses for their employees. The town has remained much the same, except today the businesses and homes are privately owned. If you need to stop, options include the Bear County Store and the city park, by the library and history museum.

Those who prefer the Firehouse 50 (50-mile option) route should turn right on the paved shoulder of Highway 63 and head toward Grand View. The classic jogs to the west on the highway's paved shoulder, then takes a right on Delta-Drummond Road. As you pass Mill Pond Lake, on the south side of the highway, look over along the shoreline to the mill operation that gave many people their livelihoods in those early years. Now riding north, on the far side of Drummond Lake you will find a peaceful place to stop and relax by the dam, but there are no amenities.

For the next 5 miles you will discover the road surface is abnormally porous, demanding a little extra effort as you ride the undulating roadway. Soon the ride passes the old Delta CCC Camp that operated from 1933 to 1942, and the road surface becomes smooth again. At the 28-mile mark you're in Delta. The town was known for its extensive logging operations in the early 1880s, when logs were floated down from Flynn's Dam to Delta. In 1890 the Duluth South Shore & Atlantic Railroad named the town Delta because it is the meeting place (or delta) of the south fork, west fork, and main fork of the White River. This is a great place to stop and have lunch at the Delta Diner, located at the site where the old Delta Store once stood. It is a classic East Coast diner, built on the frame of a 1940 Silk City railroad car. The new shiny establishment offers a great menu that fits the needs of any touring cyclist.

Now traveling east, the rolling countryside offers patches of farm meadows among the forest. Soon the timber stands open up to a valley, and for the next 8 miles you ride along open fields with old farm settings until you reach the village of Mason. The town was established by John Allen Humbird and named for the Freemasons by an enthusiastic surveyor who platted the town in 1882. You will find the historic railroad Depot Museum here, along with the White River Saloon.

The ride leaves Mason heading south on Highway 63 and returns to the Firehouse 50 route in Grand View. When the railroad came through this village in 1882, the settlement and station was named Gibbons for James P. Gibbons, who owned the land here. A year later he sold out to the Pratt Lumber Company and the town was renamed Prattsberg. It wasn't until 1905 that the name was changed to Grand View, perhaps because after the area was logged off, great vistas were unveiled. In town you will find a couple rest stop options, the Grand View Food Market and Grand View City Park. In the park, check out the statue of Chief Namekagon and the tale of his hidden silver mine treasure.

Now riding south, you will come to your first major climb. For the next 4 miles the county road climbs at a steady 4 to 6 percent until you hit the wall before the Divide. The last half mile will call for some of those stored calories as you dance on your pedals up the last stretch of the Divide. At the top you are at the crest of the Penokee Range that forms the Continental Divide. Take a breather here and catch the details on this geographic point of interest at the sign at the top.

It's now time to shift out of granny and jump into your high ring for a fabulous cruise down past Pioneer Road, where the 37-mile option returns. Riding along the shoreline of Namekagon Lake, you will soon cross the bridge onto Anderson Island. Andrew Nels Anderson, who came here from Sweden, homesteaded this lake community in 1890. After discovering the island, which reminded him of the island he grew up on back in his home country, he built a floating bridge and raised his family here. Today the homestead has been platted into a lake home community, which the route passes through.

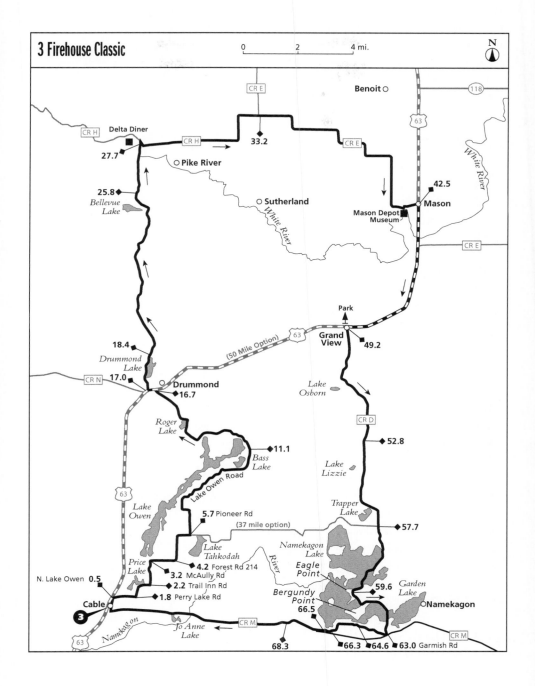

3 Firehouse Classic

0   2   4 mi.

N

CR E

Benoit ○

118

63

CR H

Delta Diner

CR H

33.2

White River

27.7◆

○ **Pike River**

CR E

25.8◆

CR E

42.5

Bellevue Lake

○ **Sutherland**

White River

Mason

Mason Depot Museum

CR E

Park

(50 Mile Option)

63

Grand View

49.2

18.4◆

Drummond Lake

Lake Osborn

CR N

17.0■

○ **Drummond**

◆**16.7**

Roger Lake

CR D

52.8◆

63

Bass Lake

◆**11.1**

Lake Lizzie

Lake Owen Road

Trapper Lake

5.7 Pioneer Rd

(37 mile option)

57.7◆

Lake Owen

Lake Tahkodah

Namekagon Lake

Price Lake

4.2 Forest Rd 214

3.2 McAully Rd

Eagle Point

N. Lake Owen **0.5**

◆**2.2** Trail Inn Rd

59.6

Garden Lake

◆**1.8** Perry Lake Rd

Bergundy Point

Namekagon ○

Cable

66.5

3

Namekagon River

Jo Anne Lake

CR M

CR M

63

68.3

66.3■ **64.6** **63.0** Garmish Rd

At the 63-mile mark, just before County Road M, take a right on Garmish Road. Here a little energy boost will add to your riding enjoyment. The next 3 miles offer a roller coaster of twists and turns as you pass by the Garmish Resort and then the Forestview Lodge Nature Trail. After turning on County Road M and passing Lakewoods Resort, the route rolls west as you cross over the Namekagon River a couple times before passing Telemark Resort Road. Look off to the south and you can see the ski slopes carved into the hillside. Two more miles and a small climb, and you are back in Cable.

Miles and Directions

0.0 Head north on First Street out of Cable.

0.5 Take a right on North Lake Owen Road.

1.8 Turn right on Perry Lake Road.

2.2 Turn left on Trail Inn Road.

3.2 Take a right on McAully Road.

4.2 Turn left on Forest Road 214.

5.2 Take a right on Forest Road 214.

5.7 Turn left on Lake Owen Road. **Option:** The 37-mile option continues east on Forest Road 214 over to Pioneer Road.

11.1 Pass Two Lakes Campground.

16.7 Turn left on Highway 63 in Drummond. **Option:** Turn right on Highway 63 for the 50-mile option.

17.0 Take a right on Delta-Drummond Road.

18.4 Pass Dam Road (wayside).

25.8 Pass Delta CCC Camp 2622.

27.7 Take a right on County Road H . **Side-trip:** Turn left 0.3 mile to the Delta Diner for lunch.

33.2 Straight ahead on County Road E.

42.1 Pass through Mason.

42.5 Take a right on Highway 63.

49.2 Turn left on County Road D in Grand View. (Note: The 50-mile option returns here.)

52.8 Ride over the Great Divide.

57.7 Pass Pioneer Road. (Note: The 37-mile option returns here.)

59.6 Arrive on Anderson Island on Namekagon Lake.

63.0 Take a right on Garmish Road, before County Road M.

64.6 Pass Garmish Resort on your right.

65.4 Pass Forestview Lodge Nature Trail on your left.

66.3 Take a right on County Road M.

66.5 Pass Lakewoods Resort.

68.3 Pass Dam Road.

72.6 Pass Telemark Lodge Road.

75.0 Return to First Street in Cable.

Local Information

Cable Chamber of Commerce; (800) 533-7454; www.cable4fun.com.
Bayfield County Tourism and Recreation; (715) 373-6125 or (800) 472-6338; www.travel bayfieldcounty.com.

Local Events/Attractions

Firehouse 50, Grandview; first Saturday in August; (715) 763-3333; www.firehouse50.org.
CAMBA Fat Tire Festival, Cable; mid-September; (715) 798-3599; www.cambatrails.org.

Restaurants

Brickhouse Cafe and Catering, 13458 Reynolds Street, Cable; (715) 798-5432.
Corner Cafe, 43465 Highway 63, Cable; (715) 798-3003.
Delta Diner, County Road H, Delta; (715) 372-6666; www.deltadiner.com.

Accommodations

Telemark Resort, 42225 Telemark Road, Cable; (877) 798-4718.

Namekagon Campground, County Road D, Namekagon; (877) 444-6777; www.reserveus.com.

Bike Shops

Riverbrook Bike & Ski Shop, 13493 North Highway 63, Seeley; (866) 297-7687; www.riverbrookbike.com.

Restrooms

Start/finish: Visitor center or library.
11.1: Two Lakes Campground.
16.9: Drummond library or park.
28.0: Delta Diner.
42.1: Depot Museum or White River Saloon in Mason.
49.4: Grand View City Park.
66.5: Lakewoods Resort.

Maps

DeLorme: Wisconsin Atlas and Gazetteer: Page 94 C2.
Wisconsin State Bicycle Map (Northern Section).
Ashland and Bayfield County Bicycle Map.

4 Greg's Packer Ramble

A special place in the northern woodlands, this ride offers visitors and residents alike a genuine opportunity to enjoy the wild and scenic wonders of this diverse area. You'll have a good time on a relaxing route that some locals find a great way to shake off the stresses of everyday life, especially after an NFL game. Starting in a town settled around a sawmill on the Namekagon River and known for its World Championship Lumberjack Show, this ramble first takes you out toward the Lake Chippewa Flowage. Soon you are climbing into the rolling hills as the route circles to the west into the open meadows and stands of jack pine forest. Upon reaching Beaver Lake Park, the tour turns north and enjoys the wildflowers along the road through the spring and summer or the colorful foliage in the fall. At the top of Chippanazie Road the ride comes full circle, returning on Company Lake Road back into Hayward.

Start: Parking lot at South Dakota Avenue and Third Street in Hayward.
Length: 31 miles with longer options available.

Terrain: Rolling with a few easy climbs.
Traffic and hazards: Use caution when riding for short distances on the local highways.

Getting there: From the visitor center on Highway 63, turn northeast onto Iowa Avenue (a one-way street through the main shopping area), and after 2 blocks turn left on Third Street. You will find the parking lot and restrooms on the corner at South Dakota Avenue.

Known for having the "World's Largest Musky" and its lumberjack shows, you will find plenty of activities in Hayward before and after your ride. In 1883 a lumberman named Anthony Judson Hayward settled here and built a sawmill on the Namekagon River. From the sawmill operation emerged a town, which has grown into an important resort community.

The ramble leaves from the public parking lot at South Dakota Avenue and Third Street and heads through the downtown area. After riding around Hayward Lake, you continue on Wheeler Road, where you will enjoy the canopy over the rolling road as it meanders through the forest. Soon you are passing the Sawyer County Fair Grounds, and if you are fortunate enough to ride this ramble on the first Sunday in August, stop for a few minutes to watch the comedy of men in fire-retardant jumpsuits racing around the track on riding lawnmowers.

If you would like to add some additional miles to this ramble, consider riding some of the roads that meander around the Lake Chippewa Flowage. Pick up a Sawyer County map at the visitor center, and at mile 3.6 turn left on County Road B and pick your distance. Most of the roads around the flowage are paved, so enjoy.

After passing the fairgrounds heading south on the ramble, you will find a stretch of road that offers a series of moderate rollers through the forest flora. Soon you will cruise along Spring Lake as the road meanders along the western shoreline. At the far end, at the boat landing, the route turns to the southwest and you gradually climb up the ridge. It's worth the effort, and you'll see why when you reach Old 27 Road while riding on the ridge. From here it's a tree-lined cruise back down.

Turn onto Rainbow Road and then cross the highway; the terrain opens up to pine forests and open meadows as you head west. In a couple miles turn north on Half Mile Road. Here the ramble takes you up Lakeshore Road, then at the 15.5 mark turn left on Beaver Lake Road. If you are looking for a rest stop, you can continue to the right for about a half mile to Beaver Lake County Park. Enjoy a picnic lunch here or the lake's sandy beach.

Back on Beaver Lake Road, the route meanders around Loon Lake and then follows the railroad tracks before turning north up across the Namekagon River to Highway 63. Use caution here, as the paved shoulder on the highway is narrow. Turning onto Pike Road, you will start riding north. For the next 6 miles you roll over farm meadows and stands of timber. On Chippanazie Road the ramble soon passes a lake with the same name. *Chippanazie* was taken from a term used by eighteenth-century French explorers and fur traders meaning "rolling rapids."

At Highway 77 turn east on the paved shoulder and continue until you reach a sign that says PHOTOS BY MARY LOU. Take a right here; even though the street sign is missing, this is Company Lake Road. (The North Harper Road sign is across the

4 Greg's Packer Ramble

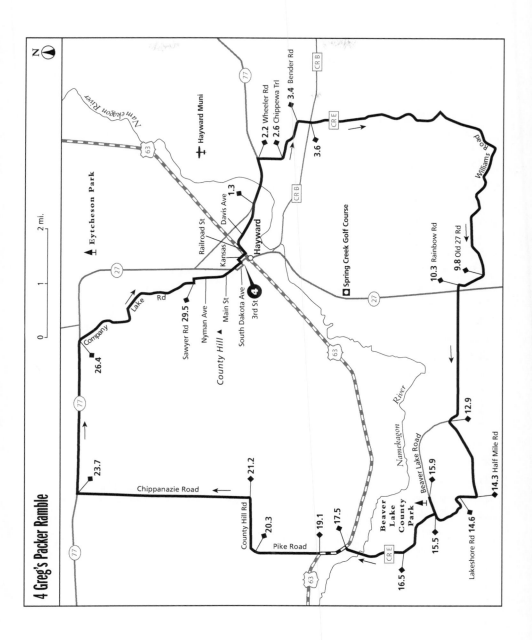

N

Eytcheson Park

Namekagon River

2 mi.

0   1

Company   26.4

Lake   Rd

Sawyer Rd **29.5**

Nyman Ave

Main St

County Hill ▲

South Dakota Ave

3rd St ▲ **4**

Hayward

Kansas

Railroad St

Davis Ave

1.3

✝ Hayward Muni

2.2 Wheeler Rd

2.6 Chippewa Trl

3.4 Bender Rd

CR B

3.6

CR B

CR E

Spring Creek Golf Course

Williams Road

10.3 Rainbow Rd

9.8 Old 27 Rd

27

63

Namekagon River

12.9

14.3 Half Mile Rd

15.9

Beaver Lake Road

15.5

Beaver Lake County Park ✝

Lakeshore Rd **14.6**

CR E

16.5

Pike Road

17.5

19.1

County Hill Rd

20.3

21.2

Chippanazie Road

23.7

77

77

63

27

77

highway.) Now circling back to the south for a mile, the road winds its way through a couple farmyards and back into town. Notice the big pines along the road; these are some of the last remnants of the forest before the logging era. In Hayward turn left on Sawyer Road and enjoy some of the town's early homes along the boulevard on your way back.

Miles and Directions

0.0 From the parking lot, head northeast on Third Street crossing Main Street.

0.1 Take a right on Kansas Avenue.

0.3 Cross Highway 63.

0.4 Turn left on Railroad Street.

0.5 Take a right on Davis Avenue.

1.3 Turn right on the paved shoulder of Highway 77.

2.2 Take a right on Wheeler Road.

2.6 Turn left on Chippewa Trail.

3.4 Turn right on Bender Road at the Sawyer County Fair Grounds.

3.6 Cross County Road B onto County Road E.

6.5 Take a right on Williams Road at the Spring Lake Boat Landing.

9.8 Turn right on Old 27 Road.

10.3 Turn left on Rainbow Road.

10.4 Cross Highway 27.

12.9 Pass Beaver Lake Road.

14.3 Take a right on Half Mile Road.

14.6 Turn left on Lakeshore Road.

15.5 Turn left on Beaver Lake Road. **Side-trip:** Head 0.4 mile east to Beaver Lake County Park.

16.5 Take a right on County Road E.

17.6 Turn left on the paved shoulder of Highway 63. Use caution—traffic can be heavy.

19.1 Take a right on Pike Road.

20.3 Take a right on County Hill Road.

21.2 Turn left on Chippanazie Road.

23.7 Take a right on the paved shoulder of Highway 77.

26.4 Take a right on Company Lake Road (at the PHOTOS BY MARY LOU sign).

29.5 Turn left on Sawyer Road.

29.6 Take a right on Nyman Avenue.

30.3 Turn left on Main Street.

30.4 Take a right on Fifth Street.

30.5 Turn left on South Dakota Avenue.

31.0 Return to parking lot.

Local Information

Hayward Chamber of Commerce; (800) 724-2992; www.haywardareachamber.com.

Local Events/Attractions

Firehouse 50, Grandview; first Saturday in August; (715) 763-3333; www.firehouse50.org.
CAMBA Fat Tire Festival, Cable; mid-September; (715) 798-3599; www.cambatrails.org.

Restaurants

Norske Nook Restaurant and Bakery, 10536 Highway 27 South, Hayward; (715) 634-4928.
The Original Famous Dave's, 12355 West Richardson Bay Road, Hayward; (888) 774-2674.
Coop's Pizza, 10588 California Avenue, Hayward; (715) 634-3027.

Accommodations

Best Northern Pine Inn, 9966 North Highway 27 South, Hayward; (715) 634-4959.
Nelson Lake Landing and Campground, 13045 North Dam Road, Hayward; (715) 634-4175.

Bike Shops

New Moon Bike Shop, 15569 Highway 63, Hayward; (800) 754-8685; www.newmoonski.com.

Restrooms

Start/finish: Public restroom at the corner of Third and South Dakota.
15.9: Beaver Lake County Park.

Maps

DeLorme: Wisconsin Atlas and Gazetteer: Page 94 D1.
Wisconsin State Bicycle Map (Northern Section).
Sawyer County Sportsmen's Map.

5 Tranquil County Cruise

In an area that borders the Chequamegon-Nicolet National Forest, discover the peace and serenity of riding through parcels of forest while circling around the area's lakes. Located between Hayward and Minocqua, this route departs from a community surrounded by flowages created from dams built in the logging era. The town suffered a major fire in its early years but was rebuilt with the red brick and sandstone architecture you see today. Leaving from a grotto park full of concrete statues that some say are haunted, the cruise travels back into town and then west to the Phillips chain of lakes. You'll luxuriate in the chain's tranquil setting as you meander along the south shore of Long Lake. You will soon approach and circle another lake fed by the Elk River, called Lac Sault Dore. After crossing the river the route circles up to the north then jets to the east along the northern shore of the lake. Soon you cross the highway and ride up and around another pristine lake setting before returning back to Phillips.

Start: Wisconsin Concrete Park in Phillips.
Length: 44 miles with a 30-mile option.
Terrain: Flat to gentle rolling hills.

Traffic and hazards: Ride with care on the paved shoulder of Highway 13.

Getting there: The park is a half mile south of town on Highway 13.

This cruise begins south of town in Fred Smith's Wisconsin Concrete Park. A grotto tucked away alongside Highway 13, this park's collection of mythical and real character pieces is an experience in itself. Smith, a self-taught artist, made more than 200 figures using concrete and broken beer bottle. A tribute to his life, his creations include soldiers, miners, cowboys, and other recognizable figures like Ben Hur and Abraham Lincoln. Some say that since Smith's death, the statues have been known to move around. Take note before leaving how the figures are standing. Haunted or not, it's a great place to start the ride.

After riding back into Phillips on the paved shoulder of Highway 13, you will have another chance to use a restroom or have breakfast. This village, located on a chain of lakes, was platted in 1876 by Elijah Phillips, the general manager of the Wisconsin Central Railroad. In the early 1890s the town was destroyed by fire but was soon rebuilt. Notice the unique buildings in the downtown area built with red brick and sandstone trim.

Head west out of town on County Road W. You will pass Sokol Park as the road lazily meanders along the south shore of Long Lake, which is part of the Phillips Lake chain and fed by the Elk River. At the 4.3-mile mark you pass the Hidden Valley Resort, a great place to stay while visiting the area. At Flemings Rapids Road you can shorten the ride to 30 miles, if you so desire, by turning right here. At about the 8-mile mark, the ride passes the Corner Connection, a convenience store at Soo Line Road. Around the next bend you travel along Lac Sault Dore. This lake, fed by the Elk River, has jagged fingers and was named by French explorers. It is commercially known today as Soo Lake.

You then cross the Elk River and turn north on County Road S. This part of the route jogs in and out of the fingers on the north side of Soo Lake and passes several little cottage resort communities. Upon reaching County Road F, jog to the right for a half mile, then turn left at the junction of Flemings Rapids Road. Here is where the 30-mile option returns from the south. As the route continues east over gentle rolling forest vegetation, you will soon come to Pine Ridge Road, where you head north before crossing Highway 13.

Now on Old 13 Road, enjoy some fun rollers until you pass Squaw Creek Road. To shorten the ride, turn right here and deduct 8.6 miles. Otherwise, continue north for another mile before the road turns to the northeast on West Solberg Lake Road. Watch for deer grazing along the way as the road twists and turns along the lake's north shoreline. At the 29.9-mile mark you will pass Solberg Lake County Park, a great place to have a picnic or enjoy the sandy beach. After circling up around one of the northern bays of the lake, you will soon come to Federal Road. Take a right here on East Solberg Lake Road and follow the gently rolling cottage lane back to the south. Before leaving the lake, you will pass Comfort Cove Resort, then Squaw Creek Road.

When you reach County Road H, jog to the east for 1 mile, then take a right on Big Elk Road, which merges into Worchester Road. Continue riding south

5 Tranquil County Cruise

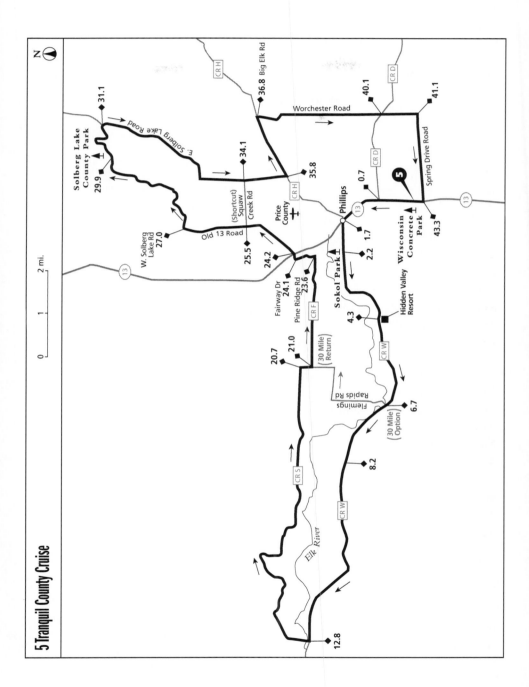

N

0   1   2 mi.

Solberg Lake County Park
31.1
29.9
E. Solberg Lake Road
34.1
35.8
Big Elk Rd
CR H
36.8 Big Elk Rd
Worchester Road
40.1
CR D
41.1
Spring Drive Road
CR D
0.7
5
Phillips
13
CR H
Price County
(Shortcut) Squaw Creek Rd
Old 13 Road
W. Solberg Lake Rd
27.0
25.5
24.2
1.7
2.2
Wisconsin Concrete Park
43.3
13
Fairway Dr 24.1
Pine Ridge Rd 23.6
CR F
Sokol Park
4.3
Hidden Valley Resort
CR W
20.7
21.0
30 Mile Return
Flemings Rapids Rd
6.7
30 Mile Option
8.2
CR S
CR W
Elk River
12.8

through open meadows with birds frolicking in the breeze, and take a right on Spring Drive Road. As you are traveling west back to the park, you will encounter a small climb. Back at the park, you be the judge: Walk around the concrete figures and see if you notice anything different.

Miles and Directions

0.0 From Wisconsin Concrete Park, take a right onto Highway 13.

0.7 Pass County Road D.

1.7 Turn left on County Road W.

2.2 Pass Sokol Park.

4.3 Pass Hidden Valley Resort.

6.7 Pass Flemings Rapids Road. **Option:** Turn right on Flemings Rapids Road for the 30-mile option.

8.2 Pass Corner Connection at Soo Line Road.

12.8 Take a right on County Road S.

20.7 Take a right on County Road F.

21.0 Turn left on County Road F. (Note: The 30-mile option returns here.)

23.6 Turn left on Pine Ridge Road.

24.1 Take a right on Fairway Drive.

24.2 Cross Highway 13 onto Old 13 Road.

25.5 Pass Squaw Creek Road. **Shortcut option:** Turn right on Squaw Creek Road to deduct 8.6 miles from cruise.

27.0 Take a right on West Solberg Lake Road.

29.9 Pass Solberg Lake County Park.

31.1 Take a right on East Solberg Lake Road.

34.1 Pass Squaw Creek Road. (Note: The shortcut option returns here.)

35.8 Turn left on County Road H.

36.8 Take a right on Big Elk Road.

37.1 Turn right on Worchester Road.

40.1 Cross County Road D.

41.1 Take a right on Spring Drive Road.

43.3 Take a right on Highway 13.

44.0 Return to park.

Local Information

Price County Tourism, Price County Courthouse, 82 Lake Avenue/Highway 13, Phillips; (800) 269-4505; www.pricecountywi.net. **Phillips Area Chamber of Commerce,** 305 South Lake Avenue, Phillips; (888) 408-4800; www.phillipswisconsin.net.

Wisconsin Concrete Park, N8236 Highway 13, Phillips; (715) 339-6475.

Local Events/Attractions

Czechoslovakian Festival, Phillips; second weekend in June; (888) 408-4800; www.phillipswisconsin.net.

Dirtfighters Classic Mountain Bike Race;
first weekend in July; (888) 408-4800;
www.phillipswisconsin.net.

Restaurants

Crystal Corner Cafe, 138 South Lake Avenue,
Phillips; (715) 779-5181.
Birch Island Resort, N8221 East Wilson
Flowage Road, Phillips; (715) 339-3151.

Accommodations

Hidden Valley Resort, W7724 County Road W,
Phillips; (715) 339-2757; www.hiddenvalley
wi.com.
Solberg Lake County Park, West Solberg Lake
Road, Phillips; (715) 339-6371.

Bike Shops

Pine Line Sports, 351 North Eighth Street,
Medford; (715) 748-3400.

Restrooms

Start/finish: Wisconsin Concrete Park
0.9: Phillips visitor center.
29.9: Solberg Lake County Park.

Maps

DeLorme: Wisconsin Atlas and Gazetteer: Page
103 B6.
Wisconsin State Bicycle Map (Northern
Section).
TREK the Northwoods Trails (www.northwoods
biking.com).

6 Pleasant Place Cruise

This route starts in a resort community that is divided by two lakes, making it almost an island city. You'll start at the Bearskin State trailhead and travel through the countryside on roads of Oneida and Vilas Counties. It's your choice: Leave this pioneer resort community on the bike trail, or follow the lakefront roads as they wind around the bays and peninsulas of Kawaguesaga Lake. Within 3 miles the bike trail meets up with the cruise as it twists and turns to the west on the rolling forested lane. After pedaling up around a couple scenic lakes, you soon visit a village named by French traders who saw the local Indian tribe fishing from their canoes at night by the light of torches. As you coast down along Fence Lake, you might see the resident eagle perched in a tree. Farther along you pass through a town named for an early lumber camp that is today home to the "Angel on Snowshoes." Coming full circle, you soon return to Minocqua.

Start: Bearskin State trailhead parking lot in Minocqua.
Length: 47 miles with 26-mile and 36-mile options.
Terrain: Gently rolling.
Traffic and hazards: Ride with caution on the

short stretches of highway, as traffic can be fast and abnormally heavy on Friday afternoons and Sunday mornings as tourists arrive and leave. There is no paved shoulder on Highway 70 from County Road F to your turn on Silver Beach Road.

Getting there: The trailhead parking lot is 2 blocks west of Highway 51 on Front Street in Minocqua.

From a resort community that is divided by two lakes, making it almost an island city, the ride begins at the Bearskin State trailhead. Early records mention a Chief

Minocquip of the Chippewa Indian tribe, who may have been the source of the city's name, though some claim that *Minocqua* means "mid-journey," "noon-day rest," or "a pleasant place to be." With its shores being in the center of the headwaters region, this was a stopping point between the Wisconsin and Flambeau Rivers for French missionaries, explorers, and early pioneers. In 1851 government surveyors found a Chippewa Indian village here called *Nin-oco-qua*. By the mid-1880s there were many lake cottage settlers and the Chicago, Milwaukee & St. Paul Railroad made its way across the lake and into this "pleasant place to be."

Here you have your first ride option: You can deduct 1.5 miles by riding the Bearskin State Trail across the railroad trestle over Minocqua Lake and south to Northern Road, then to Kawaga Road. The cruise leaves from this once-industrious railroad yard and journeys downtown on the one-way street that leads south out of town. You soon veer off on Old Highway 70, and then take a quick right on Northern Road. After another mile winding back and forth around the fingers of Kawaguesaga Lake, turn left on Kawaga Road. If you want a shorter option, turn right here on Northern Road for a 26-mile ramble.

Soon you are crossing the Bearskin State Trail as it heads south toward Merrill. After turning left on Agawak Road, the route now takes you around the south shore of Blue Lake (State Rustic Road 58) and on a series of rollers until crossing the Tomahawk River. Here you turn to the right and head north around Mercer Lake, then up to Highway 70.

For the next 5 miles the route uses the paved shoulder of Highway 70. Soon you pass Florshiem Road; those who prefer the 36-mile route should turn right here and follow the shoreline of Shishebogama Lake. The cruise continues traveling along the highway. After passing County Road F and for the next mile, use caution as the paved shoulder disappears as you ride into Vilas County. At Silver Beach Road the route heads north again and meanders around the southwest shore of Crawling Stone Lake up to Lac du Flambeau.

Now at about the 24-mile mark, this is a great place for lunch in a community that offers several rest stop options. In 1745 Chief Sharpened Stone led his Ojibwa band here from the east in fulfillment a prophecy that said that their journey would end when they found food that grew on water. It was in this area that they found wild rice growing in abundance. The name *Lac du Flambeau* (Lake of the Torches) comes from the French traders who observed the band's spring spearfishing ritual in which fish were attracted to the canoes with torchlight.

Every Tuesday evening during the summer, tribal members dance, sing, and drum at the Lac du Flambeau Indian Bowl. In the George W. Brown Jr. Ojibwa Museum and Cultural Center is a wonderful exhibit of the band's history in this land of plenty. When you visit you'll likely be greeted with *Boohoo,* which means "Hello," and when leaving, *Miigwetch, ga waa ba min,* or "Thank you, we'll be seeing you."

A mile north of town the cruise takes a right on Thorofare Road. For the next couple miles, enjoy the road's even descent, at a 5 percent grade, to the creek that

6 Pleasant Place Cruise

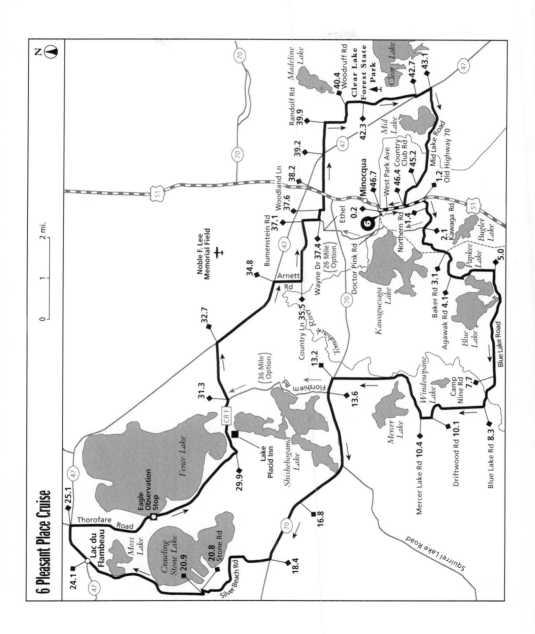

connects Crawling Stone and Fence Lakes. If you stop at the boat landing on Fence Lake, look along the south shore for the resident eagle perched in a nearby tree. At the 29.9-mile mark you turn left on County Road F and soon pass through the towering pines between Fence Lake and Placid Twin Lakes. If you haven't had lunch yet, the Lake Placid Inn makes a good place to stop.

Those who chose the 36-mile option will rejoin the cruise in another half mile at Florshiem Road. Now, reaching Highway 47, head southeast to Arnett Road. After turning left on Country Lane, step down to Wayne Drive, where the 26-mile option rejoins the cruise as it arrives in Woodruff.

When the Chicago & Northwestern Railroad built its line north, a terminal was established in 1905 next to the lumber camp of the Woodruff-McGuire Company. The railroad men became accustomed to using the phrase "for Woodruff," and the name was adopted. Today this area is part of the Minocqua community and is home to the Dr. Kate Museum and Historical Society. Called the "Angel on Snowshoes," her dream was to build a hospital in Woodruff. Dr. Kate needed one million pennies to build this medical facility, and with the help of area schoolchildren, donations came in from every state in the U.S. and from some foreign countries.

As you cross Highway 47 on County Road J, if you are in need of some ice cream or a little snack, stop at Hoggie Doggie's Snack Shack. At the 40-mile mark, leave County Road J and head south past the Art Ochmke State Fish Hatchery before reaching Clear Lake Forest State Park, where you will find restrooms if you need to stop. After a quick stint on the paved shoulder of Highway 47, find harmony on Mid Lake Road on your way back to explore downtown Minocqua.

Miles and Directions

0.0   From the Bearskin State trailhead, turn left on Front Street.

0.2   Take a right on Highway 51 in downtown Minocqua.

1.2   Take a right on Old Highway 70.

1.4   Take a right on Northern Road.

2.1   Turn left on Kawaga Road. **Option:** Turn right on Northern Road for the 26-mile option.

2.2   Turn left on Baker Road. (State Rustic Road 58 continues up to Highway 70.)

3.1   Cross Bearskin State Trail.

4.1   Turn left on Agawak Road.

5.0   Take a right on Blue Lake Road.

7.7   Pass Camp Nine Road.

8.3   After crossing the Tomahawk River, the route turns to the right and heads north.

10.1   Take a right on Driftwood Road.

10.4   Take a right on Mercer Lake Road.

13.2   Turn left on Highway 70.

13.6   Pass Florshiem Drive. **Option:** Take a right on Florshiem Road around Shishebogama Lake for the 36-mile option.

16.8 Pass County Road F.

18.4 Take a right on Silver Beach Road.

20.8 Turn left Stone Road.

20.9 Take a right on County Road O.

23.7 Arrive at Lac du Flambeau, with lunch and rest stop options.

24.1 Take a right on Highway 47.

25.1 Take a right on Thorofare Road.

27.3 Pass boat landing on Fence Lake.

29.9 Turn left on County Road F.

31.3 Pass Florshiem Road. (Note: The 36-mile option returns here.)

32.7 Take a right on Highway 47.

34.8 Take a right on Arnett Road.

35.5 Turn left on Country Lane.

37.1 Take a right on Bumenstein Road.

37.4 Turn left on Wayne Drive. (Note: The 26-mile option returns here.)

37.6 Take a right on Woodland Lane.

37.8 Turn left on Townline Road/County Road J.

38.2 Cross Highway 51.

39.2 Cross Highway 47.

39.9 Take a right on Randolf Road.

40.4 Turn left on Woodruff Road.

41.1 Pass Art Ochmke State Fish Hatchery.

42.3 Pass Clear Lake Forest State Park.

42.7 Turn left on Highway 47.

43.1 Take a right on Mid Lake Road.

44.4 Turn right on Thoroughfare Road.

45.2 Take a right on Country Club Road

46.4 Turn right on Highway 51.

46.7 Turn left on West Park Avenue.

47.0 Return to trailhead.

Local Information

Minocqua-Arbor-Vitae-Woodruff Area Chamber of Commerce, 15124 South Highway 51, Minocqua; (800) 446-6774; www .minocqua.org.
Lac du Flambeau Area Chamber of Commerce, 602 Peace Pipe Road, Lac du Flambeau; (877) 588-3346; www.lacduflambeau.com.

Local Events/Attractions

Dr. Kate Museum and Historical Society, 923 Second Avenue, Woodruff; (715) 356-6896; www.minocqua.org.
Northwoods Wildlife Center, 8683 Blumenstein Road/Highway 70, Minocqau; (715) 356-7400; www.northwoodswildlifecenter.com.
George W. Brown Jr. Ojibwa Museum and Cultural Center, 603 Peace Pipe Road, Lac du Flambeau; (715) 588-3333; www.ojibwe.com.

Restaurants

Tula's Cafe, 70 West Center, Minocqua; (715) 356-2847.

Hoggie Doggie's Snack Shack, Highway 51 and County Road J, Woodruff; (715) 356-5938.

Lake Placid Inn, 1520 County Road F, Lac du Flambeau; (715) 356-4202.

Accommodations

AmericInn, 700 Highway 51 North; (800) 634-3444.

Clear Lake Forest State Park, Woodruff Road, Woodruff; (715) 356-3668.

Bike Shops

Adventure Bicycles, 301 Front Street, Minocqua; (715) 356-1618.

Z Best Bikes, 329 Front Street, Minocqua; (715) 356-4224.

Restrooms

Start/finish: Bearskin State trailhead.

23.7: Lac du Flambeau Visitors Center.

38.2: Hoggie Doggie's Snack Shack in Woodruff.

42.3: Clear Lake Forest State Park.

Maps

DeLorme: Wisconsin Atlas and Gazetteer: Page 88 A3.

Wisconsin State Bicycle Map (Northern Section).

7 Musky Cruise

Blessed with the largest concentration of freshwater lakes in the world—and a large population of eagles—the roads in this area make it a wonderful place to enjoy cycling. This cruise leaves from a town with the same name as the river and follows its banks to the southwest. After crossing the Eagle River before it flows into the Wisconsin River, travel up to the Otto Hydro Dam for a self-guided tour. A couple more miles along the river and the route turns north, up past Snipe Lake Park. Enjoy the twists and turns on the undulating Musky Road. As the cruise meanders around the north shore of Lost Lake, make a sharp left and head over to Weber's Wildlife Family Bar. In another mile you are in a village named after a gentleman who moved here to manage a summer home for a Confederate colonel and became its first postmaster. Now swinging up to the northeast through the hardwoods, you will have the option to stop for ice cream in a town named in memory of Harry Star. Coming full circle, the route turns to the southeast and winds its way around several lakes, back through the pine forests, and returns to Eagle River.

Start: River Park in Eagle River.

Length: 48 miles with 18-mile and 33-mile options.

Terrain: Rolling.

Traffic and hazards: Extra care should be taken when leaving town on the paved shoulder of Highway 70.

Getting there: From eastbound Highway 70 turn left (north) on Highways 17/32/Highway 45 (Bridge Street) at the stoplight. Go 0.1 mile north and turn left on Willow Street. Cross Division

Gentle rollers like these await riders on the Musky Cruise.

Street and merge right onto West Riverview Drive to park. Downtown Eagle River is across the highway for your pre-ride supply needs.

This cruise leaves from River Park in a town with the same name as the river on which it is situated. Because there were so many eagles nesting in the area when platting the village in 1885, the Milwaukee, Lakeshore & Western Railroad took the name of the river. The Indian word for eagle is *mi-gis-iwis-ibi*.

After following the one-way lane from the park, you will take a right on Division Street and follow it around the county fairgrounds. At the four-lane Highways 17/70, take a right along its shoulder. After crossing the Mud Creek Bridge, where the Eagle River flows into the Wisconsin River and Highway 17 turns south, the cruise continues west on Highway 70.

As the Wisconsin River runs toward the Rainbow Flowage, you will soon pass the Otto Hydro Dam on your left. A self-guided tour is available here if you want to cross the highway onto Cloverland Drive. Another mile west and you will pass Hawks Nest Outfitters, which offers paddling and tubing opportunities on the river—a great way to cool off after the ride. At the 6-mile mark take a right on Wilderness Trail. For the next 4 miles the road grade gradually rises with many gentle rollers. Watch for deer as you meander up through the rich vegetation to Snipe Lake.

As you pass the southwest side of Snipe Lake, there is a wilderness park if you need to stop. After taking a right on Musky Road, for the next couple miles you will find a number of undulating rollers as you weave to the north. When you reach County Road G, the cruise heads northwest. Those who prefer the 18-mile ramble option turn right here and head east back to Eagle River.

For the next 5 miles the cruise continues its northerly course and then turns left on Four Corners Lane, which twists and turns along Lost Lake's north shore as you follow the route west. Those who prefer the 33-mile option should continue on County Road G. On the main ride, the road starts to dip south, making a sharp right at Lost Lake Road and then heading west to the paved shoulder of Highway 155. Eventually you pass Weber's Wildlife Family Bar. This is your best option for lunch, but if you prefer, it's only another mile to Sayner, where you will find a convenience store and a bar and grill.

This town was named for Orrin W. Sayner, who with his family arrived by train in Eagle River to take a job as caretaker for a summer home belonging to Confederate Colonel Tatum. Mr. Sayner built a summer resort and became the town's first postmaster in 1891. It was here in 1927 that Carl Eliason invented and patented the snowmobile. Today you can see the snowmobile exhibit while strolling down memory lane at the Vilas County Historical Museum.

As you ride east on County Road N, notice that the flora has change to rolling hardwoods. When you reach County Road K at the 25.7-mile mark, you have a side-trip option: Add an extra mile round-trip if you wish to go west to the store in Star Lake. This little community was developed in 1894 by the William and Salisch

7 Musky Cruise

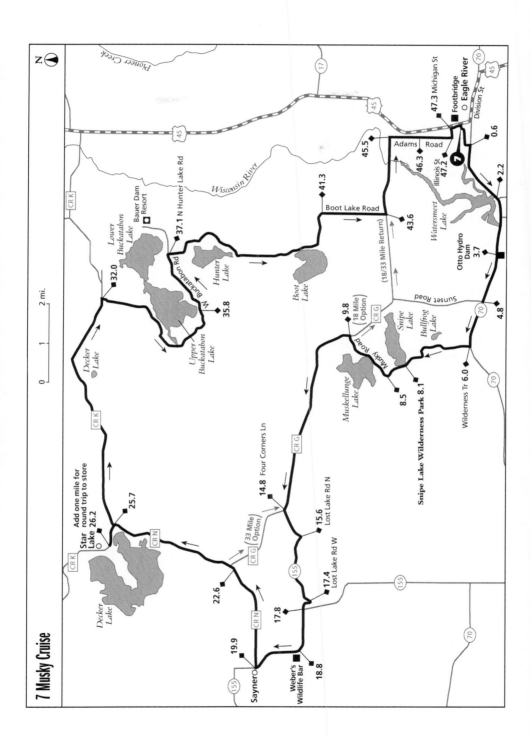

N

0   1   2 mi.

Pioneer Creek

CR K

Wisconsin River

17

45

45

47.3 Michigan St

Footbridge O Eagle River

70

45

Division St

47.2 Illinois St

0.6

Adams Road

46.3

45.5

2.2

Lower Buckatabon Lake

Bauer Dam Resort

Watersmeet Lake

Otto Hydro Dam 3.7

37.1 N Hunter Lake Rd

32.0

W Buckatabon Rd

Hunter Lake

41.3

Boot Lake Road

43.6

4.8

Boot Lake

(18/33 Mile Return)

70

35.8

Upper Buckatabon Lake

9.8

Snipe Lake

Sunset Road

CR K

Decker Lake

18 Mile (Option)

CR G

Bullfrog Lake

Wilderness Tr 6.0

25.7

Add one mile for round trip to store

Musky Road

8.5

70

Star Lake 26.2

CR N

Muskellunge Lake

Snipe Lake Wilderness Park 8.1

Decker Lake

22.6

CR G

14.8 Four Corners Ln

CR K

33 Mile Option

CR G

15.6

155

Lost Lake Rd N

19.9

17.4 Lost Lake Rd W

Sayner O

CR N

17.8

Weber's Wildlife Bar

18.8

155

70

70

155

Lumber Company and named in memory of Harry Star, who was killed by a pile driver as the tracks were being laid across a small bay to connect the railroad's roundhouse with the sawmill. Today the general store, a quarter mile off the route, is a good place to stop for ice cream, and you'll also find restrooms at the campground next door, if needed.

For the next 5 miles, as the cruise travels east on County Road K, the road meanders through a reforested area. Once you reach West Buckatabon Road, ride south and follow the route around Lower Buckatabon Lake. At the southern end, after passing the boat landing, it's just a short distance until you pass Camp Ramah. This camp was established in 1947 to offer children ages eleven to sixteen an opportunity to feel a part of the "great outdoors," while offering learning opportunities in the Hebrew language.

Now following the twisting lake road to the southeast, turn south on North Hunter Lake Road at the 37.1-mile mark. If you need a rest stop, the Bauer Dam Resort is 1 mile farther northeast. Continue south through pine forests to where the road merges onto Boot Lake Road and takes you all the way to County Road G, where the 18-mile and 33-mile options return.

As you ride east you will soon cross the Wisconsin River, at Dr. Oldfield Memorial Park. Take a right here on Adams Road and head south back into town. As Michigan Street approaches the highway, take a right onto the footbridge that crosses the Eagle River and head back to the park.

Miles and Directions

0.0 Head west on the one-way lane from River Park.

0.2 Take a right on Division Street.

0.6 Turn right on the four-lane Highway 17/70 through town.

2.2 At the junction of Highway 17, continue west on the paved shoulder of Highway 70.

4.8 Pass Sunset Road.

6.0 Take a right on Wilderness Trail.

8.1 Pass Snipe Lake Wilderness Park.

8.5 Take a right on Musky Road.

9.8 Turn left on County Road G. **Option:** Turn right on County Road G for the 18-mile option.

14.8 Turn left on Four Corners Lane.

15.6 Take a right on Lost Lake Road North.

17.4 Take a sharp right on Lost Lake Road West.

17.8 Turn onto the paved shoulder of Highway 155.

18.8 Pass Weber's Wildlife Family Bar.

19.9 Take a right on County Road N in Sayner.

22.6 Pass County Road G. **Option:** Turn right on County Road G for the 33-mile option.

25.7 Take a right on County Road K. **Side-trip:** Add 1 mile round-trip to go to the store in Star Lake.

32.0 Turn right on West Buckatabon Road.

35.8 Pass Camp Ramah.

37.1 Take a right on North Hunter Lake Road.

41.3 Take a right on Boot Lake Road.

43.6 Turn left on County Road G. (Note: The 18-mile and 33-mile options return here.)

45.5 After crossing the Wisconsin River, take a right on Adams Road.

46.3 Pass the airport.

47.2 Turn left on Illinois Street.

47.3 Take a right on Michigan Street.

47.7 Cross footbridge over Eagle River.

48.0 Return to park.

Local Information

Eagle River Area Chamber and Visitor Center, 201 North Rail Road Street, Eagle River; (800) 359-6315; www.eagleriver.org.

Three Eagle Trail Foundation, www.3eagletrail.com.

Local Events/Attractions

Eagle River Historical Museum, 519 East Sheridan Street, Eagle River; (715) 479-2396.

Vilas County Historical Museum, 1584 Highway 155, Sayner; (715) 542-3388.

Restaurants

Donna's Cafe, 4356 East Wall Street, Eagle River; (715) 479-6697.

Soda Pop's, 125 South Railroad Street, Eagle River; (715) 479-9424.

Weber's Wildlife Family Bar and Animal Park, 2649 Highway 155, Sayner; (715) 542-3781.

Accommodations

Wild Eagle Lodge, 4443 Chain O' Lakes Road, Eagle River; (877) 945-3965; www.wildeagle lodge.com.

Chain O' Lakes Campground, 3165 Campground Road, Eagle River; (715) 479-6708.

Bike Shops

Chain of Lakes Cyclery, 107 Railroad Street, Eagle River; (715) 479-3920.

Restrooms

Start/finish: River Park.

2.2: Wayside rest, junction of Highway 17.

8.1: Snipe Lake Wilderness Park (no water).

18.8: Weber's Wildlife Family Bar.

19.1: Vilas County Historical Museum in Sayner.

26.2: Star Lake Campground.

45.5: Dr. Oldfield Memorial Park.

Maps

DeLorme: Wisconsin Atlas and Gazetteer: Page 89 A6.

Wisconsin State Bicycle Map (Northern Section).

Eagle River Area Visitors Map.

8 Hodag Cruise

"Don't let the Hodag scare you!" That's what the local community stresses, even though it was a hoax created in 1868. The folklore surrounding this frightening monster with razor-sharp claws has turned the local legend into a celebration throughout the years. Like the Hodag's backbone, bristling with dozens of gleaming white horns, the route you are soon to embark on is filled with hairpin curves that reach up into the fingers of the lakes you pass. You will enjoy rolling through the forest at the north end of the cruise on Gypsy Road, where black squirrels are common. On River Road you ride into a town where baseball is played on snowshoes. On the homestretch you will follow a route with jagged right and left turns. It is like you were stepping down the beast's back as you follow along the flowage of the Wisconsin River back to Hodag Park in Rhinelander.

Start: Hodag Park in Rhinelander.
Length: 54 miles with 28- and 38-mile options.

Terrain: Rolling with a couple moderate climbs.
Traffic and hazards: Beware of heavy traffic on County Road W.

Getting there: From the east side of Rhinelander on Highway 8, head north on Highway 17. At Stevens Avenue turn west and take a right on West Monica Street. As you enter the park, follow the one-way Hodag Park Drive to the parking area.

In an area with vast forests and crystal clear lakes, this cruise starts in the city of Rhinelander. Originally platted in 1872 as Pelican Rapids, the name was changed when the railroad company came through. That fall the town was renamed to honor the president of the Milwaukee, Lakeshore & Western Railroad, F. W. Rhinelander of New York City. The town was already unofficially known as the City of the Hodag, a mythical creature invented by the famous cruiser, surveyor, and prankster, Eugene Shepard.

Leave from Hodag Park, on the shores of the Rhinelander Flowage, and head northwest on County Road W. When you come to the Kozy Korner Supper Club, turn left on Pine Lake Road and follow this semi-flat lane north. Those who prefer the 28- or 38-mile options should turn left at Spider Lake Road, about 3 miles ahead. The Hodag Cruise continues north for 7 more miles to County Road D. Now traveling west, you pass the Menonomie Sports Camp for Boys, which was established in 1928, and in another 3 miles you pass a cranberry farm at North Nokomis Lake.

Turn onto Gypsy Road and watch for black squirrels as you meander past several lakes as you ride south. At River Road turn right and continue west. Here the 38-mile ramble option returns as you take a left. Before crossing the Wisconsin

Don't let the Hodag Monster scare you!

River at the 30-mile mark, you will pass Newbold Memorial Park, and in another 3 miles you will turn north into the village of Lake Tomahawk, with several rest stop options.

This community was settled on the east shore of the lake after the Milwaukee, Lakeshore & Western Railroad came through on its way from Rhinelander. Many years earlier, according to an Indian peace council tradition, somewhere on the shores of the lake, a tomahawk was buried to symbolize that the two warring tribes had settled their differences. Today the town is famous for its snowshoe baseball. At a custom-built ballpark, with an infield covered with a heavy mat of wood chips, the locals play baseball with snowshoes on their feet. It's a town highlight that happens every Monday at 7:00 p.m. and is a great story to share with your friends after visiting the area.

From the ballpark the cruise leaves on the back streets through town and jogs to the right on County Road D. After riding a short distance on Kildare Road, travel 3.4 miles on the paved shoulder of Highway 47 to McNaughton. Here you will discover when you turn left on Bridge Road that the only thing left in this town is the general store. Originally called Hazelhurst Junction, it was renamed McNaughton for the foreman of a large sawmill operation. At the same time the Milwaukee, Lakeshore & Western Railroad created a spur line to Hurley.

8 Hodag Cruise

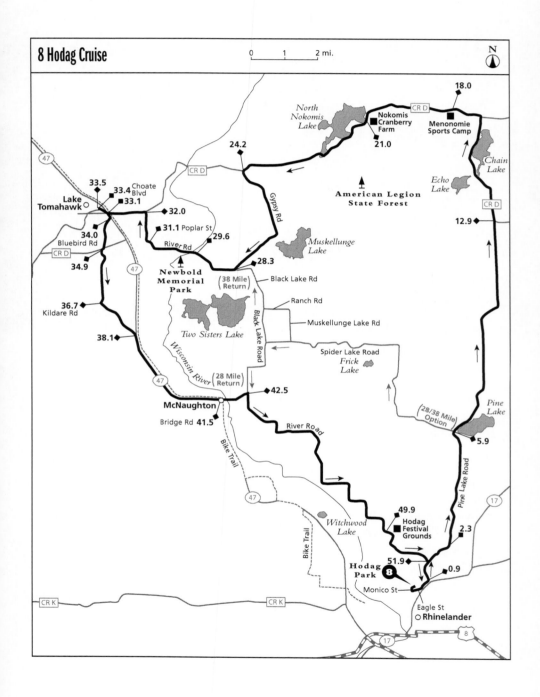

0   1   2 mi.

N

North Nokomis Lake

Nokomis Cranberry Farm   18.0

Menonomie Sports Camp   21.0

Chain Lake

Echo Lake

CR D

24.2

Gypsy Rd

American Legion State Forest

CR D

12.9

47

33.5
33.4 Choate Blvd
33.1
Lake Tomahawk
32.0

31.1 Poplar St
29.6

34.0
Bluebird Rd
River Rd

CR D

34.9

Muskellunge Lake

28.3

47

Newbold Memorial Park

(38 Mile Return)   Black Lake Rd

Ranch Rd

Muskellunge Lake Rd

36.7
Kildare Rd

38.1

Two Sisters Lake

Black Lake Road

Spider Lake Road
Frick Lake

Pine Lake

Wisconsin River

(28 Mile Return)

(28/38 Mile) Option

47

42.5

5.9

McNaughton

Bridge Rd   41.5

River Road

Bike Trail

17

Pine Lake Road

Bike Trail

Witchwood Lake

47

49.9
Hodag Festival Grounds

2.3

51.9

0.9

Hodag Park

8

Monico St

CR K

CR K

Eagle St
Rhinelander

17

8

Now riding on River Road again, the cruise follows the Rhinelander Flowage southeast, past the Hodag Festival Grounds, on route back to the park in Rhinelander. After returning, enjoy a refreshing dip in Boom Lake or explore the town with the self-guided Historic Walking Tour that starts at the tourism office.

Miles and Directions

0.0   Leave Hodag Park on Hodag Park Drive.

0.3   Turn left on Monico Street.

0.5   Turn left on Eagle Street.

0.9   Turn left on County Road W. (**Note:** There is a BP station a block to the left.)

1.6   Pass River Road.

2.3   Turn left on Pine Lake Road at Kozy Korner Supper Club.

5.9   Pass Spider Lake Road. **Options**: Turn left on Spider Lake Road for the 28- and 38-mile options. For the 28-mile route, take Spider Lake Road to Black Lake Road and head west/southwest on Black Lake Road. For the 38-mile route, go right on Muskellunge Lake Road at 8.5 miles, then left on Ranch Road, then right (north) on Black Lake Road to River Road where you join the main ride.

12.9   Turn left on County Road D.

18.0   Pass Menonomie Sports Camp for Boys.

21.0   Pass Nokomis Cranberry Farm.

24.2   Turn left on Gypsy Road.

28.3   Take a right on River Road.

29.6   Pass Newbold Memorial Park.

31.1   Take a right on Poplar Street.

32.0   Turn left on County Road D.

33.1   Take a right on Highway 47 into Lake Tomahawk.

33.4   Turn left on Choate Boulevard.

33.5   Turn left on Iris Street at Lake Tomahawk Ballpark.

33.6   Turn left on Rainbow Road.

33.7   Take a right on Lilly Street.

34.0   Take a right on Bluebird Road.

34.9   Jog to the right on County Road D.

36.7   Turn left on Kildare Road.

38.1   Take a right on the paved shoulder of Highway 47.

41.5   Turn left on Bridge Road at McNaughton.

42.5   Take a right on River Road (Note: The 28-mile option returns here.)

49.9   Pass Hodag Festival Grounds.

51.9   Take a right on County Road W.

52.5   Turn right on Eagle Street.

52.9   Take a right on Monico Street.

53.2 Turn left on Thayer Street.

53.4 Take a right on Madison Street.

53.8 Take a right on Hodag Park Drive.

54.0 Return to park.

Local Information

Rhinelander Chamber of Commerce, Highway 8 and Sutliff Avenue, Rhinelander; (800) 236-4386; www.rhinelanderchamber.com.

Local Events/Attractions

Hodag County Fest; second weekend in July; (800) 762-3803; www.hodag.com.

Smokin Spoke Race, Camp Tesomas, Rhinelander; last Sunday in April; (715) 369-1999; www.bike-n-board.com.

Logging Museum in Pioneer Park, 124 Oneida Avenue, Rhinelander; (715) 365-8625; www.rhinelanderchamber.com.

Restaurants

The Garden of Eatin', 46 North Brown Street, Rhinelander; (715) 369-5333.

Three Coins Restaurant, 4060 South Shore Drive, Rhinelander; (800) 261-1500; www.holidayacres.com.

Happy Daze, 7247 Bradley Street, Lake Tomahawk; (715) 277-2523.

Accommodations

Holiday Acres Resort, 4060 South Shore Drive, Rhinelander; (800) 261-1500; www.holidayacres.com.

West Bay Camping Resort, 4330 South Shore Drive, Rhinelander; (715) 362-2481.

Bike Shops

Bikes & Boards, 1670 North Stevens Street, Rhinelander; (715) 369-1999.

Mel's Trading Post, 105 South Brown Street, Rhinelander; (800) 236-6357.

Restrooms

Start/finish: Hodag Park.

0.9: BP station.

29.6: Newbold Memorial Park.

33.5: Lake Tomahawk Ballpark.

41.5: McNaughton General Store.

49.9: Hodag Festival Grounds.

Maps

DeLorme: Wisconsin Atlas and Gazetteer: Page 89 C5.

Wisconsin State Bicycle Map (Northern Section).

9 Rib Falls Challenge

In the center of Wisconsin you will find a beautiful area of rolling plains, hills, and a couple geographic wonders. First is Rib Mountain, now the home of Granite Peak Ski Area. To the east of this magnificent rock formation, which has withstood millions of years of glacial movement and floods, is a town whose name means "far away." As the route departs from this town on the Wisconsin River, it gradually climbs the ridge. Rolling past plots of ginseng, you soon arrive in another river town that was named by Indians for a set of falls. Farther east visit a town "halfway to the North Pole and halfway around the Western Hemisphere" and join the 45 x 90 Club—it's one of only four such spots on the globe. Circling through rolling farmland, the ride turns north and passes through a village that settlers felt had similar topography to Athens, Greece. As you turn back to the east, you pass a crossroads settlement named for the moonshine sold there during the Prohibition era. Now heading south, ride down a rolling lane back to Wausau.

Start: Marathon Park in Wausau.
Length: 54 miles with a 37-mile option.
Terrain: Rolling with a couple steep hills.

Traffic and hazards: Use caution riding on Stewart Avenue out of Wausau and Highway 97 into Athens, as traffic can be moving fast.

Getting there: From Highway 51 in Wausau, take exit 192 to Highway 52 east. At 17th Avenue the highway mergers into Stewart Avenue; the park entrance is another block on your right.

Surrounded by waterways, woods, and valleys, you will find the roads around Rib Mountain's lurking shadows a challenge, but fun. Here, next to Wisconsin's second-highest elevated point, the ride leaves from Wausau.

Early voyageurs traveling north from the Indian station at Dubay originally called this place Big Bull Falls, for the roar of the falls that sounded like the lowing of a bull. George Stevens, of Stevens Point, acquired land from the Indians here so he could use the waterpower to build a sawmill. Then in 1841 the Honorable W. D. McInode selected the pretty Indian word *Wausau* as a more fitting name for the town. This Chippewa word means "far away" and speaks of the place a long distance from their ancestral hunting grounds in eastern Canada.

As you leave from Marathon Park, you will find a community of six villages that have come together, offering many pre- and post-ride opportunities. Use caution turning left out the park as you pass through the regulated intersection and merge into the left turn lane to continue on Stewart Avenue. Traveling west on the paved shoulder of Stewart Avenue, you will pass several cafes and a convenience store before riding under Highway 51 and then Highway 29, which brings visitors into town.

9 Rib Falls Challenge

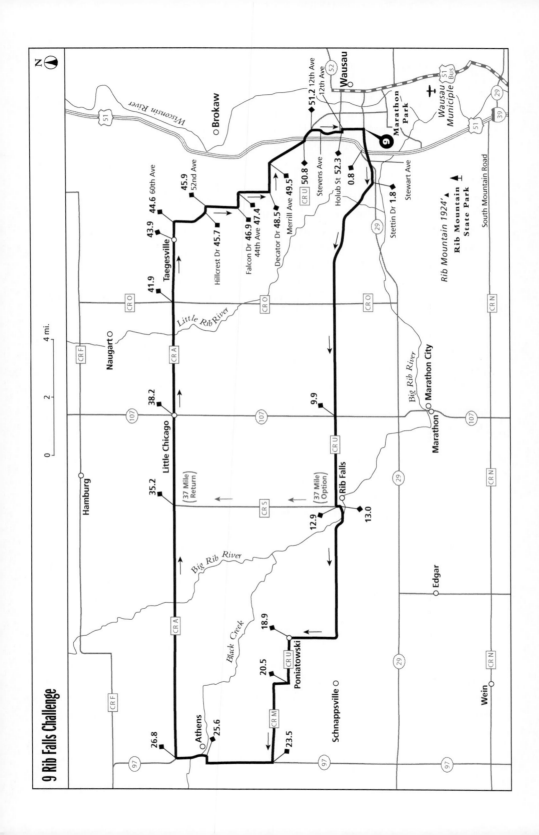

N

4 mi.

2

0

Hamburg

CR F

CR F

Naugart

CR A

CR A

Little Rib River

CR O

CR O

CR O

CR O

Taegesville

41.9

43.9

44.6 60th Ave

45.9 52nd Ave

Hillcrest Dr 45.7

Falcon Dr 46.9
44th Ave 47.4

Decator Dr 48.5

Merrill Ave 49.5

CR U 50.8

Stevens Ave

Holub St 52.3

51.2 12th Ave
12th Ave

Wausau

51 Bus

52

Brokaw

Wisconsin River

51

Little Chicago

38.2

107

107

35.2

(37 Mile Return)

CR S

(37 Mile Option)

Rib Falls

9.9

CR U

12.9

13.0

Big Rib River

Marathon City

Marathon

107

29

Big Rib River

0.8

29

Stettin Dr 1.8

Stewart Ave

Rib Mountain 1924'
Rib Mountain
State Park

South Mountain Road

Marathon Park

Wausau
Municiple

39

29

51

9

Athens

26.8

25.6

97

CR M

20.5

23.5

Poniatowski

CR U

18.9

Schnappsville

Black Creek

Edgar

29

CR N

CR N

Wein

CR N

97

97

Jut to the right on Stettin Drive and head in a northwest direction with a moderate incline. After crossing the Little Rib River, the road starts to undulate as you pass several ginseng farms. Ginseng is a plant used for medicinal and energy-enhancing purposes that once grew wild here. Due to a huge worldwide demand, especially in Asia, in 1880s farmers started cultivating the plant by shading it. Today the crop is grown in plots in a contoured field, with a black web fabric shading the plants until harvest.

Soon you pass through Stettin, which in 1860 was settled by immigrants who took the name from a town in their northern Poland homeland. The village is now a part of Wausau. Continuing west, you soon cross Highway 107 onto County Road U for some more rollers. At County Road S turn south and cross the Rib River into Rib Falls. Those who prefer the 37-mile option will turn right here.

Settled in 1876, the town took its name from the river, which winds down from a mountain that was also named Rib by the Indians. Here you will find a park next to the falls and a couple of taverns at the south end of the village. After passing these establishments turn on County Road U and continue riding west. Here the terrain levels out, and at about the 19-mile mark you enter Poniatowski.

The immigrants that settled here named the village after King Stanislaw August Poniatowski, the last king of Poland in the late 1700s. Today, with only two bars, a cemetery, and a few houses, the town is visited regularly by thousands of people from all over the world and receives occasional media attention because its location is "halfway to the North Pole and halfway around the Western Hemisphere." This is where the principal latitude and longitude crosshairs on most maps and globes intersect at 45 and 90 degrees. Of the four spots like it on the planet, two are underwater and the other is in the middle of China. To see the actual USGS benchmark, you will have to travel a half mile east of town on Cherry Lane to Robin Road (both gravel). When you return to Wausau, stop by the visitors center and join the 45 x 90 Club. It's free! Just sign the register and you will receive a shiny 45 x 90 medallion.

For the next 3 miles the challenge continues west over rolling corn fields and then turn right on Highway 97. Use caution on the secondary highway, as there is no paved shoulder riding north into Athens. Originally settled as a sawmill town in 1879, the village was known as Black Creek Falls but a year later was renamed Athens by a townsman for his love of classic Greek and the similar topography of Athens, Greece. You will find several options for lunch here, including the Hamburger Hopper and Country Cafe, in addition to a tranquil park setting if you packed a lunch.

After heading north out of town, you will soon come to County Road A and turn east. For the next 18 miles the route offers a semi-rolling cruise as you ride by several old farm sites and a couple small villages along the way. You will pass County Road S, where the 37-mile option returns to the route, and then cross Highway 107 and pass through the village of Little Chicago. Here at the crossroads a settlement with a couple of taverns was established in the early 1900s. The name was reportedly given to one of the site's taverns during Prohibition, allegedly because moonshine was sold at or near the corner. There is still a tavern here, along with a few residences and a car dealership.

As you continue east, after crossing the Little Rib River again, you will experience another climb and soon pass through Taegesville. This village was originally established in 1870 as the town of Maine, taking the name of the township. The name was changed in 1891 when William Taege, who had a tavern here, became the postmaster. The tavern still stands today as the Schmidt Ballroom.

Past Taegesville, turn right on 60th Avenue. The route now travels south and continues to jog slightly to the east as you cruise down the rolling roads, past hobby farms and housing developments, back to Wausau.

Miles and Directions

0.0   Turn left on Stewart Avenue from Marathon Park.

0.2   Cross 17th Avenue and move into the center lane to make a right on Stewart Avenue.

0.8   Cross under Highway 51.

1.2   Cross under Highway 29.

1.8   Take a right on Stettin Drive.

9.9   Cross Highway 107 onto County Road U.

12.9   Turn left on County Road S into Rib Falls. **Option:** Turn right on County Road S for the 37-mile option.

13.0   Take a right on County Road U.

18.9   Turn left on County Road U in Poniatowski.

20.5   Take a right on County Road M.

23.5   Take a right on Highway 97.

25.6   Pass through Athens.

26.8   Take a right on County Road A.

35.2   Pass County Road S. (Note: The 37-mile option returns here.)

38.2   Cross Highway 107 in Little Chicago.

41.9   Cross County Road O.

43.9   Pass Taegesville.

44.6   Take a right on 60th Avenue.

45.7   Turn left on Hillcrest Street.

45.9   Take a right on 52nd Avenue.

46.9   Turn left on Falcon Drive. (Note: There is no sign.)

47.4   Take a right 44th Avenue.

48.5   Turn left on Decator Drive.

49.5   Take a right on Merrill Avenue.

50.8   Turn left on County Road U.

50.9   Cross Highway 51.

51.2 Take a right on 12th Avenue/Stevens Avenue.

52.3 Turn left on Hulub Street.

52.4 Take a right on 12th Avenue.

54.0 Cross Stewart Avenue and arrive back at the park.

Local Information

Wausau/Central Wisconsin Convention and Visitors Bureau, 10204 Park Plaza, Wausau; (888) 948-4748; www.visitwausau.com.

Local Events/Attractions

Leigh Yawkey Woodson Art Museum, Franklin and 12th, Wausau; (715) 845-7103.

Yawkey House Museum, Marathon County Historical Society, 403 McInoe Street, Wausau; (715) 848-0378.

Rudy Rack Big Ring Classic; first weekend in June; (715) 592-5095; www.wors.org.

Restaurants

Annie's American Cafe, 305 South 18th Avenue, Wausau; (715) 842-0846.

Wausau Mine Company, 39th and Stewart Avenues, Wausau; (715) 845-7304.

Athens Country Cafe, 220 Alfred Street, Athens; (715) 257-7477.

Accommodations

Lodge At Cedar Creek, 805 Creske Avenue, Wausau; (888) 365-6343; www.lodgeatcedar creek.com.

Marathon County Park, 1201 Stewart Avenue, Wausau; (715) 261-1566.

Rib Mountain State Park, 4200 Park Road, Wausau; (715) 842-2522; www.wiparks.net.

Bike Shops

Builer's Cycle & Fitness, 215 South Third Avenue, Wausau; (715) 842-4185.

City Bike Works, 908 Third Avenue, Wausau; (715) 845-1656.

Jammer Sports, Inc., 4600 Rib Mountain Drive, Wausau; (715) 355-4844.

Rib Mountain Cycles, Inc., 3716 Rib Mountain Drive, Wausau; (715) 359-3925.

Shepard & Schaller Sporting Goods, 324 Scott Street, Wausau; (715) 845-5432.

Restrooms

Start/finish: Marathon Park.

12.9: Rib Falls Park.

25.6: Athens City Park.

Maps

DeLorme: Wisconsin Atlas and Gazetteer: Page 64 A3.

Wisconsin State Bicycle Map (Central Section).

Wausau Wheelers Bike Loops (www.wausau wheelers.org).

Western Wisconsin

10 Mound Builders Challenge

Situated along the Red Cedar River, this challenge begins in a town where mystery and questions still exist on what exactly happened to the area's first residents in AD 1200. You leave along a lake created by a logging-era sawmill and pass by some of the mounds the early inhabitants left behind. As you cruise over the countryside, the route passes through a town with a beautiful historic church before passing a herd of buffalo. Reaching the upper end of Red Cedar Lake, you arrive in a town named for the white birch growing along the lake's north shore. Now traveling south, the terrain becomes more rugged. Riding by Murphy's Flowage, the route soon rolls through the Blue Hills before visiting a village named after a successful lumber baron. Circling to the east, you will pass the intersection where a town once stood that counted on the railroad to pass through, but the line went south leaving only some ghost lore. The residents of the next town you come to also moved when the railroad came through 3 miles to the north. As you come full circle, the route passes over the flowage of the Red Cedar River back to the park in Rice Lake.

Start: Narrows Park in Rice Lake.
Length: 66 miles with 30-mile and 46-mile options.
Terrain: Rolling with a couple moderate climbs.

Traffic and hazards: Traffic on county roads can be fast. Care should be taken when riding on Highway 48 up to Birchwood.

Getting there: From Highway 53 take the County Road O exit into Rice Lake. At County Road SS (Old Highway 53), turn left and travel north to County Road C/Sawyer Street and take a right a half mile to the park.

In 1935 an archaeologist discovered that the first inhabitants in this area were Mound Builders. After the discovery of two clay death masks, the Wisconsin Historical Society estimated that a tribe was here around AD 1200. Those masks are now at the Museum of Science in Milwaukee. We know the Mound Builders made large earthen structures in perfect squares or circles without the benefit of levels or T squares, but who were they, and where did they go? It's still a mystery, and some speculate that they assimilated into other tribes like the Santee Sioux, who moved into the area in the mid-1500s. Check the facts, and you be the judge!

The Knapp Stout Lumber Company established its logging center south of the Red Cedar River in 1868. Along the river's edge at the time were wild rice pools, rush swamps, and an Indian village called *Manominikaning*, Chippewa for "wild rice," or the "wild rice place." After building the logging camp here, the lumber company built a dam, which transformed the rice pools into the lake. Then in 1887 the Chippewa Falls & Northern Railroad came through, and the city was granted a municipal charter and named Rice Lake.

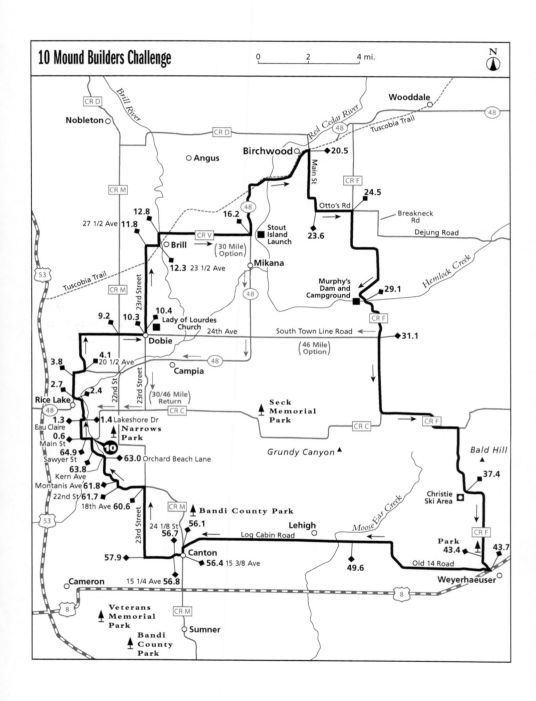

10 Mound Builders Challenge

0   2   4 mi.

N

After leaving from Narrows Park, on Rice Lake, the route takes you north on Main Street. Along the way stop at the visitor center at 37 South Main Street and pick up a Historic Walking Guide of Downtown Rice Lake to stretch you legs after the ride. Three blocks north of the chamber office, the route jogs over to Lakeshore Drive and rides up along Rice Lake past Indian Mound Park, where the Mound Builders' death masks were discovered. After taking a right at the corner, you'll come to Miller Cheese House, where Highway 48 travels east. Ride the paved shoulder to 20 ½ Avenue and head north up along Stump Lake. For the next 8 miles the route offers easy riding as you roll through farm fields on your way to Dobie.

In 1878 Father Dole arrived here and established the community along with the historic Our Lady of Lourdes Catholic Church. This small village at the 11.3-mile mark offers a beautiful church, a few homes, and an eating establishment if you need to stop. As you leave town, watch for buffalo grazing on your right. You will soon arrive in Brill as you continue north. This little village was named after Judge Brill of St. Paul, who was a railroad attorney, and was established back when the Rice Lake, Dallas & Menomonie Railroad (Soo Line) reached north, from Rice Lake up to the timber areas.

As you ride east over lightly rolling terrain, the route soon turns left on the paved shoulder of Highway 48. Here at the corner is the parking lot for the ferry that takes visitors over to Stout Island on Red Cedar Lake. Frank D. Stout inherited part of his father's lumber fortune in 1900, moved to Chicago, and became one of the wealthiest men in the country. In 1903 he moved his family and servants to the island for the summer months. Modeled after the famous Adirondack camps, the lodge was built with plank flooring, carved beams from Germany, and cedar logs from Idaho. This beautiful island sanctuary is now an inn with a restaurant and thirty-one guest rooms. If you are in the area for a couple days, the author highly recommends that you call them to make a dinner reservation and take a tour of the property.

If you prefer the 30-mile option, take a right on Highway 48 and head south. Otherwise, the challenge travels north up along the shore of Red Cedar Lake to Main Street in Birchwood. This village was named by George M. Huss, who was the president of the Soo Line Railroad. As he was buying up plats along the right-of-way from Ridgeland to Reserve, he noticed that white birch was prevalent along the lakeshore here so he named the village Birchwood. You can stop here at Grumpy's Grill or the Porch Restaurant if you are ready for lunch.

Now heading south on Main Street, the challenge jogs to the southeast on Otto's Road before taking a right on County Road F. As the terrain becomes more rolling, you will pass Murphy's Dam and Campground from the Murphy Flowage. At the 31.1-mile mark the route passes South Town Line Road. Here the 46-mile option turns right and heads back to the west.

The terrain become more rugged and forested as the challenge continues south, and soon you are rolling past the entrance of Christie Ski Area in the Blue Hills. This beautiful swath of hill country runs from Rusk County to Rice Lake and is well-known for its Alpine and Nordic skiing in the winter. For the next 5 miles shift into your high ring and cruise down to Weyerhaeuser. Fredrick Weyerhaeuser, founder of Weyerhaeuser Lumber Company, developed his fortunes by harvesting the virgin white pine timber in Wisconsin. One of his headquarters was located here, and in 1870 the village took his name. As you cruise into town, you will pass a community park and a couple taverns if you need to stop.

After leaving town on Railroad Avenue, the route rolls east and passes several little lakes. If it is a hot day and you need to cool off, there is a nice beach and tavern on Bass Lake. Continuing along, pass Log Cabin Road. On the north side of this intersection once stood a village, settled in 1887, called Strickland. When the rail line was built to the south and Lehigh was made a stopping point, the town was abandoned. It is said that the area where the settlement once stood is haunted. Legend has it that one of the founding fathers suffered a tragic death after losing his investment building the town.

As you continue east, the route rolls up to County Road M, crosses the railroad tracks, and jogs south onto 15 ⅞ Avenue in Canton. Around 1870 this village was settled with the name Sumner, but when the St. Paul & Sault Ste. Marie Railroad built tracks through Barron County in 1884, the town had to be moved 3 miles to the north, to its present location. After platting the new site, a post office was established and it was discovered that there was already a town named Sumner in the state. Because most of the townspeople were from Canton, Ohio, they renamed it for their hometown. The challenge shuffles through this bedroom community with fractions in its street names and continues east out of town.

After another mile, the route circles to the north on 23rd Street and jogs back to the park in Rice Lake. After loading up your bike, pull out the historic walking tour brochure of the downtown area and stretch those legs.

Miles and Directions

0.0 From Narrows Park, turn right onto Sawyer Street.

0.6 Take a right on Main Street/County Road SS.

1.0 Pass the Rice Lake chamber after crossing the river.

1.3 Take a right on Eau Claire Street.

1.4 Turn left on Lakeshore Drive.

2.4 Take a right on Highway 48.

2.7 Turn right on Lakeshore Drive.

3.8 Take a right on Highway 48.

4.1 Turn left on 20½ Avenue.

7.7 Take a right on 24th Avenue.

9.2 Cross County Road M.

10.3 Turn left on 23rd Street in Dobie.

10.4 Pass Our Lady of Lourdes Catholic Church.

11.7 Watch for buffalo to your right.

11.8 Take a right on 27½ Avenue into Brill.

12.3 Turn left on 23½ Street.

12.8 Take a right on County Road V.

16.2 Take a left on Highway 48 at the Stout Island Launch. **Option:** Turn right on Highway 48 for the 30-mile option.

20.5 Take a right on Main Street in Birchwood.

23.6 Turn left on Otto's Road.

24.5 Take a right on County Road F.

29.1 Pass Murphy's Dam and Campground.

31.1 Pass South Town Line Road. **Option:** Turn right on South Town Line Road for the 46-mile option.

37.4 Pass Christie Ski Area.

39.0 Pass Blue Hills.

43.4 Pass city park in Weyerhaeuser.

43.7 Take a right on Railroad Avenue (changes to Old 14 Road).

49.6 Pass Strickland (ghost town) at Log Cabin Road intersection.

56.1 Turn left on County Road M.

56.4 Take a right on 15⅜ Avenue in Canton.

56.7 Turn left on 24⅛ Street.

56.8 Take a right on 15¼ Avenue.

57.9 Take a right on 23rd Street.

60.6 Turn left on 18th Avenue.

61.7 Take a right on 22nd Street.

61.8 Turn left on Montanis Avenue.

63.0 Turn left on Orchard Beach Lane.

63.8 Take a right on Kern Avenue.

64.9 Take a right on Sawyer Street.

66.0 Return to park.

Local Information

Rice Lake Tourism Commission, 37 South Main Street, Rice Lake; (800) 523-6318; www.ricelaketourism.com.

Local Events/Attractions

Pioneer Village Museum, 15132 County Road West Cameron; (715) 458-2841.

Tuscobia State Trail and Ice Age National Trail, north on County Road SS, Rice Lake; (715) 266-3511; www.tuscobiatrail.com.

Blue Northern 50; second week in June; Northroads Bicycle Club; (715) 234-4127.

Return to Forever; first Sunday in August; Northroads Bicycle Club; (715) 234-4127.

Tour de Color; third Saturday in September; Barron Electric; (800) 322-1008; www.barron electric.com.

Restaurants

Lehman's Supper Club, 2911 South Main Street, Rice Lake; (715) 234-9911.

Leroy's Bakery & Coffee Shop, 630 South Main Street, Rice Lake; (715) 234-3066.

Stout's Lodge, boat landing at Highway 48 and County Road V, Mikana; (715) 354-3646; www.stoutslodge.com.

Accommodations

AmericInn of Rice Lake Lodge & Suites; 2906 Pioneer Avenue South, Rice Lake; (715) 234-9060.

Shady Rest Campground, 2883 17 ¾ Street, Rice Lake; (715) 234-7339.

Bike Shops

Back Road Bike Too, 17 East Messenger Street, Rice Lake; (715) 736-6969.

Restrooms

Start/finish: Narrows Park.
1.0: Rice Lake chamber after crossing river.
20.5: Park in Birchwood.
29.1: Murphy's Dam and Campground.
43.4: City park in Weyerhaeuser.

Maps

DeLorme: Wisconsin Atlas and Gazetteer: Pages 72 A2 and 84 D3.

Wisconsin State Bicycle Map (Northern and Mississippi River Sections).

11 Step Back in Time Challenge

Recapture those memories of visiting grandma on the farm, and step back to a time when life was much simpler. This challenge leaves from a river town named in honor of Ulysses S. Grant, at a location where Snow Flake Flour was once milled. As you ride north, you follow a trail of golden geese up through the Crex Meadows State Wildlife Area, where you discover what the area looked like when the pioneers first laid eyes on this land. Now, as you make your way east, the route takes you up to Balcome Bridge and crosses over the Clam Lake Flowage. You then turn southeast and discover a French fort on the Yellow River where you are greeted with a sign that says BOOZ HOO. After riding around a lake with the same name as the river, step back fifty years and visit a town with the 1950s Americana look. Turning to the southwest, enjoy an ice-cream cone in a village named after a cream separator. As you come full circle, you pass Crex Meadows one more time before the golden geese guide you back to Grantsburg.

Start: Memorial Park in Grantsburg.
Length: 62 miles with 22-mile and 43-mile options.
Terrain: Rolling with a few small hills.

Traffic and hazards: Traffic can be fast when riding on County Road F and on the shoulder of Highway 70.

Getting there: From Highway 70 turn north on South Russell Street in Grantsburg. At West Olson Drive, turn left and follow the road to the park.

This challenge leaves from Grantsburg, a village the Indians originally named "the great cranberry place." The Honorable Canute Anderson came to the area in 1851 and established a post office called Burnett, the same name as the county is today, which was named for the early Wisconsin legislator Thomas P. Burnett. Fifteen years later Anderson built a sawmill and laid out the village, naming it in honor of General Ulysses S. Grant, who was popular at the time because of his victory at the Battle of Vicksburg.

John Deere Crossing is a fine place to stretch your legs.

On the west side of town in Memorial Park, where the ride begins, is the site where the Hickerson Roller Mill once stood. The mill produced Snow Flake Flour and ran from 1860 to 1917. If you have an interest, there is a stone marker next to the dam on the Wood River that details the story of the mill.

As you head north out of town, follow the golden geese painted on the pavement. This trail of geese will lead you out to the Crex Meadows Visitor Center. Crex Meadows is a 30,000-acre state wildlife management area that was drastically altered by settlers in the 1800s. Around 1912 the Crex Carpet Company purchased a large amount of the acreage here to produce grass rugs, a popular floor covering before linoleum flooring was developed. The company went out of business around the time of the Great Depression, but the Crex name remained. Through prairie and wetland restoration, this area today is a spectacular wildlife showplace offering bicycling opportunities. Before heading north, you may want to stop at the visitor center and pick up some useful information about the meadows and what you might see there.

For the first 15 miles this tour circles up and around the northwest end of the meadows, where you can see what the area must have looked like when the early settlers first arrived. The first 5 miles is fairly flat as you head north on County Road F along the western boundary of the refuge. After turning on North Refuge Road into the wildlife area, the paved lane offers moderate rollers and is a good place to see songbirds in the tree-lined windbreaks. Soon you pass Reigel Overlook, where deer, cranes, and geese are easy to spot. This overlook is about 0.1 mile south on a gravel road. At the 9.6-mile mark is Currey Road. If you are low on supplies, you can go 1 mile north to County Road F and then 1 block west to the Ekdall Country Store.

As the tour continues east on Refuge Road, you will pass a historical marker that gives information on the Crex Meadows. A little farther is the park's wayside rest area, with picnic tables and primitive restrooms. It's a great place to stop, listen, and reflect on the area's past. Soon you will reach Town Hall Road, where the route turns to the north. Those who prefer the 22-mile option will continue east for a short distance and then turn south on East Refuge Road. This shortcut route heads south and passes refuge fields that are planted with grains to attract wildlife, including sandhill cranes, sharp-tailed grouse, and sandpipers.

As the challenge reconnects with County Road F, in less than a quarter mile, turn east on Reed Lake Road. In another 3 miles the road jogs to the south past the parking area for Sand Blow, an area that late nineteenth-century settlers attempted to farm. Because of the sterile, sandy soil up to 80 feet deep, farming was discontinued, and today asparagus and box elder trees are the only evidence remaining that a farmstead once stood here. The lane then turns east again and heads toward High Line Road. As you ride north you will again reconnect to County Road F, which you follow over the Balcome Bridge to get around the Clam Lake Flowage. You will notice that the forest is more prevalent as you continue east.

If you prefer the 43-mile option, at the 20.7-mile mark turn right on South River Road. Otherwise, continue east for 3 more miles to County Road FF. Turn right and head south through gentle rolling terrain down to County Road U, where you turn left. You will pass Fort Folle Avoine, a historic park and museum on the banks of the Yellow River. This is the actual site where the fur-trading companies bartered with the native Ojibwe in the early 1800s. If you stop by, you will be greeted with a sign that says BOOZ HOO, meaning "welcome," while costumed interpreters conduct tours in the reconstructed trading post and Ojibwe Indian village.

When leaving the fort another sign says MIGWECH ("thank you") as you turn south on North Lake Road to Yellow Lake. Like the town just to the east, the Chippewa Indians named the lake and river here for their yellow sand bottoms. After passing Yellow Lake Lodge, test you lower gears for a short climb up the lake road. At the top of the ridge, ride the lane between Yellow Lake and Little Yellow Lake. Soon you will take a short ride on County Road FF down to Beach Street. This country lane follows the south shoreline of Yellow Lake, where you pass John Deere Crossing. Reconnecting to County Road FF, continue east into Webster.

This town was originally established as Clam River in 1896. Soon one of the community's leading pioneers, J. D. Rice, applied to have the name changed to Webster after Noah Webster, the great lexicographer. Today, when you reach Highway 35 at the 32.8-mile mark, you will be greeted by a simpler time. Have lunch at the

11 Step Back in Time Challenge

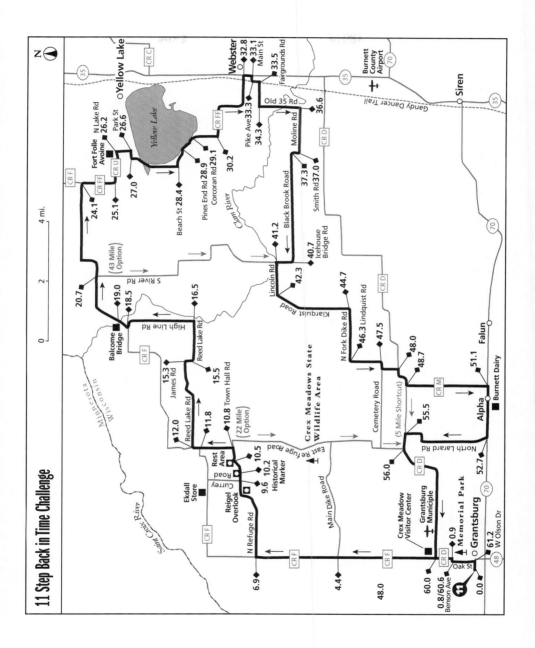

drive-in restaurant at the corner or continue on downtown. As you ride down Main Street, notice the 1950s Americana look. A block down from the local cafe, at the end of the street, you will find the Gandy Dancer Trail. Departing from this quaint little downtown community, turn left on Pike Avenue and head south along the trail.

The route soon jogs to the southwest on its return back toward the wildlife area on Fairgrounds Road. After turning onto Icehouse Bridge Road, you soon turn left again on Lincoln Road, where the 43-mile option returns. Riding south on Klarquist Road, you reenter Crex Meadows for another visit. Continue southwest on North Fork Dike Road, and soon you are on County Road M and leaving the meadows once again for Alpha.

The first postmaster here was Guy E. Noyes, a butter maker, who originally requested the name Smoland Prairie for the town because many of the settlers were from Smoland, Sweden. The postal department, however, said the name was too long. Frustrated and looking for a shorter name, the budding postmaster glanced at his cream separator, which was an Alpha Number One De Laval, and christened the town Alpha.

As you ride the paved shoulder of Highway 70, in about 1.5 miles you will find Burnett Dairy to your left, a great place to sample some cheese and enjoy an ice-cream cone. Across the road is the Smoland Prairie Homestead Inn, just a short ride up from the highway on a gravel driveway and well worth the visit. Take a step back in time to the nineteenth century at this two-story, hand-hewn log farmhouse, now a bed-and-breakfast. If you appreciate antiques, plan on making a reservation to stay here when you visit the area. They also sell fresh bread, eggs, and natural beef if you want to stop back after the ride.

After leaving Alpha, travel another mile on Highway 70's paved shoulder then head north on North Larard Road back towards Crex Meadows. As you riding east again on County Road D, you soon pass East Refuge Road, where the 22-mile option returns. In another 4 miles the route again passes the Crex Meadows Visitor Center. If you stop, share you meadows experience with the staff there.

Remember the trail of golden geese coming out of Grantsburg when you started the ride? Now you can look ahead, in the left lane, and follow them back to Grantsburg.

Miles and Directions

0.0 Turn left from Memorial Park onto West Olson Drive.

0.1 Turn left on North Oak Street and follow the golden geese painted on the pavement.

0.8 Take a right on East Benson Avenue. (Note: You will pass a store if you need last-minute supplies.)

0.9 Turn left on County Road D.

1.4 Go straight ahead on County Road F. **Side-trip:** The Crex Meadows Visitor Center is 1 block to your right.

4.4 Pass Main Dike Road.

6.9 Take a right on North Refuge Road.

9.4 Pass Reigel Overlook.

9.6 Pass Currey Road. **Side-trip:** The Ekdall Country Store is 1 mile north to County Road F and then 1 block west.

10.2 Pass historical marker.

10.5 Pass wayside park area.

10.8 Turn left on Town Hall Road. **Option:** The 22-mile ramble option continues east and then south on East Refuge Road.

11.8 Take a right on County Road F.

12.0 Turn right on Reed Lake Road.

15.3 Take a right on James Road and pass parking area for Sand Blow.

15.5 Turn left again on Reed Lake Road.

16.5 Turn left on High Line Road.

18.5 Take a right on County Road F.

19.0 Cross Balcome Bridge.

20.7 Pass South River Road. **Option:** Turn right on South River Road for the 43-mile option.

24.1 Take a right on County Road FF.

25.1 Turn left on County Road U.

25.9 Pass Fort Folle Avoine Historical Park.

26.2 Turn right on North Lake Road.

26.6 Turn right on Park Street.

26.7 Turn left on Yellow Lake Road.

27.0 Pass Yellow Lake Lodge.

27.7 Turn left on County Road FF.

28.4 Turn left on Beach Street.

28.9 Take a right on Pines End Road and pass John Deere Crossing.

29.1 Turn left on Corcoran Road.

30.2 Turn left on County Road FF.

32.8 Take a right on Highway 35 in Webster.

33.1 Take a right on Main Street.

33.3 Turn left on Pike Avenue, which runs parallel with the Gandy Dancer Trail.

33.5 Take a right on Fairgrounds Road.

34.3 Turn left on Old 35 Road.

36.6 Take a right on Moline Road.

37.0 Take a right on Smith Road.

37.3 Turn left on Black Brook Road.

40.7 Take a right on Icehouse Bridge Road.

41.2 Turn left on Lincoln Road. (Note: The 43-mile option returns here.)

42.3 Turn left on Klarquist Road.

44.7 Take a right on North Fork Dike Road.

46.3 Turn left on Lindquist Road.

47.5 Turn left on Cemetery Road.

48.0 Take a right on County Road D.

48.7 Turn left on County Road M.

51.1 Take a right on Highway 70.

51.7 Pass through Alpha.

52.7 Take a right on North Larard Road.

55.5 Turn left back on County Road D.

56.0 Pass East Refuge Road. (Note: The 22-mile option returns here.)

60.1 Turn left on County Road D at the Crex Meadows Visitor Center.

60.6 Take a right Benson Avenue.

60.7 Turn left on North Oak Street.

61.2 Take a right on West Olson Drive.

62.0 Return to park.

Local Information

Village of Grantsburg, 316 South Brad Street, Grantsburg; (715) 463-2405; www.grantsburg wi.com.

Burnett County Tourism Information Center, at the corner of Highways 35 and 64, Siren; (800) 788-3164; www.burnettcounty.com.

Local Events/Attractions

Crex Meadows Wildlife Area, corner of County Roads D and F, Grantsburg; (715) 463-2739; www.crexmeadows.org.

Burnett Dairy Cheese Store, 11677 Highway 70, Alpha; (715) 689-2748; www.burnette dairy.com.

Fort Folle Avoine Historical Park, Burnett County Historical Society, 8500 County Road U, Danbury; (715) 866-8890.

Restaurants

Dale's Restaurant, 133 Highway 70, Grantsburg; (715) 463-2640.

Northview Drive Inn, 26595 Lakeland Avenue North, Webster; (715) 866-7642.

Yellow Lake Lodge, 27924 Yellow Lake Road, Webster; (715) 866-4354.

Accommodations

Smoland Prairie Homestead Inn, 11658 Highway 70, Alpha; (715) 689-2528; www.smolandinn.com.

James N. McNally Campground, 1259 West Olson Drive, Grantsburg; (715) 463-2405.

Bike Shops

Hayes Pro Bike & Ski, 25209 Old 35, Siren; (715) 866-8101.

Restrooms

Start/finish: Memorial Park.

1.4: Crex Meadows Visitor Center.

25.9: Fort Folle Avoine Historical Park.

27.0: Yellow Lake Lodge.

33.3: Gandy Dancer trailhead in Webster.

51.7: Burnett Cheese Store and Dairy in Alpha.

60.1: Crex Meadows Visitor Center.

Maps

DeLorme: Wisconsin Atlas and Gazetteer: Page 82 B3.

Wisconsin State Bicycle Map (Northern Section).

12 Stardig's Co-Motion Cruise

This cruise starts in a river town, named in honor of a Seminole Indian chief, that still offers passage up the valley on railcars powered by a steam engine. If you are fortunate enough to hear old No. 328's whistle blowing as you depart, it should get your adrenaline rolling. The route takes advantage of the valley's landscape as it travels counterclockwise. For the first 16 miles you will enjoy the lush scenery as you pass through the rolling farmland. Circling to the east, you will soon cruise down along the Apple River to a town established in the 1850s with a working trout farm. As you travel north, you will encounter your first of two major climbs. At the top of the first hill, pick up your cadence a bit as you enjoy several true Wisconsin rollers. As you meander from one scenic lake to another, you will soon hit that second wall. Here at the top of this ridge you will have a great view of the St. Croix River valley before descending to a town known for its traprock and downhill skiing. Now back in the valley, enjoy a few more rollers as you cruise back to the park in Osceola.

Start: Oakley Park in Osceola.
Length: 47 miles with 25-mile and 36-mile options.
Terrain: Rolling terrain with a couple of climbs.

Traffic and hazards: Traffic on county roads can be fast. Care should be taken as you turn left on Highway 65 in Star Prairie and cross Highway 35 in Dresser.

Getting there: From Highway 35 in Osceola, head east on Sixth Street to the park.

As you begin your ride in this river town in the St. Croix Valley, you may hear in the distance the stream engine of the Scenic Osceola & St. Croix Valley Railway as it blows its whistle. The cruise departs from Oakley Park and begins by touring through downtown Osceola. After riding under the railroad trestle where Old No. 328 crosses, the route juts off the paved shoulder of Highway 35 and turns west into the lush valley.

In the spring of 1844 William Kent and several young entrepreneurs who came from Maine settled in the area now known as Osceola. The town was originally called Leroy, after the first white man to die here, and then renamed Bluffsville for the sandstone cliffs above the river. But it was Kent who owned the entire claim of what is now Osceola, utilizing the waterpower at Osceola Creek and Cascade Falls to build a sawmill, and he decided he wanted to change the name of the flourishing river town. In 1855 it was reported that he traded the privilege of renaming the community to James Livingston in exchange for some sheep. Livingston chose the name Osceola in honor of the great Florida Seminole Indian chief, and in 1858 the name was officially changed.

After taking a right on Ridge Road, follow the St. Croix River valley while enjoying moderate rollers through lush agricultural land. As you pass 30th Avenue, those who prefer the 25-mile or 36-mile option should turn left here. The cruise continues south and turns east on County Line Avenue. After turning you will pass a couple marshes. If the bugs are thick and you're lucky, you will be greeted by a flock of swallows acrobatically maneuvering below the power lines to gather some pesky insects.

After crossing Highway 35 you will have another 4 miles of harmonious rollers before your next turn. Now turning south, you will cross into St. Croix County and cruise down along the shores of Cedar Lake. Turn left on County Road C, a designated bike route with a posted speed limit of 45 mph, as it follows the Apple River into Star Prairie. This town was established in 1854 when Trueworthy and Thomas Jewell migrated here from New Hampshire. Enamored by the Apple River and the easily accessible prairie farmland, they entered into a contract with the government and established Jeweltown. Within four years of their arrival, the brothers had erected a sawmill and gristmill and the town took off and prospered.

Some years later, Trueworthy's son-in-law, Major Edmond Otis, observed one evening, "How beautiful the stars are tonight over the prairie." His comment spurred the town's name change to Star Prairie, which became official in 1900. Many of the buildings and the mill from that time are long gone, but you can still see remnants of the mill's foundation along the banks of the Apple River, in River Island Park. The trout farm next to the park was established a few years after the town was founded and is still in operation today. In addition to full restroom facilities in the park, the town also offers several eating establishments if you make this a stopping point.

As you leave town you will cross the Apple River and encounter your first climb. A steady 8 percent grade for the first quarter mile puts you on a rolling spree, typical of Wisconsin, for the next several miles. Crossing back into Polk County at the 22.5-mile mark, the rollers continue. Soon the route turns onto Church Road, and those who selected the 36-mile option return at 190th Street as the cruise turns north again.

Up along the east shore of Church Pine Lake, you soon ride by a country store as you pass between Big Lake and Wind Lake. Now pedaling to the northwest, turn north again on County Road Y and cross over an abandoned railroad bed, then head up along the east shore of Horse Lake. Here you may want to stop and enjoy the lakeside scenery for a couple minutes before the fun really begins.

As you turn to the west again, the cruise jogs back and forth and takes you past Lotus Lake County Park on 90th Avenue, then jogs south on County Road MM for a quarter mile. After turning west again on 90th Avenue, the road starts to climb at a steady 8 percent pace for the next mile. Enjoy the view at the crest before coasting all the way down to Dresser. At the edge of the city, jog over to County Road F (Trollhaugen Road), then roll into the downtown area.

The town was established in 1861, and on September 2, 1887, the first railroad line was completed. Sam Dresser, one of the original settlers, named the site Dresser Junction because of a junction of two sections of railroad. Then in 1914 the Dresser Trap Rock mines were established for the excavation of traprock, a fine-grained volcanic rock. This is the hardest rock in North America and is still being mined for railroad bed use. As the community continued to grow, in 1950 Trollhaugen Ski Area was established. It is still in operation today.

12 Stardig's Co-Motion Cruise

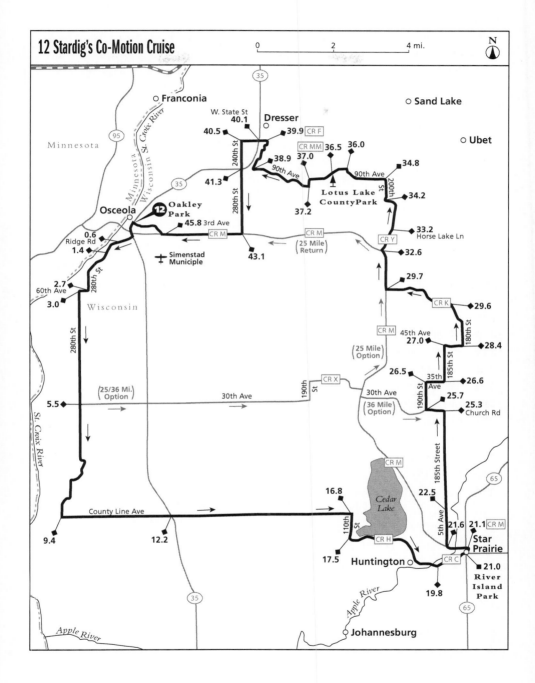

0   2   4 mi.

N

○ **Franconia**

○ **Sand Lake**

W. State St
40.1
Dresser ○
40.5   **39.9** CR F

○ **Ubet**

Minnesota

95

CR MM   **36.5**   **36.0**

38.9   **37.0**   **34.8**

90th Ave   90th Ave   200th St

41.3

35

*Lotus Lake
CountyPark*   **34.2**

Osceola ○   **Oakley
Park**
12

37.2

45.8 3rd Ave

0.6
Ridge Rd
1.4

CR M

33.2
Horse Lake Ln

+ Simenstad
Municiple

43.1

(25 Mile
Return)

CR Y

32.6

2.7
60th Ave

29.7

3.0

CR K   **29.6**

Wisconsin

280th St

CR M

180th St

45th Ave
27.0   **28.4**

(25 Mile
Option)

185th St

26.5   35th **26.6**
190th St   Ave

280th St

190th St   CR X

30th Ave

25.7

5.5

30th Ave

(25/36 Mi.)
Option

30th Ave

(36 Mile
Option)

25.3
Church Rd

CR M

185th Street

*Cedar
Lake*

65

16.8

22.5

St. Croix River

County Line Ave

110th St

5th Ave

21.6   **21.1** CR M

9.4

12.2

CR H

**Star
Prairie**

17.5

Huntington ○

CR C

21.0
**River
Island
Park**

35

19.8

65

Apple River

○ **Johannesburg**

After crossing Highway 35 onto West State Street, you will find a couple rest stop options, if needed, before leaving town. Soon you are in the St. Croix Valley, with many productive irrigated farm fields along the way as you ride south. As you turn west on County Road M, the 25-mile option returns. After you turn onto Third Avenue back into Osceola, you will discover the ride isn't over yet. Muster your energy reserve as the road into town snakes over rolling terrain before jogging to the northwest. You will pass several city blocks onto Chieftain Street and will soon be back at the park.

Miles and Directions

0.0 Leave from Oakley Park on Sixth Street.

0.1 Turn left on Highway 35 through downtown Osceola.

0.6 Take a right on Ridge Road.

1.4 Merge onto 280th Street.

2.7 Take a right on 60th Avenue.

3.0 Turn left back on 280th Street.

5.5 Pass 30th Avenue. **Option:** Turn left on 30th Avenue for the 25-mile and 36-mile options.

9.4 Turn left on County Line Avenue.

12.2 Cross Highway 35.

16.8 Take a right on 110th Street.

17.5 Turn left on County Road H.

19.8 Continue on County Road C into Star Prairie.

21.0 Turn left on Highway 65/Main Street.

21.1 Turn left on County Road M.

21.6 Take a right on Fifth Avenue.

22.5 Cross back into Polk County onto 185th Street.

25.3 Turn left on Church Road.

25.7 Take a right on 190th Street. (Note: The 36-mile option returns here.)

26.5 Take a right on 35th Avenue.

26.6 Turn left on 185th Street.

27.0 Take a right on 45th Avenue.

28.4 Turn left on 180th Street.

29.6 Turn left on County Road K at the country store.

29.7 Take a right on County Road M.

32.6 Take a right on County Road Y, passing over an old abandoned railroad bed.

33.2 Take a right on 200th Street.

34.8 Turn left on 90th Avenue.

36.0 At the Rod & Gun Club, 90th Avenue turns left.

36.5 Pass Lotus Lake County Park.

37.0 Turn left on County Road MM.

37.2 Take a right back on 90th Avenue,

38.9 Take a right on 235th Street into Dresser.

39.1 Merge onto Garfield Street.

39.3 Turn left on Lincoln Avenue.

39.5 Take a right on South Street.

39.6 Turn left on Blaisdelle Avenue.

39.7 Take a right on Warren Street.

39.8 Turn left on Polk Avenue.

39.9 Turn left on County Road F (Trollhaugen Road) over the railroad tracks.

40.1 Cross Highway 35 onto West State Street.

40.5 Turn left on 240th Street.

41.3 Cross Highway 35 onto 280th Street.

43.1 Take a right on County Road M. (Note: The 25-mile option returns here.)

45.8 Take a right on Third Avenue back into Osceola.

46.5 Take a right on Hill Street.

46.6 Turn left on Fourth Avenue.

46.7 Take a right on Fifth Avenue

46.8 Take a right on Chieftain Street.

46.9 Take a right on Sixth Street

47.0 Return to park.

Local Information

Osceola Main Street Chamber, 310 Chieftain Street, Osceola; (800) 947-0581; www.osceola chamber.org.

Polk County Tourism, Highway 8 and Highway 35 South, St. Croix Falls; (800) 222-7655; www.polkcountytourism.com.

Local Events/Attractions

The Osceola & St. Croix Valley Railway, Osceola; train rides and historic depot; (800) 643-7412.

Cascade Bike Classic; first Sunday in June; (800) 947-0581; www.osceolachamber.org.

Restaurants

Adventures Restaurant & Pub, 1020 North Cascade Street, Osceola; (715) 755-2797.

Mainstreet Pizza, Subs & Ice Cream, 106 Highway 65/Main Street, Star Prairie; (715) 248-7447.

Trap Rock Inn, 736 Highway 35 South, Dresser; (715) 755-3549.

Accommodations

River Valley Inn & Suites, Highway 35 North/Cascade Street, Osceola; (888) 294-4060; www.osceolavalleyinn.com.

Popular Point Rentals and Park, 2102 120th Avenue, Dresser; (715) 485-3561.

Bike Shops

Russell's Sport N' Bike, 703 Jewell Street, Star Prairie; (715) 248-3644.

Smitty's Bike Shop, 402 Delmar Avenue, Osceola; (715) 755-3494.

Restrooms

Start/finish: Oakley Park.

21.0: River Island Park in Star Prairie.

36.5: Lotus Lake County Park.

40.1: BP station, Dresser.

Maps

DeLorme: Wisconsin Atlas and Gazetteer: Page 70 B3.

Wisconsin State Bicycle Map (Mississippi River Section).

13 Leinenkugel Classic

This classic ride mirrors the excellent Chippewa Valley Century Ride established as an annual Memorial Day weekend bike event that serves great beer and brats at the end. The route leaves from a city that at one time had the largest sawmill operation under one roof, and circles around to the north, passing the Old Abe Recreational Trail, which runs parallel to the Chippewa River. You will visit a village that was originally named for its red clay banks, and after passing the historic Cobban Bridge, you enter a town that was named for the president of a university. After crossing over the Holcombe Flowage, the route takes you into Rusk County to the confluence of the Flambeau and Chippewa Rivers, then turns away from the river and follows the rolling terrain around several lakes before crossing over the Ice Age Trail. You then circle back to the south along the verdurous irrigated farm fields running through the Chippewa Valley and discover several little towns along the way. Upon your return to Chippewa Falls, the route passes through the zoo and then back to sample a brew at the Leine Lodge.

Start: Bernard Willi Pool in Chippewa Falls.
Length: 101 miles with 35-mile, 50-mile, and 75-mile options.
Terrain: In between open stretches of farm fields, there are many rolling sections and a few challenging hills.

Traffic and hazards: Roads on this route are paved with low to medium traffic. Care should be taken when riding on the highways, as the shoulders are generally narrow and traffic can be fast.

Getting there: From Eau Claire travel north on Highway 53 to Highway 124 through Chippewa Falls. After crossing the Chippewa River, take a right on Jefferson Avenue/Highway 124. At Bridgewater Avenue, just past Leinenkugel's Brewery, turn left and go 1 block; the Bernard Willi Pool is on the left across from Irvine Park.

This classic leaves from the parking lot of the community pool, where a dip and showers await your return, and takes you through Irvine Park before leaving town. In 1836 pioneer Jean Burnet named the city for the large falls on the Chippewa River at this site. Those falls, at one time, supplied the power for the world's largest sawmill operation under one roof.

After riding through the south end of Irvine Park, turn onto Highway 124's wide shoulder for a short distance, then turn east and pass the Old Abe trailhead. Those who choose to ride this paved trail north along the route will need to purchase a wheel pass. The classic continues east and soon merges onto Wissota Green Boulevard, passing through a new development with a roundabout and clock tower. Here you can synchronize your watch before traveling up County Road S.

As you cross the Chippewa River as it flows into Lake Wissota, if you look off to your left you can see the Old Abe Trail running parallel. After passing the Native

Riders taking in the view of the Chippewa River.

Bay Restaurant, turn left on 97th Avenue and cross the trail. If you have a desire to visit Lake Wissota State Park, it is 3 miles to the east on County Road O. As the classic heads north again, both the trail and the road follow the east bank of the Chippewa River. Soon the roadbed rolls northeast through farm fields with the familiar dairy-operation aroma. Turning to the north, you will run into your first hill with a 6 percent grade before approaching Jim Falls.

James Ermatinger, a native of Canada, was the first to settle the area. The village was originally named Vermillion Falls because the clay banks were so red, but the name was later changed to Ermatiger Falls and then shortened to Jim Falls. If you need a rest stop, you will find a couple options here. Leaving to the north, you will have a photo opportunity and a mileage decision. At the intersection where the statue of the bald eagle stands, the classic turns right on County Road S; those who prefer the 35-mile option turn left on County Road Y.

The challenge continues east for the next 3 miles over rolling roads that border farm fields and lowlands. After turning north again on County Road K, you will cruise into Cobban. In 1867 Joseph Cobban, a farmer and industrialist who owned land here, platted the town. After leaving town you will pass County Road T at the historic Cobban Bridge. If you prefer the 50-mile option, cross the bridge and ride the paved shoulder of Highway 178, then head west on 180th Avenue.

Once again the classic veers to the north up along moderate rolling ridges that border the banks of the Chippewa River. At about the 29-mile mark you will have a couple options for lunch as you roll into Cornell. This town was originally named Burnet's Falls for Jean Burnet, who opened a portage and trading post here after moving from Chippewa Falls, but was soon renamed for Ezra Cornell, the president of Cornell University. In town, if you take a left at the Holiday Station on Highway 64, you will find a couple options for lunch in town.

Back on the ride the road starts to undulate while twisting and turning in and out of the river bottom, then up a rocky ridge. After jogging to the east one more time, you soon head north again and cross the Fisher River before arriving in the town of Holcombe. This early settlement was first known as Little Falls, but when the village was platted a few years later, the surveyor changed the name to his own. While in town take a side-trip down Main Street and visit Albrecht's Cheese. Along with many types of cheeses and sausages to sample, their homemade donuts are a great treat if you left some room from lunch.

At the 34.1-mile mark you now turn onto County Road M and head west across the Holcombe Flowage. Use caution here, as the shoulder is minimal and weekend traffic in the summer can be busy. For the next 5 miles you will pass many resorts and marinas lively with summer tourists. After passing the road to Pine Point Campground, in a couple more miles you will turn north again. This stretch of road is fairly flat, touching the Holcombe Flowage fingers that reach out like waterway cul-de-sacs and support the lake homes here. If you are not up to a century today, turn left when you reach 290th Avenue for the 75-mile option. The classic takes a

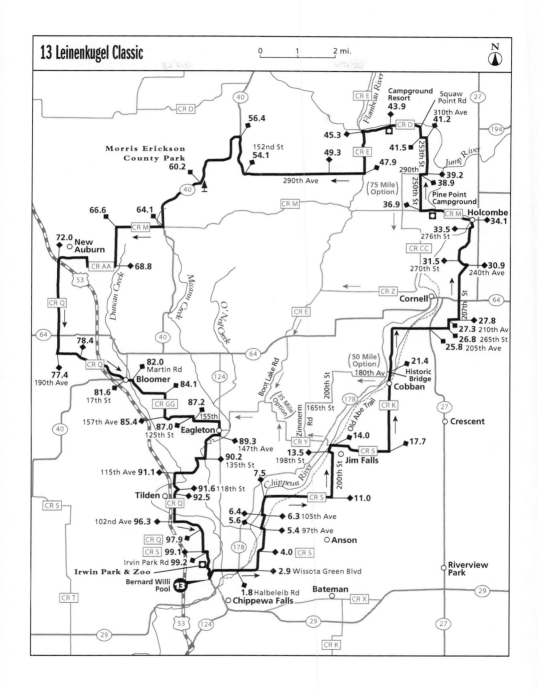

13 Leinenkugel Classic

0   1   2 mi.

N

Campground Resort 43.9
Squaw Point Rd
CR E
Flambeau River
CR D
310th Ave 41.2
45.3
41.5
253rd St
Jump River
194
56.4
152nd St 54.1
49.3
47.9
290th
39.2
250th St
38.9
Pine Point Campground
Morris Erickson County Park 60.2
290th Ave ←
(75 Mile Option)
36.9
CR M
Holcombe
CR M
34.1
66.6
64.1
CR M
33.5
276th St
72.0 New Auburn
CR CC
31.5
270th St
30.9
240th Ave
CR AA 68.8
53
CR Z
Cornell
64
CR Q
Duncan Creek
Mecan Creek
O'Neil Creek
CR E
27.8
207th St
27.3 210th Av
26.8 265th St
25.8 205th Ave
64
78.4
40
77.4 190th Ave
CR Q
82.0 Martin Rd
(50 Mile Option)
180th Av
21.4 Historic Bridge
Cobban
Boot Lake Rd
84.1
Bloomer
81.6 17th St
87.2
CR GG
CR K
27
Crescent
157th Ave 85.4
155th
125th St 87.0
Eagleton
89.3
147th Ave
(35 Mile Option)
165th Rd
Zimmerm Rd
178
Old Abe Trail
14.0
17.7
90.2 135th St
CR Y
200th St
CR S
115th Ave 91.1
13.5 198th St
Jim Falls
Chippewa River
7.5
91.6 118th St
Tilden
92.5
200th St
11.0
CR Q
CR S
6.4
6.3 105th Ave
102nd Ave 96.3
5.6
97.9
CR Q
5.4 97th Ave
CR S
99.1
178
Anson
Irvin Park Rd 99.2
4.0 CR S
Irwin Park & Zoo
Bernard Willi Pool
13
2.9 Wissota Green Blvd
Riverview Park
CR T
1.8 Halbeleib Rd
Bateman
CR X
29
Chippewa Falls
29
53
124
29
27
CR K

124
40

right and then left on its way up to Squaw Point on the Chippewa River. This tranquil stretch along the south bank of the river soon merges onto County Road D next to the church by the bridge.

In less than a half mile, you will pass Adee's Flambeau Resort and Campground. Close to the 44-mile mark, this venue makes a great place to spend the night if you want to make this classic into a two-day trip. Following the west bank, where the Flambeau River flows into the Chippewa River, the ride turns south and you will have your first major climb. For close to a mile the grade gets steeper, and you may have to dance on those pedals when hitting the wall. At the top, coast all the way down to 290th Avenue—you've earned it!

Turn west here and enjoy the road as it rolls over the glacial ridges. Once you pass Warden Lake, the route jogs north again and passes Lakes One, Two, Three, and Four before circling back around Sand Lake. Turn south onto the wide paved shoulder of Highway 40, and then cruise along the north shore of Long Lake. Take a well-deserved break at Morris Erickson County Park, where Cedar Creek flows into the lake at the 60-mile mark.

After passing the shores of Larrabee Lake and then Salsbury Lake, you will travel southwest into New Auburn. In 1858 this town was known as Cartwright's Mill, but in 1902 it took the name of the township, Auburn, which in turn was named by early settlers for their hometown in New York . Now cutting across Highway 53 and then south again, the route follows Lake Como into Bloomer.

Originally this town was named Vanville in honor of Sylvester Van Loon, who acquired a homestead along beautiful Duncan Creek. As more settlers moved in and the railroad came through, the name was officially changed to Bloomer for Bloomer's Prairie, which was named after an ambitious merchant who several years earlier had sent his men in search of hay in this prairie area.

As you leave Bloomer you will pick up the designated bike route on County Road SS/Martin Road. This route winds through irrigated farmlands and cuts over to the town of Eagleton. Settled in 1876 in the township of Eagle Point, the village was name for the many eagle sightings around the area at the time. As you ride south through this town, you will find a great park pavilion on Highway 124. At the 89.3-mile mark the route heads southwest. Riding over rolling agricultural croplands, the classic soon arrives in the town of Tilden on County Road Q. This town separated from Eagle Point in 1883 and was named for Samuel J. Tilden.

About a mile south of town, turn left and head southeast past the Tilden Millpond. When you reach County Road S, you will be at the 99.1-mile mark, and here you jog to the east and then south on Irvine Park Road. This road winds through the park past the zoo before returning to the parking lot at the municipal swimming pool.

Miles and Directions

0.0 From Bernard Willi Pool, cross Bridgewater Avenue onto Irvine Park Road.

0.2 Take a right on Wolf Drive in the park.

0.3 Turn left on Highway 124.

0.6 Take a right on First Avenue.

1.8 Take a right on Halbeleib Road.

1.9 Turn left on Kennedy Road.

2.1 Cross Highway 178 onto Highway 1 and pass trailhead.

2.9 Merge onto Wissota Green Boulevard.

3.0 Head north on Green Parkway at roundabout.

3.1 Resume travel on North Highway 1.

4.0 Take a right on County Road S.

5.4 Turn left on 97th Avenue and cross Old Abe Trail.

5.6 Take a right on 162nd Street.

6.3 Turn left on 105th Avenue.

6.4 Take a right on 161st Street.

7.5 Take a right on 115th Avenue.

8.9 Cross trail.

10.1 Trail crosses County Road S.

11.0 Turn left on 200th Street.

13.5 Turn left on 198th Street in Jim Falls.

13.6 Take a right on County Road S.

14.0 Take a right on County Road S at the junction of County Road Y. **Option:** Turn left on County Road Y for the 35-mile option.

14.1 Cross trail.

17.7 Turn left on County Road K.

20.7 Cross trail.

21.4 Arrive in Cobban.

21.7 Pass County Road T at the historic Cobban Bridge. **Option:** For the 50-mile option, cross the bridge and ride the paved shoulder of Highway 178, then head west on 180th Avenue.

25.8 Cross Highway 27 onto 205th Avenue.

26.8 Turn left on 265th Street.

27.3 Take a right on 210th Avenue.

27.8 Turn left on 270th Street.

28.8 Cross Highways 27/64 in Cornell.

30.9 Turn left at 240th Avenue.

31.2 Cross the Fisher River.

31.5 Take a right on 270th Street.

33.5 Take a right on 276th Street.

33.8 Pass Main Street in Holcombe.

34.1 Turn left on County Road M.

34.3 Cross the Holcombe Flowage.

36.5 Pass Pine Point Campground.

36.9 Take a right on 250th Street.

38.9 Take a right on 290th Avenue. **Option:** Turn left on 290th Avenue for the 75-mile option.

39.2 Turn left on 253rd Street.

41.2 Turn left on 310th Avenue.

41.5 Take a right on Squaw Point Road.

42.0 Turn left before the Chippewa River.

43.7 Turn left on County Road D by the church.

43.9 Pass Adee's Flambeau Resort and Campground.

45.3 Turn left on County Road E.

47.9 Take a right on 290th Avenue.

49.3 Pass Worden Lake.

54.1 Take a right on 152nd Street.

56.4 Turn left on Highway 40.

60.2 Pass Morris Erickson County Park.

64.1 Take a right on County Road M.

66.6 Turn left on 90th Street/Duncan Creek Road.

68.8 Take a right on County Road AA.

72.0 Turn left on County Road Q.

72.4 Cross Highway 53.

76.4 Cross Highway 64.

77.4 Turn left on 190th Avenue.

78.4 Take a right on County Road Q.

80.0 Cross Highway 53.

81.6 Cross Highway 40 onto 17th Street in Bloomer.

82.0 Take a right on County Road SS/Martin Road.

84.1 Take a right on County Road GG/110th Street.

85.4 Turn left on 157th Avenue.

87.0 Take a right on 125th Street.

87.2 Turn left on 155th Avenue.

88.6 Take a right on Highway 124.

89.0 Pass Eagleton Road. (Note: The 35-mile, 50-mile, and 75-mile options return here.)

89.1 Pass Eagleton City Park.

89.3 Take a right on 147th Avenue.

90.2 Take a right on 135th Street.

91.1 Turn left on 115th Avenue.

91.6 Turn left on 118th Street.

92.5 Turn left on County Road Q.

95.2 Arrive in Tilden.

96.3 Take a right on 102nd Avenue.

97.4 Pass Tilden Millpond.

97.9 Turn left on County Road Q.

99.1 Turn left on County Road S.

99.2 Take a right on Irvine Park Road.

101.0 Return to pool parking lot.

Local Information

Chippewa Falls Area Chamber of Commerce, 10 South Bridge Street, Chippewa Falls; (888) 723-0024; www.chippewachamber.org.

Local Events/Attractions

Leinenkugel Leine Lodge & Tours, 1336 Highway 124 North, Chippewa Falls; (888) 534-6437; www.leinie.com.

Sierra Century Bike Ride; first weekend in May; 12-, 30-, 60-, 80-, or 100-mile options; (715) 835-4829; www.wisconsin.sierraclub .org/chippewa.

Chippewa Valley Century Ride; Sunday preceding Memorial Day; 35-, 50-, 75-, or 100-mile options; (715) 720-1439; www.chippewa valleyride.us.

Restaurants

Bake and Brew Cafe, 117 North Bridge Street, Chippewa Falls; (715) 720-2360.

Loopy's Saloon & Grill, 10691 Business Highway 29, Chippewa Falls; (715) 664-8600.

Accommodations

AmericInn, 11 West/South Avenue, Chippewa Falls; (715) 723-5711.

Lake Wissota State Park, 18127 County Road O, Chippewa Falls; (715) 382-4574.

Ardee's Flambeau Resort, W10355 County Road D, Holcombe; (715) 595-4738.

Bike Shops

Anybody's Bikeshop, 411 Water Street, Eau Claire; (715) 833-7100.

Spring Street Sports, 12 West Spring Street, Chippewa Falls; (715) 723-6616.

Restrooms

Start/finish: Bernard Willi Pool.

13.6: Cenex station in Jim Falls.

28.8: Holiday station in Cornell.

36.5: Pine Point Campground.

60.2 Morris Erickson County Park.

66.6: BP station in New Auburn station.

81.6: Bloomer Park.

89.1: Eagleton Park Pavilion.

Maps

DeLorme: Wisconsin Atlas and Gazetteer: Page 61 A5.

Wisconsin State Bicycle Map (Mississippi River Section).

14 Red Cedar Challenge

This route begins in one of Wisconsin's early settlements and makes a circle tour around the Red Cedar Trail. After traveling the city streets past the Stout College campus, the route takes you south for a rest stop option in a town with a jail cell in the backyard of the museum. You continue south and cross the Red Cedar River to an early town where the county courthouse once stood. After passing through this village of yesteryear, ride west. Here the terrain becomes lush green, and you will find a number of rollers as you approach a town that the French explorers named for the gravel banks of the river that flows through it. The route circles to the north and comes back briefly east to the Red Cedar Trail before veering off to the northwest, where the fun really begins. For those who love the adrenaline rush of Wisconsin's hills, this section of the challenge offers two major climbs. As you turn back to the northeast after the second climb, you will enjoy several miles of easy riding as you slide into another sleepy little river town before passing the Devil's Punch Bowl. You then ride north along the river and soon return to Menomonie.

Start: Riverside Park and Red Cedar trailhead in Menomonie.
Length: 53 miles with 18-mile, 28-mile, and 42-mile options using trail.
Terrain: Rolling with a few climbs.

Traffic and hazards: Use caution riding on or crossing Highway 25 and for the first couple miles of County Road Y, as traffic can move fast.

Getting there: From Interstate 94 travel south to Menomonie on Highway 25. Turn left at Highway 29; the park and trailhead is a half mile ahead on the left.

Here at the trailhead of the Red Cedar State Trail in Menomonie, visit the original railroad freight depot that now houses an interpretive center. At the center you can gain some additional information on the various natural and historic highlights before riding this route. If you plan to use the crushed limestone trail for one of the shorter options back, this is a great time to pick up a trail pass. Leaving the park, ride the paved shoulder of Highway 29 as it enters Menomonie.

The city's name, though spelled differently than the Chippewa word *mano-minikaning,* also means "wild rice." From its early beginning in 1822, Menomonie has continued to grow and develop around the shores of beautiful Lake Menomin. Harding Perkins, representing James H. Lockwood and Joseph Rolette, erected a lumber mill at the confluence of Wilson Creek and Red Cedar River. Then in 1830, after a flood forced the rebuilding of the mill and dam, the city's first permanent settlement was established.

As you take a right on Highway 25, look to the north a few blocks. After your ride, experience downtown Menomonie, where many of the stores and shops have

Bovine spectators are common in Wisconsin.

been providing a wide variety of goods and services for more than a hundred years. One of the area's most famous landmarks, the Mabel Tainter Memorial Theater, was built in 1890.

Now turning left on 13th Avenue, you will pass the Stout College campus as you head out of town. Turn right onto County Road Y and ride single-file for the next 3 miles, as traffic can be fast at times and there is no paved shoulder. After turning left at 410th Avenue, continue south as the road becomes more rolling.

After jogging to the west on County Road C, you soon turn south again on 510th Street. Those who prefer the 18-mile option will continue on County Road C into Downsville and pick up the trail. The challenge continues south and meanders through the rolling countryside on Hardscrabble Road (510th Street). Upon reaching County Road Y, take a right, coast down the hill, and cross the Red Cedar River into Dunnville. Before crossing the bridge over the river or turning north on the Red Cedar Trail for the 28-mile option, see the foundation where the Knapp, Stout Company Store once stood. Or, south of the trailhead parking lot, visit the Tainter House, which provided lodging for visitors to Dunnville who traveled by river steamer. Today all that is left of Dunnville is a few remnants of a once-thriving river town.

After crossing the bridge, you will pass on your right the site where the hotel stood when Dunnville was known as Colburn's Landing. A War of 1812 veteran by the name of Lamb founded the town in 1840, choosing the site because of the junction of the Red Cedar and Chippewa Rivers. The community was named after Charles Dunn, then a state senator and former chief justice of the Wisconsin Territory. When the prosperous lumber town became the seat of Dunn County in 1854, in addition to Lamb's Inn, there were warehouses, log cabins, a trading post, and a wooden courthouse. In 1858 the courthouse burned down and the county seat was moved to a more central location, Menomonie. With the community in chaos and the loss of the county seat, the town reverted back to its wilderness state, except for the sandstone that is still quarried just north along the river bluff.

Up the road you will pass an old schoolhouse that is now converted into a residence. To the west on the wooded rise, which is private land, is where the first county courthouse and jail stood. Now traveling west, the road is fairly flat until crossing Highway 25. On Flick Road you will start enjoying some fun Wisconsin rollers as the route travels southwest down into Eau Galle. Settled in 1856, the town was named by French voyageurs and means "gravel banks." At the 22-mile mark climb up the river bluff in the village, where you will find Pine View Park and a local bar and grill that you can use as a rest stop.

The route then heads north over lush green rolling hills and soon turns east, twisting and turning through the valley as you make your way back to Downsville. At the 34.2-mile mark the cruise crosses Highway 72 onto 440th Street/River Road and heads northwest. If you need to go into Downsville for one of its several rest stop choices or to pick up the Red Cedar Trail for the 42-mile option, take a right and follow the highway a quarter mile into town.

This village was named after Captain Burrage E. Downs, who built a dam here around 1858 to run a sawmill. In addition to lumber, the first cut sandstone was extracted shortly after the town was established. The Red Cedar Trail originated as a rail line to haul the quarried stone to Menomonie, where it was used in several buildings, including the Mabel Tainter Memorial Theater.

Now aiming north, the cruise encounters a few more hills before meandering through another valley floor and climbing up the ridge, where you take a left on 340th Avenue/Hartfield Road. At the top look off to the west and see the beautiful rolling countryside. The view is spectacular as the hawks soar over the valley below. Ride down into another valley and enjoy a couple miles of lush green fields before turning on 430th Avenue. Now its time to dance on those pedals again.

At the top you will take a right on County Road K and coast for the next 4 miles into the little river town of Irvington. The town was settled around 1880 by George Irving and is now a bedroom community of Menomonie. Turn left here and ride along the river's edge, up past the Devil's Punch Bowl County Park. Designated a "Scientific Study Area," this picturesque gorge is an undisturbed retreat for both humans and wildlife.

14 Red Cedar Challenge

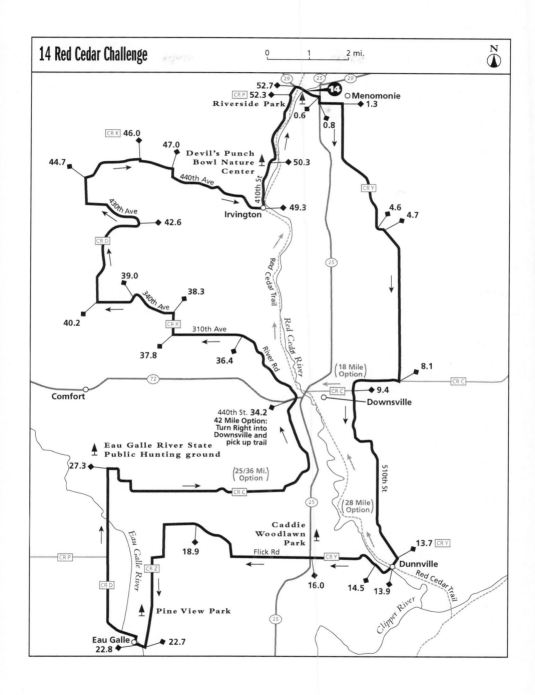

0   1   2 mi.

N

52.7 ◆
CR P 52.3 ◆
Riverside Park
0.6

14
○ Menomonie
1.3
0.8

CR K 46.0 ◆
47.0 ◆
Devil's Punch
Bowl Nature
Center
◆ 50.3

44.7 ◆
440th Ave
410th St
◆ 49.3
Irvington

430th Ave
42.6 ◆

CR Y
4.6
4.7

CR D
25

39.0 ◆
340th Ave
38.3 ◆

40.2 ◆

CR K
310th Ave
37.8 ■
36.4 ■
River Rd
Red Cedar Trail
Red Cedar River

8.1 ■

72
(18 Mile)
Option
CR C
9.4 ◆ Downsville
CR C

Comfort ○

440th St. 34.2 ◆
42 Mile Option:
Turn Right into
Downsville and
pick up trail

Eau Galle River State
Public Hunting ground
27.3 ◆

(25/36 Mi.)
Option
CR C

510th St

25

(28 Mile)
Option

18.9 ◆
Caddie
Woodlawn
Park
Flick Rd
CR Y

13.7 CR Y
Dunnville
Red Cedar Trail

Eau Galle River

CR P
CR Z
CR D

16.0
14.5 13.9 ◆

25
Clipper River

Pine View Park

Eau Galle ○ ◆ 22.7
22.8 ◆

With only 3 miles left at this point, enjoy the river bluff scenery as you continue north. At County Road P take a right and another right on Highway 29 before crossing the river and returning to the park.

Miles and Directions

0.0 Take a right on Highway 29 from Riverside Park.

0.6 Take a right on Highway 25 in Menomonie.

0.8 Turn left on 13th Avenue and pass Stout campus.

1.3 Take a right on Ninth Street/County Road Y.

4.6 Turn left on 410th Avenue (County Road Y).

4.7 Take a right and resume south on County Road Y.

8.1 Take a right on County Road C.

9.4 Turn left on 510th Street (Hardscrabble Road). **Option:** Continue on County Road C into Downsville to pick up the Red Cedar Trail for the 18-mile option.

13.7 Take a right on County Road Y.

13.9 Cross the Red Cedar Trail and River. **Option:** Turn north on the trail for the 28-mile option.

14.5 Pass through Dunnville.

16.0 Cross Highway 25 onto 130th Avenue/Flick Road.

18.9 Turn left on County Road Z.

22.7 Take a right onto County Road D into Eau Galle.

22.8 Cross river.

27.3 Take a right on County Road C.

34.2 Cross Highway 72 onto 440th Street. **Option:** Turn right into Downsville to pick up the Red Cedar Trail for the 42-mile option.

36.4 Turn left on 310th Avenue.

37.8 Take a right on County Road K.

38.3 Turn left on 340th Avenue/Hartfield Road.

39.0 Note the great vistas off to the west at the top.

40.2 Take a right on County Road D.

42.0 Pass 410th Avenue.

42.6 Turn left on 430th Avenue and climb some more.

44.7 Take a right on 470th Avenue.

46.0 Take a right on County Road K.

47.0 Turn left on 440th Avenue.

49.3 Turn left on 410th Street in Irvington.

50.3 Pass Devil's Punch Bowl County Park.

52.3 Take a right on County Road P.

52.7 Take a right on Highway 29.

53.0 Return to park.

Local Information

Greater Menomonie Area Chamber of Commerce, 342 East Main Street, Menomonie; (800) 283-1862; www.menomoniechamber.org.
Red Cedar Trail, Department of Natural Resources, 941 Brickyard Road, Menomonie; (715) 232-1242.

Local Events/Attractions

Empire in Pine Museum, County Road C, Downsville; (715) 232-8685.
Weekend On Wheels (WOW); second weekend in August; Twin City Bicycling Club; www.mtn .org/tcbc/wow.

Restaurants

Kernel Restaurant, 1632 North Broadway, Menominie; (715) 235-5154.
The Creamery Restaurant and Inn, 1213 County Road C, Downsville; (715) 664-8354.
Tillis Cafe & Store, 12104 County Road C, Downsville; (715) 664-8600.

Accommodations

The Holiday Manor, junction of I–94 and Highway 25, Menomonie; (800) 622-0504.

Twin Springs Resort & Campground, 3010 Cedar Falls Road, Menomonie; (715) 235-9321.

Bike Shops

Bad Cat Bikes, 327 Main Street East, Menomonie; (715) 231-2453.
Brickyard Cyclery, Highway 29, Red Cedar Trail, Menomonie; (715) 231-8735.

Restrooms

Start/finish: Riverside Park/Red Cedar trailhead.
9.8: Red Cedar trailhead, Downsville.
22.9: Pine View Park, Eau Galle.
34.5 Red Cedar trailhead, Downsville.

Maps

DeLorme: Wisconsin Atlas and Gazetteer: Page 60 A1.
Wisconsin State Bicycle Map (Mississippi River Section).
Menomonie Chamber of Commerce Bicycle Tour Map.

15 Pepin County Challenge

One of the smaller counties in Wisconsin, Pepin is a rider's diamond in the rough tucked away between the bluffs and the mighty Mississippi River. This challenge starts in a community with a museum housed in the last wood-frame courthouse in Wisconsin and takes you on an exhilarating countryside tour. After crossing the Chippewa River, the route aims to the west to a town named for a stream that passes through. Here, stop at a park where you can follow the sparkling water of Arkansaw Creek as it cascades over the rocks and pools below the limestone wall. The route then travels south between the Chippewa River and the foot of the bluffs before passing through another village on the river's bank, once known as Shoo Fly. After winding down the valley floor you encounter your first major climb, over a ridge, before reaching the Mississippi. At the top, enjoy the twisty-turny descent to a Mississippi River town with one of the oldest names on Wisconsin maps. Here you can visit the Laura Ingalls Wilder Museum. Now riding east along the Great River Road, you pass the Lower Chippewa River State Natural Area before circling back to the north. The last leg of this challenge will test your riding ability and stamina as you make your way back to Memorial Park in Durand.

Start: Memorial Park in Durand.
Length: 50 miles.
Terrain: Rolling with four major climbs.
Traffic and hazards: Use caution when riding over the bridge on the paved shoulder of Highway 10 from Durand and then riding on the paved shoulder of Highway 35 between Pepin and Nelson, as traffic can be fast.

Getting there: From Highway 10 turn into Durand on Sixth Avenue, then go west on Wells Street for 4 blocks. Park on the left side of the street.

To maximize the amount of cruising versus climbing time, the route travels counterclockwise, leaving from Memorial Park. As you depart from this well-preserved river town, enjoy the scenery from a simpler time. Originally known as Bear Creek, in the winter of 1857, the snow was so deep that the town flooded in the spring and had to be moved. Miles Durand Pindle purchased the land at the new location, surveyed and platted the town, and renamed it Durand, his mother's maiden name. As you leave town on Highway 10, use caution as you cross the Chippewa River and turn east on County Road P. Now cruising over rolling farmland, you will soon be in Arkansaw.

When you arrive in this little village, which stands along a narrow gorge, you can see why the site was ideally suited for lumber and grain milling. In 1852

Riders meandering along the bluffs on ▶
the Pepin County Challenge.

Willard F. Holbrook took a day off from the sawmill he worked at to go trout fishing with a friend. Walking over Gap Hill, they discovered a small stream that he named Arkansaw after the river. Later he came back and built a log cabin and established a furniture factory, and a town grew. Today, at the scenic Arkansaw Creek Park, you can see the sparkling water for a quarter mile as it rushes through the beautiful sandstone gorge.

Now turning to the south, the route follows the valley floor as the Chippewa River flows to the confluence of the Mississippi through the Tiffany State Wildlife Area. With spectacular bluffs to your right and an occasional paved country lane winding into the tree-lined distance, you will soon be at Silver Birch Park and Holden Park Campground. If you choose to stop here, the park is off the road about a quarter mile and borders Silver Birch Lake.

For the next 5 miles enjoy the quiet beauty of this area as you cruise down the valley floor before reaching the river town of Ella. Originally called Shoo Fly by settlers who came by water, it was renamed Ella after the first child born in the settlement. Today there are only a few residences left and a picnic area along the river. As you pass Bear Pen Road on County Road N, the route veers away from the river, sidestepping Fivemile Bluff and continuing through a couple valleys before turning south again. After looking to the west toward Devil's Corner, you will encounter your first major climb. Here the gorge on your right becomes visible as the road grade peaks at 13 percent over the next winding mile. At the crest you can see miles of rolling ridges and many lush valleys while picking up the pungent aroma of the mossy highland vegetation. After taking in the views for a second, it is time to enjoy the fruits of your labor as you cruise down into Pepin.

This village was named for the enlargement, or lake, of the Mississippi River in front of the village. Pepin is one of the oldest labels on Wisconsin maps, being mentioned by that name when the French explorer Duluth passed through. It is noted in his journal of 1679 that he crossed paths with the Pepin brothers, who were trapping in the area. Shaped by the lake, this village was an important shipping port in its early days; today it's a great place to have lunch or just enjoy the river activity. You will find several restaurants a block east of the route, down by the river's edge. Those who cherish the "Little House on the Prairie" series will enjoy stopping at the Pepin Historical/Laura Ingalls Wilder Museum. Here you can also find information on the exact site Laura was born, 7 miles north up in the bluffs.

Now leaving to the east on the paved shoulder of Highway 35, or the "Great River Road," the designated bike route follows the Mississippi River for the next 7 miles. The ride along the highway at the rivers' confluence will be especially interesting if you enjoy wildlife viewing. As you cross the Lower Chippewa River State Natural Area, you will find the largest intact floodplain forest and savanna in the upper Midwest. Because of the superb habitat, 75 percent of Wisconsin's nesting bird species can be found in this area. As you travel over the many bridges through this flowage area, even with the traffic noise, you are sure to see many interesting bird and plant species.

The highway curves south as you leave the floodplain, and the route then turns east onto County Road D. Here you have an option: If you want to explore the town of Nelson and pack in some extra energy for what lies ahead, follow the highway for another 0.75 mile south. An Englishman by the name of James Nelson settled here around 1843 and opened Nelson's Landing, a popular stopping place for river travelers. Just north of the landing, where the business district lies today, was a growing commerce center called Fairview, but when the post office was established in 1858, the combined villages took the name Nelson. Before leaving town, enjoy lunch or an ice-cream cone at the Nelson Cheese Factory—you are going to need the energy for the three major climbs that lie ahead.

Back on the route, after rolling through wild meadows where many colorful flowers heighten the landscape, you will turn to the north. After passing Center Creek Road you encounter the second of the four major hills on this ride. Shifting into granny, this first climb twists and turns for the next couple miles. At the crest, peek over the bluff to the northeast and enjoy the vista. You'll see the deep wooded ravine between you and the lush green valley ahead. Now shift back to your high ring and enjoy cruising down several miles of mountainous lanes.

After switching from one road to another to get to Lindstrom Valley Road, your body will be summoned to tap into that energy reserve once again. You'll pass a farm field with hundreds of little white huts housing young calves, and then the lane starts to climb up the outer edge of the ridge. Now circling around the lane, turn into the bluff and in your lowest possible gear, take on the heightening grade. Soon you are hitting the wall of the bluff and dancing on those pedals at 17 percent. Whether you rode or walked up this hill, you will need to stop and catch your breath before turning right on County Road V, which doesn't have a street sign. You will enjoy several miles of ridge running before your next descent.

Savor the rolling countryside for the next 5 miles as you jog from one valley road to another. As you approach the outskirts of Durand on the paved shoulder of PP, this challenge tests your stamina one more time as you approach a 0.75-mile hill with a 15 percent grade. At the top you will have a beautiful view of the city before enjoying a well-deserved cruise into town. Once you return, explore the Old Courthouse Museum or enjoy dinner on Durand's Main Street.

Miles and Directions

0.0 From Memorial Park, travel west on First Avenue and Wells Street.

0.2 Take a right on Third Avenue.

0.3 Take a right on Main Street.

0.7 Turn left on Sixth Avenue.

0.8 Cross the new Highway 10 bridge.

1.3 Turn left on County Road P.

3.1 Take a right on County Road O.

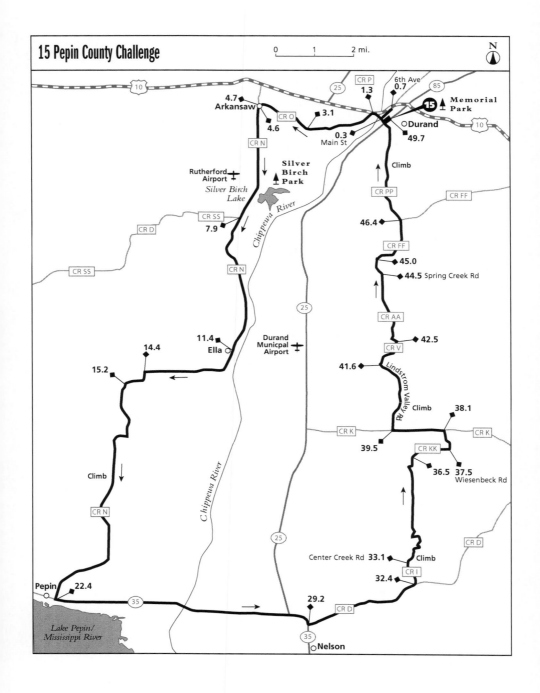

15 Pepin County Challenge

0   1   2 mi.

N

CR P
1.3

6th Ave
0.7

85

4.7
Arkansaw

CR O

3.1

15

Memorial
Park

4.6

CR N

0.3
Main St

Durand

10

49.7

Climb

Rutherford
Airport

Silver
Birch
Park

CR PP

CR FF

Silver Birch
Lake

46.4

Chippewa River

CR SS

CR FF

CR D

7.9

45.0

44.5 Spring Creek Rd

CR N

CR SS

CR AA

25

42.5

Durand
Municpal
Airport

CR V

11.4

41.6

Ella

14.4

15.2

Lindstrom Valley Rd

Climb

38.1

CR K

CR K

39.5

CR KK

Climb

CR N

Chippewa River

36.5 37.5
Wiesenbeck Rd

CR D

Center Creek Rd 33.1

Climb

CR I

32.4

Pepin

22.4

29.2

CR D

35

35

Lake Pepin/
Mississippi River

35

Nelson

4.6	Pass through Arkansaw.
4.7	Turn left on County Road N.
7.3	Pass Silver Birch Park.
7.9	Pass County Road SS.
11.4	Pass through the village of Ella.
14.4	Pass Boyd Spring Road.
15.2	Pass Plum Valley Road.
22.4	Turn left on Highway 35 in Pepin.
29.2	Turn left on County Road D. **Side-trip:** To visit the town of Nelson, take Highway 35 south for 0.75 mile.
32.4	Turn left on County Road I.
33.1	Take a right on Center Creek Road.
36.5	Take a right on County Road KK.
37.5	Turn left on Wiesenbeck Road.
38.1	Take a right on County Road K.
39.5	Turn right on Lindstrom Valley Road.
41.6	Take a right on County Road V at the top of the hill (no sign).
42.5	Turn left on County Road AA.
44.5	Pass Spring Creek Road.
45.0	Take a right on County Road FF.
46.4	Turn left onto County Road PP.
49.2	Take a right on Montgomery Street in Durand.
49.7	Turn left on Second Avenue.
50.0	Return to park.

Local Information

Pepin County Development Office, 740 Seventh Avenue, Durrand; (715) 672-5709; www.co.pepin.wi.us.
Pepin Area Community Club, 1468 Highway 35, Pepin; (715) 442-3011; www.pepin wisconsin.com.

Local Events/Attractions

Old Courthouse Museum, Washington Square, Durand; (715) 672-5423.
Pepin Historical/Laura Ingalls Wilder Museum, 306 Third Street/Highway 35, Pepin; (715) 442-2142.
Tiffany State Wildlife Area, DNR Office, 18428 Second Street, Alma; (608) 685-6222.

Restaurants

Ana's Russain Bakery & Coffee Shop, 311 Main Street, Durand; (715) 672-4888.
Durand House, 214 West Main Street, Durand; (715) 672-5975.
Garden Pub & Grill, 210 Third Street/Highway 35, Pepin; (715) 442-5500.
Nelson Cheese Factory and Restaurant, 38 Highway 35 South, Nelson; (715) 673-4725.

Accommodations

Audrey Boehn's House Inn, 402 West Prospect Street, Durand; (715) 495-8880.
Holden Park, off County Road N in Arkansaw; (715) 672-8665.

Bike Shops

Bad Cat Bikes, 327 Main Street East, Menomonie; (715) 231-2453.

Brickyard Cyclery, at Highway 29 next to the Red Cedar Trailhead in Menomonie; (715) 231-8735.

Brone's Bike Shop, 615 South Main Street/Highway 35, Fountain City; (608) 687-8601.

Restrooms

Start/finish: Memorial Park.

4.6: Arkansaw Creek Park.

7.8: Silver Birch Park (0.5 mile in from the road).

22.4: Pepin Historical/Laura Ingalls Wilder Museum.

29.9: Nelson Cheese Factory.

Maps

DeLorme: Wisconsin Atlas and Gazetteer: Page 60 C1.

Wisconsin State Bicycle Map (Mississippi River Section).

16 Trempealeau County Classic

In a land with majestic bluffs, meandering waterways, and rich Wisconsin history, this classic tour will give you a taste of areas with many riding possibilities. It is a biker's oasis of touring routes, so just pick up a free county bike map and decide. Starting in a centrally located Trempealeau County town, your next decision will be whether to ride the route as a century or as a two-day adventure. As you travel counterclockwise to gain the most momentum from the hills, you will encounter the route's first town, which was named after the centennial celebration of America's independence. After your first climb, enjoy ridge riding for several miles until you hit the Alligator Slide that drops you down to a town with two villages. You then roll through several fertile valleys, pass Chicken Breast Bluff, and enter a historic river town first settled in the early 1650s. Now circling back to the north, you will visit several villages, each with their own story, while relishing the rolling terrain. Along the way learn about the legend of Princess Marie Nounko and view the Amish way of life before returning to Whitehall.

Start: LaFollette/Melby Park in Whitehall.
Length: 104 miles with a 57-mile option.
Terrain: Rolling with several major climbs. Most roads in the county are paved, making it easy to customize rides.

Traffic and hazards: Ride with care, as some county roads and highways on the route can be heavy with traffic at times.

Getting there: From Highway 53 in Whitehall, turn west on Highway 21. After 1 block turn south on Park Street and go 2 blocks to Lincoln Street. The park is on the left and offers plenty of free street parking.

Start this classic in a community nestled in the rolling hills and lush landscape along the Trempealeau River, in the center of a bike-touring paradise. The arrival of the

A barge heads down the Mississippi past downtown Trempealeau.

railroad in 1873 brought settlement and commerce here. A year later the town was founded and named by early English settlers for Whitehall, Illinois, which in turn was named after Whitehall, New York, to honor Whitehall in England. After leaving LaFollette Park, turn south and roll out of town. Four miles of rolling prairie land later, turn to the west up through Kirth Valley into the village of Independence.

Situated at the confluence of Elk Creek and the Trempealeau River, this community was established in 1876, the year of the centennial celebration of America's independence. While here, swing by the restored 1902 City Hall and Opera House. The city park is just behind the Opera House, if needed. Looking for an old-fashioned protein road snack? Stop at Bushy's Meat Market for their snack sticks and homemade coffee cake. Leave town on the paved shoulder of Highway 93 for 1 mile, then turn west on County Road X.

For the next 8 miles enjoy rolling through Traverse Valley, then Hunt Valley. After passing Pape Valley, you will encounter your first climb. At the top of County Road X, make a sharp left onto Montana Ridge Road, and for the next 14 miles revel in the many scenic vistas as this classic rolls along the top of the ridge. After turning onto Konkell Valley Road, you will jog over to Bremer Ridge Road and take a right on Pansy Pass. At mile 32.7 there is a photo/rest stop option as you pass a bar and restaurant with a giant arrow sticking into the ground.

Now turning to the southeast, cruise down Alligator Slide. If you prefer the 57-mile option, watch for River Road about a half mile on the left of your descent. River Road will take you to the south side of Arcadia, then use the free county bike map to get back to Whitehall. Arcadia was formerly known as Bishop's Settlement and, because of the number of barns erected here by the early settlers, Barntown. Noah Comstock suggested the name of Arcadia, for its real or fancied resemblance to the valley of Arcadia in ancient Greece.

As the classic continues down River Road to Upper River Road, you will follow the banks of the Trempealeau River and for the next 3 miles travel through the lush green Doelle Valley. Then as you meander over the rolling terrain on Barth Road, you will pass through Buchler Valley, then Bohns Valley, before crossing the Trempealeau River into two villages at the 44.4-mile mark.

Known as the twin cities of Trempealeau County, stopping here is like stepping back in time. These two rural villages offer you peace and serenity with the look and feel of years gone by. The settlement was originally named Pine Creek for the towering pines that stood here, but when the Green Bay & Western Railroad came through, some of the residents wanted to rename the town Dodge after William E. Dodge, the prominent financier and philanthropist from New York who was involved with the construction of the railroad. Because the settlement was never incorporated, they kept both names.

About 3 miles south of town, turn onto Whistle Pass Road and cross Pine Creek, at which time the road will summon you to shift down into your lower gears for your next climb. At the crest you cruise down toward Perrot State Park. After crossing the Great River State Trail, you'll notice Chicken Breast Bluff to your right as you ride into the town of Trempealeau.

The first settlement in the area was a trading post established in 1685 by Nicolas Perrot, a mile north of where the city is today. The original settlement was at a high elevation completely surrounded by water and was known to the early French voyageurs as *la montagne qui trempe a l'eau,* or "the mountain that is steeped in the water." This, in turn, seems to have been a translation of *pah-hah-dak,* the Sioux word for "mountain separated by water." In 1840 several log cabins were built at the present site by French trappers. The trapper James Reed built a spacious two-story inn for river travelers, and the settlement became known as Reed's Landing. Then in 1852 the town was surveyed and platted as Mountainville, or Montoville. Due to several disagreements, it was resurveyed and given the name Trempealeau.

At the 56.2-mile mark, you will find the city park as you enter town. If you want to visit this riverfront village or spend the night, making this a two-day ride, continue south on Pine Street. Here at the river's edge is the Historic Trempealeau Hotel, Restaurant & Saloon, established in 1871. There is another hotel on Main Street, so you have plenty of options for your visit.

The classic turns onto 10th Street after leaving the park and heads east through the residential district before departing town. The terrain here is flat as you jog north and then east until you turn onto McGilvery Road. Over the next 4 miles the road becomes more rolling as you approach Galesville. Also called Gales, the town was named for Judge George Gale, who in 1853 purchased a large tract of land that includes the present site of the city. He also built a mill here on Beaver Creek and gave his name to the college. With a beautiful town square in the downtown district, you will want to stop and take a look around. Ride past "Old Main," the Historic Gale College, or when you leave on West Ridge Road, check out all the stately Victorian homes built by the prominent residents of an earlier time.

Now turning on Fourth Street, ride around Marinuka Lake. This beautiful body of water was given its name from the legend of Princess Marie Nounko, who was the granddaughter of the great Chief Decorah. Three miles up the road, discover more about this Indian legend as you pass by the Arctic Springs Supper Club and Galesville Trout Club and Park, which is just off the road and has rearing pens for trout. Down by the park shelter is the grave site of the Indian princess who died in 1889 at the age of thirty-two. At the request of her tribe, she was buried at midnight, with her head facing toward the rising sun.

On the road a mile farther east, you will pass through Abraham Coulee, and in another mile as the route approaches Highway 53, turn to the north in Frenchville. This village was settled by Henery French, who came from Pennsylvania with his wife in 1856. The route now follows French Creek and gradually turns east as the road starts to climb. After reaching the top, enjoy the next couple miles as you coast into Ettrick. John Cance (or Chance), who came here in 1855 and became the postmaster, got the town's name from Sir Walter Scott's *Marmion*. The Ettrick forest was a mountainous region of Scotland.

After leaving this little village, follow the north fork of Beaver Creek on County Road C. The route crosses the highway and creek a couple times before you arrive at Beach's Corners, named for Charles Beach, who owned most of the land here in 1870. Today you will find it a great place to stop for a Beach's Burger.

At the 82.7-mile mark, as you continue east, you pass through Hegg. This village was named for Colonel Hegg, the Civil War commander of the Fifteenth Wisconsin Norwegian Regiment, which brought fame to Wisconsin. If you need to stop for a bite to eat, you'll find the Hillbilly Fun Grill & Saloon and the D. S. Diner here. A mile from town, the classic turns north on Joe Coulee Road and runs parallel to the creek of the same name. You will soon pass Tenba Ridge Winery as you pedal up the valley floor.

As you ride along Tappen Coulee Creek on South River Road, you will be greeted by a sign saying VELKOMMEN TIL BLAIR ("Welcome to Blair") as you roll into this Scandinavian village nestled in the scenic, unglaciated hills. The village was originally known as Porterville, but after the Green Bay & Western Railroad came through in 1873, it began to develop and took the name of John Insley Blair, of Blairtown, New Jersey, who was a stockholder of the railroad. Today, what would a town with a Scandinavian heritage be if it didn't have a plant that produced leftse (thin potato pancakes) that you could enjoy?

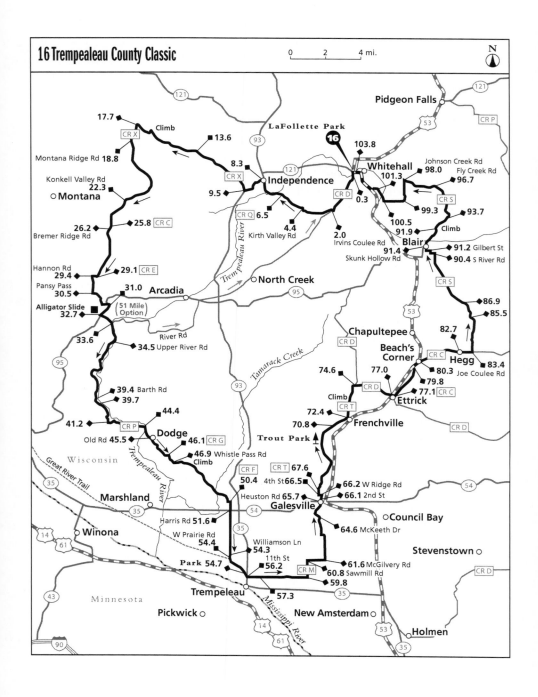

16 Trempealeau County Classic

0   2   4 mi.

N

Pidgeon Falls

121

53

CR P

17.7

Climb

13.6

CR X

LaFollette Park

Montana Ridge Rd **18.8**

93

103.8

16

Johnson Creek Rd **98.0**

Fly Creek Rd

8.3

121

Whitehall

101.3

Konkell Valley Rd

CR X

22.3

9.5

Independence

CR D

0.3

CR S

96.7

○ **Montana**

CR Q 6.5

4.4

99.3

93.7

26.2

25.8 CR C

100.5

Kirth Valley Rd

91.9

Bremer Ridge Rd

2.0

Irvins Coulee Rd

Climb

Blair

91.2 Gilbert St

Hannon Rd

29.4

29.1 CR E

Skunk Hollow Rd

91.4

90.4 S River Rd

Pansy Pass

30.5

31.0 **Arcadia**

○ **North Creek**

95

CR S

Alligator Slide

(51 Mile

Option)

86.9

32.7

85.5

33.6

River Rd

Chapultepee

82.7

34.5 Upper River Rd

CR D

Beach's

CR C

Hegg

Corner

83.4

74.6

77.0

80.3 Joe Coulee Rd

79.8

39.4 Barth Rd

93

CR D

77.1 CR C

39.7

Climb

Ettrick

72.4

CR T

44.4

70.8

Frenchville

CR D

41.2

CR P

Dodge

Old Rd **45.5**

46.1 CR G

67.6

66.2 W Ridge Rd

Wisconsin

46.9 Whistle Pass Rd

CR F

CR T

Climb

50.4

4th St 66.5

66.1 2nd St

Marshland

Heuston Rd **65.7**

54

Galesville

35

Harris Rd **51.6**

54

64.6 McKeeth Dr

○ **Council Bay**

○ **Winona**

W Prairie Rd

Williamson Ln

14

61

54.4

54.3

Stevenstown ○

11th St

61.6 McGilvery Rd

Park 54.7

56.2

CR M

60.8 Sawmill Rd

43

Trempeleau

59.8

CR D

57.3

35

Pickwick ○

New Amsterdam ○

14

53

Holmen

90

61

35

Now turning left on Skunk Hollow Road around the west side of Lake Henry, the Trempealeau River pauses as it flows through the lake. A mile out of town, you will be summoned again to shift to a lower gear as the road grade increases over Gransberg Hill, then one more time as you start riding on County Road S. At the top, shift back to your high ring and start cruising again. On Fly Creek Road you will pass many Amish farmsteads and the Fly Creek Buggy Shop along this 4-mile stretch. At the 98-mile mark the route turns west through rolling farmland where horse-drawn equipment still cultivates the soil.

Now circling back to the northwest, you soon turn onto Ervin Street/Highway 53 in Whitehall, where you will pass the lovely Oak Park Inn and Historic Hopkins House before returning to the park.

Miles and Directions

0.0 From LaFollette Park on Lincoln Street, take a right on Park Street.

0.2 Turn left on Ervin Street.

0.3 Take a right on County Road D.

2.0 Take a right on Irvins Coulee Road. (Note: The 57-mile option returns here from the south.)

4.4 Take a right on Kirth Valley Road.

6.5 Turn left on County Road Q.

8.2 Pass Hugitties Filler Road in Independence.

8.3 Turn left on Highway 93.

9.5 Take a right on County Road X in Traverse Valley.

13.6 Pass through Hunt Valley.

17.7 Turn left on County Road X.

18.8 Turn left on Montana Ridge Road.

20.5 Ride over Montana Ridge.

22.3 Take a right on Konkell Valley Road.

25.8 Take a right on County Road C.

25.9 Turn left on Montana Ridge Road.

26.2 Merge onto Bremer Ridge Road.

29.1 Take a right on County Road E.

29.4 Turn left on Hannon Road.

30.5 Take a right on Pansy Pass.

31.0 Take a right on Highway 95.

32.7 Turn left on Alligator Slide Road.

33.6 Pass River Road. **Option:** Turn left on River Road for the 57-mile option.

34.5 Take a right on Upper River Road.

39.4 Turn left on Barth Road.

39.7 Pass Buchler Valley.

41.2 Turn left on County Road P.

44.4 Turn left and cross the Trempealeau River.

45.5 Take a right on Old Road in Dodge.

46.1 Take a right on County Road G.

46.9 Turn left on Whistle Pass Road.

50.4 Take a right on County Road F.

51.6 Cross Highway 35 onto Harris Road.

54.3 Take a right on Williamson Lane.

54.4 Turn left on West Prairie Road.

54.7 Turn left at Perrot State Park.

55.6 Pass Chicken Breast Bluff.

56.1 Pass city park in Trempealeau.

56.2 Turn left on 11th Street.

56.3 Take a right on Highway 35.

57.3 Turn left on Freemont Road (Shubert Road).

58.0 Take a right on 11th Street (Bulawa Road).

59.8 Turn left on County Road M.

60.8 Take a right on Sawmill Road.

61.6 Turn left on McGilvery Road.

63.4 Take a right on Cooper Road.

64.6 Turn left on McKeeth Drive.

65.7 Cross Highway 54 into Galesville on Heuston Road.

66.1 Turn left on Second Street.

66.2 Turn left on West Ridge Road.

66.5 Take a right on Fourth Street.

67.6 Take a right on County Road T.

70.8 Pass Abraham Coulee.

72.4 Turn left on County Road T in Frenchville.

74.6 Take a right on County Road D.

77.0 Cross Highway 53 onto First Street in Ettrick.

77.1 Turn left on County Road C.

79.8 Take a right on Highway 53.

80.3 Take a right on County Road C at Beach's Corners.

82.7 Pass through Hegg.

83.4 Turn left on Joe Coulee Road, which runs parallel to creek.

85.5 Turn left on Silverson Road.

86.9 Take a right on County Road S.

90.4 Turn left on South River Road.

90.5 Take a right on Louberg Road in Blair.

91.2 Turn right on Gilbert Street.

91.3	Take a right on Highway 95.
91.4	Turn left on Skunk Hollow Road.
91.9	Ride over Gransburg Hill.
93.7	Go straight on County Road S.
96.7	Turn left on Fly Creek Road.
98.0	Turn left on Johnson Creek Road.
99.3	Take a right on Rat Road.
100.5	Take a right on Schwansberg Road.
101.3	Turn left on Wade Road.
101.7	Take a right on Highway 53.
103.6	Turn left at the intersection of County Road D and follow Ervin Street.
103.7	Take a right on Park Street.
103.8	Turn left on Lincoln Street.
104.0	Return to park.

Local Information

Whitehall Area Chamber of Commerce, 213 Hudson Street, Whitehall; (715) 538-4353; www.whitehall-chamber.com.

Trempealeau County Tourism Council, County Office, Highway 53 and Hobson Street, Whitehall; (800) 927-5339; www.trempealeau countytourism.com.

Local Events/Attractions

Trempealeau Hip Breaker Spring Tour; second Saturday in May; Bike Club of Trempealeau County; (715) 538-2168; www.ridebctc.com.

Acadia Memorial Tour; Saturday of Memorial Day weekend; Bike Club of Trempealeau County; (715) 538-2168; www.ridebctc.com.

Trempealeau Catfish 50 Tour; Saturday of weekend after the Fourth of July; Bike Club of Trempealeau County; (715) 538-2168; www.ridebctc.com.

Whitehall's Top of the World; second full weekend in September; Bike Club of Trempealeau County; (715) 538-2168; www.ridebctc.com.

Galesville Apple Affair Tour; first Saturday in October; Galesville Chamber of Commerce; (608) 582-2444.

Restaurants

Alternative Ground Coffee Shop, 36396 Main Street, Whitehall; (715) 538-1440.

City Cafe, 36375 Main Street, Whitehall; (715) 538-2249.

The Historic Trempealeau Hotel, 150 Main Street, Trempealeau; (608) 534-6898.

Accommodations

Oak Park Inn, 18224 Ervin Street/Highway 35, Whitehall; (877) 479-7024; www.oak parkinn.com.

Bike Shops

Brone's Bike Shop, 615 South Main Street/Highway 35, Fountain City; (608) 687-8601.

Restrooms

Start/finish: LaFollette Park.
8.3: Independence City Park.
32.6: Tavern just before Alligator Slide Road.
44.9: Taverns in Dodge.
56.1: Trempealeau City Park.
66.1: Galesville City Park.
91.2: Riverside Memorial Park in Blair.

Maps

DeLorme: Wisconsin Atlas and Gazetteer: Page 49 B6.

Wisconsin State Bicycle Map (Mississippi River Section).

Trempealeau County Connected Bicycle Loop Map.

17 Cranberry Cruise

This ride starts on the east side of Monroe County and circles up around the edge of rugged coulee terrain before passing through colorful cranberry fields. The route starts in a Lemonweir Valley community named for a great Indian chief with strong character and high ideals, and rolls to the north. The first town you come to was originally known as Blue Ridge, but the name was changed once a tunnel was built through the bluffs here. After climbing up the ridge, enjoy 10 miles of roller coaster fun before the cruise levels out on its way to the "Cranberry Capital of Wisconsin." As you turn south, you'll travel through a colorful marsh area with patches of jack pine forest before reaching an old railroad village. Now circling back to the west, continue to enjoy scenes of productive berry farms as you make your way back to Tomah.

Start: Winnebago Park in Tomah.
Length: 42 miles with a 33-mile option.
Terrain: The first 10 miles offer a few challenging climbs before leveling out for a cruise through Wisconsin's cranberry marsh country.

Traffic and hazards: Use caution riding on Highway 12 and Highway 173, as traffic can move fast.

Getting there: From Highway 12/Superior Avenue in Tomah, turn west on Juneau Road and go 5 blocks. Take a right on Butts Avenue; the park is 3 blocks north. Turn left on Lakeside Drive to the park, which has plenty of free parking.

Here, where the interstate splits in western Wisconsin, you are at the "Gateway to Cranberry Country," Tomah. In the spring of 1856 Robert Gilbert and his son climbed the ridge from the south to a knoll in the Lemonweir Valley and came upon a sight few white men had yet seen. Choosing this site to make their home, with natural meadows around them, they had a dream to build a city and took the name of a great Menominee Indian chief from a legend they had heard. Fifty years earlier Chief Tomah had reigned over this area, with the Winnebago tribe just to the south. The chief was described as a strong character with high ideals, and the settlers felt it was an honor to use his name, linked as it was to the rich story of Wisconsin's past.

The Gilberts' dream wouldn't come true for two more years, when the city gained its charter and the long-awaited railroad also came through to enhance Tomah's growth. Today this community offers all the necessary amenities and attractions to make your visit memorable. The cruise leaves from Winnebago Park on Lakeside Drive and follows the south shore around Lake Tomah. Now heading north on Gondola Road, the first 6 miles zigzag to the northwest, over the rolling countryside and up to Tunnel City.

This was the first settlement on the stagecoach trail, known as the Blue Ridge Road. By 1850 the village consisted of several homes and a livery, which supplied

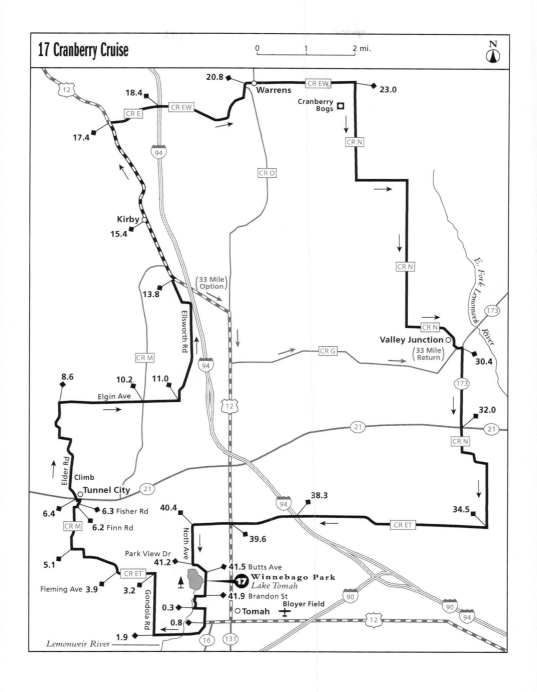

17 Cranberry Cruise

0   1   2 mi.

N

20.8
Warrens
23.0
CR EW
18.4
CR EW
12
CR E
Cranberry Bogs
17.4
94
CR N
17.4
CR O
Kirby
15.4
CR N
13.8
(33 Mile Option)
E. Fork Lemonweir River
173
Ellsworth Rd
CR N
Valley Junction
CR G
(33 Mile Return)
30.4
8.6
10.2 11.0
CR M
94
173
32.0
21
Elgin Ave
12
21
CR N
Elder Rd
Climb
Tunnel City
21
38.3
34.5
6.4
6.3 Fisher Rd
40.4
94
CR ET
CR M
6.2 Finn Rd
Noth Ave
39.6
Park View Dr
5.1
41.2
41.5 Butts Ave
CR ET
17 Winnebago Park
Fleming Ave 3.9
3.2
Lake Tomah
Gondola Rd
41.9 Brandon St
0.3
Bloyer Field
Tomah
90
0.8
90
94
1.9
12
Lemonweir River
16   131

fresh horses. Several years later the La Crosse & Milwaukee Railroad, which later became the Chicago, Milwaukee, St. Paul & Pacific, sent surveyors out to choose a new route for a rail line. The ridge was impassable, so they ran tracks up to each side and hauled freight and passengers over the ridge by teams of horses and carts to continue the journey. Then in 1861 a tunnel was built through the ridge with picks and wheelbarrows, and the town took the name Tunnel City.

Upon crossing Highway 21 onto Elder Road, you will encounter your first major climb up the Blue Ridge. Here, twisting and turning, with spectacular view of the countryside, the road grade will have you dancing on your pedals. At the top the road begins to roll, as if the bear and bull from the stock market had something to do with the terrain. Now turning to the north on Ellsworth Road, the terrain mellows as you roll through the meadows. Soon you are on the paved shoulder of Highway 12 and riding north. Those who prefer the 33-mile option will turn right and follow the highway south for 2 miles, then turn left on County Road G. As the cruise travels up the highway's paved shoulder, you will soon pass through Kirby.

This was once a thriving little community, established around 1850 by a butcher named Kirby. He departed the area shortly thereafter, but left his name to the settlement. As you continue to ride up the valley floor, you will soon reach County Road E at the 17.4-mile mark. Here at the corner you will find the River View Bar if you need to stop. Now heading east, after crossing under Interstate 94, the road turns into County Road EW. In a little over 2 miles, you will be in the "Cranberry Capital of Wisconsin," Warrens.

In 1868 the West Wisconsin Railroad Company built their line to this site, and George Warren unloaded a small sawmill and started sawing pine logs into lumber. Originally the village was call Warren's Mill, but then the post office was established and the name was shortened. After the majestic timber stands were depleted, around 1870 cranberry farming took off in the area's marshes. Today you will find the largest concentration of cranberry marshes in the state here, around 1,850 acres of bright red berries producing more than 28.5 billion pounds each year.

While here plan a stop at the Wisconsin Cranberry Discovery Center for lunch, a cranberry ice-cream cone, or just to browse around the museum. See, touch, and taste Wisconsin's number one fruit crop, and learn how the Native Americans harvested the berries in the wild and the unique growing and harvesting methods used today.

As you continue east the road flattens out as it passes several cranberry farms. Approaching County Road N, you will notice a large berry operation with an 8-foot-high fence around the perimeter to keep the deer out of the fields. The berries grow like any other irrigated crop, except they are planted on rich beds of sphagnum moss and the fields are flooded for harvest. In between cranberry marshes, you will pass through stands of jack pine forest and pastureland. At the 30.3-mile mark, turn left on County Road G and then onto Highway 173 into Valley Junction. Those who chose the 33-mile option merge back with the cruise here.

This town was established in 1872 when the Valley Line was built between Tomah and Babcock for the Chicago, Milwaukee & St. Paul Railroad. By 1928 the line was abandoned, and today there are a just few homes and Smitty's Inn that help keep the community alive. For the next 1.5 miles, as you ride south along Highway 173, you will find a narrow paved shoulder to use if the road gets busy. After crossing Highway 21, resume riding on County Road N.

At County Road ET take a right and head west back into Tomah. As you pass one of the marshes, notice the trees lining the waterway. Here you will see a heron rookery (nesting area) up in the treetops. After crossing over the interstate, you will pass the large stately Veterans Administration campus on your right. Now it is only a short distance back to the park in Tomah.

Miles and Directions

0.0   Leave Winnebago Park from Brandon Street onto Lakeside Drive.

0.3   Turn left on Juneau Road.

0.5   Take a right on Butts Avenue.

0.8   Turn right on County Road CM/Hugh Dickie Road.

1.9   Take a right on Gondola Road.

3.2   Turn left on County Road ET.

3.6   Continue straight on Flatiron Avenue.

3.9   Take a right on Fleming Avenue.

4.7   Turn right at the T next to the storage units (no sign).

5.1   Take a right on County Road M.

6.0   Turn left at the T into Tunnel City

6.2   Turn left on Finn Road.

6.3   Take a right Fisher Road.

6.4   Cross Highway 21 onto Elder Road.

8.6   Take a right on Elgin Avenue.

10.2   Cross County Road M.

11.0   Turn left on Ellsworth Road.

13.8   Turn left on Highway 12. **Option:** Turn right on Highway 12 and then left on County Road G for the 33-mile option.

15.4   Pass through Kirby.

17.4   Take a right on County Road E.

18.4   Cross under I–94; road changes to County Road EW.

20.8   Take a right on County Road EW in Warrens.

23.0   Take a right on County Road N.

30.3   Turn left on County Road G. (Note: The 33-mile option returns here.)

30.4   Take a right on Highway 173 through Valley Junction.

32.0   Cross Highway 21 and resume riding on County Road N.

34.5 Take a right on County Road ET.

38.3 Cross over I-94 into Tomah.

39.6 Cross Highway 12.

40.4 Turn left on Noth Avenue.

41.2 Turn left on Park View Drive.

41.5 Take a right on Butts Avenue.

41.9 Take a right on Brandon Street.

42.0 Return to park.

Local Information

Tomah Area Chamber of Commerce, 805 Superior Avenue, Tomah; (800) 948-6624; www.tomahwisconsin.com.

Local Events/Attractions

Wisconsin Cranberry Discovery Center, 204 Main Street, Warrens; (608) 378-4878; www.discovercranberries.com.

Restaurants

Greenwood Cafe, 906 Superior Avenue, Tomah; (608) 372-4181.

Jazzberries Coffeehouse, 1115 North Superior Avenue, Tomah; (608) 372-7446.

Cranberry Ice Cream Parlor, 204 Main Street, Warrens; (608) 378-4878.

Accommodations

Cranberry Country Lodge, Highway 21 and I-94, Tomah; (608) 374-2801.

Whispering Pines Campground, 24699 Embay Avenue, Tomah; (608) 372-2480.

Mill Bluff State Park, 15819 Funnel Road, Camp Douglas; (608) 427-6692; www.wiparks.net.

Bike Shops

Brian's Bicycle Shop, 211 West Washington Street, Tomah; (608) 372-4530.

Restrooms

Start/finish: Winnebago Park.

20.8: Wisconsin Cranberry Discovery Center.

Maps

DeLorme: Wisconsin Atlas and Gazetteer: Page 41 A4.

Wisconsin State Bicycle Map (Mississippi River Section).

Cranberry Country Bicycle/Auto Tour Map.

18 Sparta/Elroy Classic

Starting at the "Bicycling Capital of America," this ride offers you the opportunity to circle around one of the most unique and scenic rail-to-trail systems established on a converted rail line. As the crushed limestone trail runs through the valley, the classic enjoys meandering in and out of the ridges and around the coulees for an invigorating tour along the dales. The route travels south through the countryside to a town named for its resemblance to a village in Mexico. Then cruising down the valley, you will encounter your first major climb before visiting a town with an Indian name meaning "a point of land." After making another loop and climbing another set of ridges, you visit another rail-to-trail town that has a historic railroad depot and museum. One more loop, circling to the southeast, will take you to the other end of this line, where the "400" and Omaha Bike Trails also meet. Now riding north up the ridge's spine, you will pass many Amish farms along this 26-mile stretch of hillside lane. After a long descent, passing a military encampment, the route takes you back to Sparta.

Start: Evans Bosshard Park in Sparta.
Length: 90 miles with 40-mile and 69-mile options, and several additional trail options.
Terrain: Rolling with several major climbs. On the return ride, the trail is on crushed limestone and requires a trail pass.
Traffic and hazards: Use caution riding on Highways 71 and 16, as traffic can move fast.

Getting there: From Interstate 90 take the Highway 27 exit and head north into Sparta. Take a right on Wisconsin Street and follow it past the statue of "Big Ben" with his bike. Turn left on East Avenue, cross the river, and turn left again onto the park road. Parking here is free and plentiful.

Starting in Sparta, a community with a Greek name, this ride offers cyclists a chance to explore the coulee region and a place to relax between rides. The town dates back to 1849, when the first settlers, the Pettit family, made a claim here. Mrs. Pettit chose the town's name two years later as a possible tribute to the "Spartan courage" of its founders. You will find this community—the seat of Monroe County, where astronaut Donald "Deke" Slayton lives—the perfect place to start your ride.

With the statute of "Big Ben" on his bike across the street from Evans Bosshard Park, where Beaver Creek spills into the La Crosse River, the classic leaves on Water Street. Soon you will pass the Sparta/Elroy trailhead at the historic depot and visitor center. As the route tours the countryside circling around the 32 miles of crushed limestone trail on the old Chicago-Northwestern rail bed, you have many ride options. Now heading south, after passing over I–90, the road merges into Ideal Road and starts undulating. Soon you turn west at the campground and ride another mile to Leon, turning left on Kansas Avenue just before the village.

Leon was named for a village in Mexico that it was said to resemble. If you need to stop, there is a tavern in town. Otherwise, you will start cruising southeast down

Fun rollers through beautiful countryside keep riders entertained on the Sparta/Elroy Classic.

the valley floor. After turning onto County Road U, your legs muscles will be summoned for your first major climb up the ridge. It is not uncommon here to see a red fox bolt out of a ditch in front of you. After reaching the top, you will drop back down on Eagle Street into Norwalk.

One of the first settlers here was S. McGary, who helped organize the village and named it Norwalk in honor of his native village back in Ohio. The name is said to derive from an Indian word meaning "a point of land." At the 19-mile mark, those who prefer to cut the ride short can pick up a Sparta/Elroy Trail wheel pass and head back to Sparta. Those who want to take the 40-mile option should leave to the east on County Road T. No matter which tour you select, you will find a park and meal options in Norwalk, including a market and bakery.

As the classic departs on Leather Street, follow the route along the Baraboo River. After crossing the bike trail, you will pass over Highway 71 and then travel south on County Road T. As you meander around several coulees, the rugged terrain circles to the east along another ridge. Here you will ride by a couple Amish farms and a sawmill dating from the turn of the twentieth century, when horses were the main source of power. At the 30.8-mile mark you have a side trip option of riding through Tunnel 1. This is the longest tunnel on the Sparta/Elroy Trail and is a mile north on County Road V. Otherwise the classic continues riding on Mockingbird Avenue to the town of Kendall.

When it was organized, the town was named in honor of its earliest settler, James Kindel Sr. As time went by, the county board changed the orthography of the name so it could be more easily written and spoken. Here at the 35.3 mile mark, if you prefer to shorten the ride to 69 miles, cross Highway 71 on Spring Street to the middle of town and then go north on County Road W. This will take you past the historic depot and museum next to the trail. The classic turns right on Highway 71 for a short distance, then goes south again into the countryside. At Ottoman Avenue the route makes a large circle and then comes back up to the north at Deadman's Hollow before climbing another ridge. After riding the spine on County Road WW, the road changes to County Road O at the county line before descending down into Elroy.

Originally called LeRoy after a town in New York, it was soon discovered that there was already a town with that name in Wisconsin, so the first two letters were reversed. Here in Elroy you will find several options for lunch and will cross the trailhead where the Sparta/Elroy and Omaha Trails meet. After leaving town, start climbing again up along the north ridge on your way back to Kendall.

In Kendall turn right on County Road W and head up the floor of Spring Valley. After riding along Kittyhawk Road, the route turns onto King Road up along Dorset Ridge. At the top enjoy spectacular vistas as you cruise the rolling roads that wind along the ridge's spine for the next 25 miles. Along the way visit the area's Amish farm community, and be sure to watch the road along this stretch, as the horses that pull the buggies don't mind dropping their waste where you ride. Passing Kiln Road, King Road continues up the ridge after turning into County Road A and soon travels past the old town of Ridgeville.

The area was originally settled by Czechoslovakians who moved here because the land "lay high" and they wouldn't experience the water problems they had elsewhere. This community was originally called Dividing Ridge because it separated Sparta and Coles Valley from Indian Creek. By the mid-1800s the village was renamed to something easier to write. In another half mile you will pass County Road T, where the 40-mile option returns. After a long descent, the route turns left on the paved shoulder of Highway 16. To your right is Coles Valley.

This valley was popular with the Winnebago Indian tribe because of the rich soil for farming. One of the first settlers to arrive here was Charles Cole. By 1870 the community had several businesses and was nicknamed Little Chicago, but today you will only find a few homes among the farm fields. As you continue to follow Highway 16 west, take a right under I–90 at the Fort McCoy entrance.

Fort McCoy is a United States Army installation established in 1909 and was a prisoner-of-war camp during World War II. Today a war training center, the fort offers a self-guided tour, but you need an ID pass to get on base. Call the Public Affairs Office at (608) 388-3456 to arrange a tour.

Now riding on County Road A again, the route takes you back to Sparta.

Miles and Directions

0.0 Leave from Evans Bosshard parking lot on East Avenue.

0.2 Cross Highway 16.

0.6 Take a right on Walrath Street.

0.7 Turn left on Cliffton Street.

1.3 Turn left on Water Street and cross trail at the historic depot/visitor center.

2.0 Cross I-90 onto Ideal Road.

5.1 Take a right on Jancing Avenue.

6.6 Turn left on Kansas Avenue just before the village of Leon.

9.1 Turn left on County Road XX.

15.4 Turn left on County Road U.

18.6 Turn left on Eagle Street in Norwalk.

18.7 Turn left on Highway 71.

19.0 Take a right on Mill Road, at the library. **Option:** Follow Highway 71 to County Road T for the 40-mile option.

19.1 Cross bike trail.

19.4 Turn left on Leather Street.

20.2 Cross Highway 71 onto County Road T.

21.1 Turn left on Mead Avenue.

24.8 Turn left on Highway 131.

25.5 Take a right on Midway/Eagle Avenue.

30.8 Pass County Road V. **Side-trip:** To ride through Tunnel 1 on the Sparta/Elroy Trail, take County Road V north 1 mile to the trail.

31.5 Turn left on Monarch Avenue.

33.7 Turn left on Mockingbird/Moccasin Avenue.

35.3 Take a right on Highway 71 into Kendall. **Option:** Turn left on County Road W for the 69-mile option eliminating the loop to Elroy and back.

36.5 Take a right on County Road W.

40.3 Take a right on County Road W at Ottoman Avenue.

43.3 Turn left on County Road WW.

45.0 Merge onto County Road O.

48.7 Turn left on Highway 80.

49.0 Turn left on County Road PP.

49.1 Take a right on County Road P.

56.4 Take a right on County Road W in Kendall. (Note: The 69-mile option starts here.)

58.2 Turn left on County Road N at Spring Valley.

60.9 Turn left on Kittyhawk Road.

62.3 Take a right on King Road at Dorset Ridge.

64.7 Take a right on King Road at Kiln Road.

67.8 Turn left on County Road A.

18 Sparta/Elroy Classic

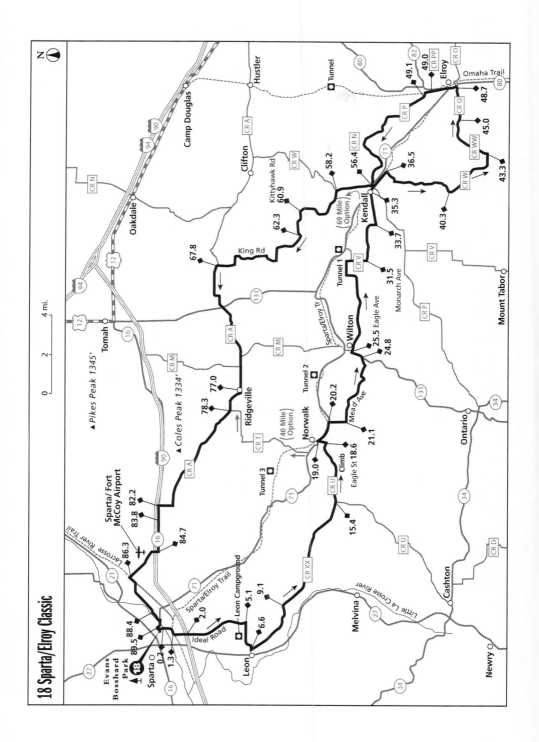

77.0 Pass Ridgeville.

78.3 Pass County Road T. (Note: The 40-mile option returns here.)

82.2 Turn left on Highway 16 at Coles Valley.

83.3 Take a right under I-90 at Fort McCoy entrance.

84.7 Turn left on County Road A.

86.3 Turn left on Hazelwood Avenue.

88.4 Cross tracks onto Milwaukee Avenue.

89.0 Take a right on the paved shoulder of Highway 16.

89.5 Take a right on East Avenue.

89.8 Turn left to park entrance.

90.0 Return to park.

Local Information

Sparta Area Chamber of Commerce, 11 Milwaukee Street, Sparta; (800) 354-2453; www.bikesparta.com.

Local Events/Attractions

Monroe County Historical Museum, 200 West Main Street, Sparta; (608) 269-8680.

Kendall Depot, 26 North Railroad Avenue, Kendall; (608) 463-7107.

Monroe County Century Challenge; last Sunday in July; (608) 584-4947; www.wisport.com.

Coulee Region Tour; second week in August; (414) 671-4560; www.wisconsinbicycletours.com.

Restaurants

Dorine's Family Inn, 215 South Water Street, Sparta; (608) 269-8258.

Leon Country Store, Highway 27, Leon; (608) 269-5224.

Gina's Pies Are Square, 400 Main Street, Wilton; (608) 435-6541.

Gins Trailhouse Cafe, 215 Main, Elroy; (608) 462-4899.

Accommodations

Country Inn, 737 Avon Road, Sparta; (608) 269-3110.

Leon Valley Campground, 9050 Jancing Avenue, Sparta; (608) 269-6400.

Bike Shops

Speed's Bicycle Shop, 1126 John Street, Sparta; (608) 269-2315; www.speedsbike.com.

Restrooms

Start/finish: Evans Bosshard Park.

5.1: Leon Campground.

18.8: Norwalk City Park.

35.3: Historic depot in Kendall.

48.7: Trailhead in Elroy.

56.4: Historic depot in Kendall.

83.8: Fort McCoy.

Maps

DeLorme: Wisconsin Atlas and Gazetteer: Page 41 A4.

Wisconsin State Bicycle Map (Mississippi River Section).

Sparta Road Tours Bicycle Map.

19 Coulee Country Challenge

This ride offers those up for the test a true taste of coulee country. The route starts in a river community along the Mississippi and uses the paved trail through the river bottom marshlands to get you in and out of town. On the road you will roll through the countryside past several Swiss Valley Farms before approaching a village named for a town in Vermont. After climbing up and riding the spine of the ridge, you will pass through a town that was named for its location on a ridge between two other ridges. Now traveling south, the route rolls past a nature center in Norwegian Valley before reaching a town with a swimming beach and park on Coon Creek. As you follow Mormon Creek to the west, the route twists and turns as several Wisconsin rollers offer you one thrill after another. You will then travel on several residential streets to Myrick Park and return to the Three Rivers Trail for the ride back to Riverside Park in La Crosse.

Start: Riverside Park in La Crosse.
Length: 57 miles with a 37-mile option.
Terrain: Very rolling with several major climbs.

Traffic and hazards: The route uses bike trails to maneuver through town. On the road use caution when riding on Highway 16 and Highway 14 as the challenge returns to La Crosse.

This route filled with natural geographic beauty leaves from La Crosse, which grew from a fur-trading post in the 1600s to a village enriched by the late 1800s lumber boom to the lively city it is today. The name *La Crosse* came from the French after early explorers saw Indians playing the game here. It wasn't until 1856 that the city charter was granted, and in 1858 the La Crosse & Milwaukee Railroad was completed, making it easier for settlers traveling from Lake Michigan to get here.

The challenge leaves from Riverside Park and uses the Three Rivers Trail to safely move cyclists to the other side of town. After meandering through the marshlands along the La Crosse River, the trail turns onto River Valley Road. Within a half mile you cross Highway 16 onto the service road and pass through a community once known as Medary. Originally called Winona Junction, it was formed when a railroad line was built to Winona, Minnesota. The town was renamed in honor of Samuel Medray, who became governor of the state of Kansas.

Now heading east on County Road O, enjoy the rolling countryside for the next 6 miles. As you ride past the stately old brick homes and farmsteads, notice that many are members of the Swiss Valley Farm group. Soon you pass Barre Mills and merge onto County Road M at 9.4 miles, still going east. This community was settled by a number of pioneers originally from Barre, Vermont. At one time there were two water-powered flour mills located on Bostwick Creek, one being the Barlow O. S. Flour Mill. If you look off to your right, you can still see the mill's foundation.

As you continue east on County Road I, at St. Joseph Coulee, the route becomes more rolling along the contoured farm fields. Those who prefer the 37-mile option will continue south on County Road M. As County Road I veers south, the challenge approaches its first climb before reaching Highway 33. You then turn east again and soon pass Highway 162, which leads to Coon Valley. After another mile you will pass Newburg Corners, which was named after a local family who settled there. Today there are only a few residences and a tavern at the corner of County Road H that opens in the afternoon.

As you continue east, you'll ride the spine of the ridge and soon pass the old Middle Ridge School House. From the school it's another mile and a half to the village of Middle Ridge and County Road G. Named in 1858 for the middle ridge between La Crosse and Bangor, the town was founded by John Becker, a wagon maker; John Schomer, who built a general store; and Frank Brown, a blacksmith. You will find a few options here for a rest break. Otherwise, if you packed a lunch, continue south on County Road G for 2.5 miles to Meadow Brook Park on Coon Creek, where you will find plenty of shade, water, and primitive restrooms.

The route continues along the valley floor, and in less than a mile County Road G turns left at the junction of County Road H. Now following Coon Creek, you will meander through the rolling farm fields in Bohemian Valley, passing a designated trout stream just before turning onto County Road P. As you pass County Road PI, notice the sign for the Norskedalen Nature & Heritage Center. This Norwegian Valley farmstead is a great place to visit for birding or nature hiking after the ride.

In another mile turn onto the paved shoulder of Highway 14 and ride into Coon Valley. The first settler here was Helge Gulbrandson, who came from Norway in 1849. For some years the valley was known as *Helgedalen,* meaning "Helge Valley." In 1865 a post office was established and it was renamed Coon Valley because so many raccoons were found in the region. At the 31-mile mark, if you didn't have lunch or are looking for an ice-cream cone, consider the Stockyard Grill and Saloon or the Up the Creek Ice Cream Shop. After leaving town on Highway 14, turn north on Highway 162 after passing the swimming beach at Coon Creek Park.

Three miles up the road, turn west again on County Road NN. Just after Roesler Coulee you will reach County Road M, where the 37-mile option returns. Now following Mormon Creek through the valley, in 3 miles turn left on Highway 14. In another mile jog west off the highway on County Road MM and climb Brinkman Ridge.

For the next 5 miles enjoy the twists and turns of these true Wisconsin rollers that offer one thrill after another. Returning to Highway 14, the route utilizes the wide paved shoulder until you veer off on the city streets in La Crosse. Once you reach Myrick Park, ride past the zoo. At East Avenue take a right onto the bike trail and head north. When you reach the T on the trail, just before the footbridge, turn left and follow the trail back to Riverside Park in La Crosse.

19 Coulee Country Challenge

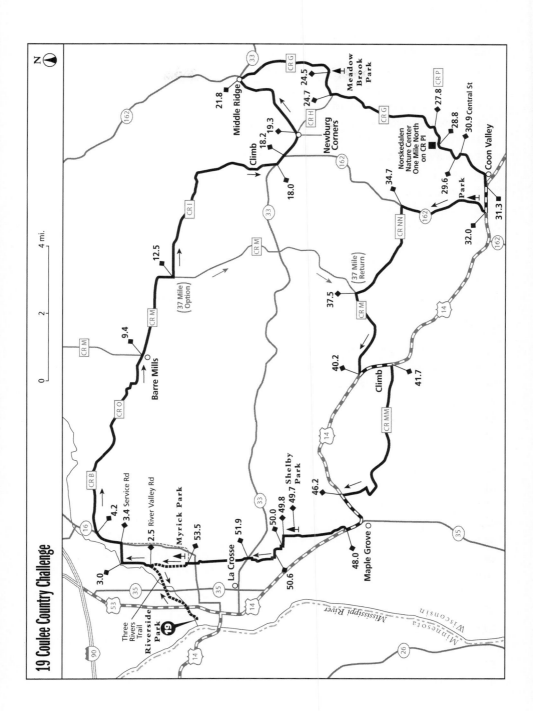

Miles and Directions

0.0 Leave Riverside Park from the Three Rivers Trail.

1.9 Turn left on trail.

2.5 Leave trail and take a right on River Valley Road.

3.0 Take a right on Gillette Street.

3.4 Turn left onto the Highway 16 service road.

4.1 Take a right onto paved shoulder of Highway 16.

4.2 Take a right on County Road B.

7.5 Take a right on County Road O.

9.4 Continue straight ahead on County Road M after passing through Barre Mills.

12.5 Turn left on County Road I. **Option:** Take a right on County Road M for the 37-mile option.

18.0 Turn left on Highway 33.

18.2 Pass Highway 162. (Note: Coon Valley is 7 miles south from here.)

19.3 Pass Newburg Corners.

21.8 Take a right on County Road G in Middle Ridge.

24.5 Pass Meadow Brook Park.

24.7 Turn left on County Road G, at County Road H, following Coon Creek.

27.8 Turn right on County Road P at Bohemien Valley.

28.8 Pass County Road PI to Norskedalen Nature Center.

29.6 Circle around Spring Coulee Ridge.

30.9 Ride into Coon Valley on Central Street.

31.3 Take a right on the paved shoulder of Highway 14.

32.0 Take a right on Highway 162.

34.7 Turn left on County Road NN.

37.5 Turn left on County Road M and follow Morman Creek. (Note: The 37-mile option returns here.)

40.2 Turn left on Highway 14.

41.7 Take a right on County Road MM up Brinkman Ridge.

46.2 Turn left on Highway 14 into La Crosse.

48.0 Take a right on 33rd Street.

49.7 Pass Shelby Park.

49.8 Turn left on Ward Avenue.

50.0 Take a right on 28th Street.

50.1 Turn left on Lincoln Avenue.

50.2 Take a right on Hoeschler Drive.

50.4 Turn left on Chase Avenue.

50.6 Cross Losey Boulevard.

50.7 Take a right on 23rd Street.

50.8 Turn left on 22nd Street.

51.3 Take a right on Green Bay Avenue.

51.4 Turn left on 22nd Street.

51.7 Take a right on Denton Avenue.

51.8 Turn left on 23rd Street.

51.9 Cross Highway 33 onto 22nd Street.

52.8 Take a right on Campell Road.

52.9 Turn left on 22nd Street.

53.0 Take a right on Myrick Park Lane.

53.2 Cross La Crosse Street onto Hillview Avenue.

53.4 Turn left on Park Drive.

53.5 Turn left on Myrick Park Drive, stay right, and pass zoo.

53.8 At East Avenue, take a right on the Three Rivers Trail north.

55.3 Before footbridge, take a left on trail.

57.0 Return to park.

Local Information

La Crosse Area Convention & Visitors Bureau, 410 Veterans Memorial Drive, La Crosse; (800) 658-9424; www.explorelacrosse.com.

Local Events/Attractions

La Crosse County Historical Society, 112 South Ninth Street, La Crosse; (608) 782-1980; www.lchs.org.

Bike 4 Trails; La Crosse River Trail and Great River Trail; (888) 540-8434; www.bike4trails.com.

City Brewery Tours, 1111 South Third Street, La Crosse; (608) 785-4820.

Restaurants

Fayze's Restaurant & Bakery, 135 Fourth Street South, La Crosse; (608) 784-9548.

Freight House Restaurant, 107 Vine Street, La Crosse; (608) 784-9548.

Grounded Specialty Coffee (with gelato ice cream); 308 Main Street, La Crosse; (608) 784-5282.

Accommodations

Grand Stay Residential Suites, 525 Front Street North, La Crosse; (877) 388-7829; www.grandstay.net.

Camp We Ha Kee, 715 28th Street South, La Crosse; (608) 787-8304.

Bike Shops

Bikes Limited, 3337 Hanson Court, La Crosse; (608) 785-2326.

Buzz's Bikes, 800 Rose Street, La Crosse; (608) 785-2737.

Gene's Bicycle Shop, 2242 State Road, La Crosse; (608) 782-7233.

Valley Ski & Bike, 321 Main Street, La Crosse; (608) 782-5500.

Restrooms

Start/finish: Riverside Park

21.8: Middle Ridge Store.

24.5: Meadow Brook Park.

49.1 Shelby Park.

53.5: Myrick Park.

Maps

DeLorme: Wisconsin Atlas and Gazetteer: Page 40 B1.

Wisconsin State Bicycle Map (Mississippi River Section).

DNR Bike 4 Trails Map.

20 Hustler Ridge Challenge

The Black Hawk War of 1832 attracted a lot of attention to what would become Wisconsin. This scenic route travels through some of the area where this tribal conflict played out, in lush valleys where creeks flow between the mountain-like hills. You will head northwest from a town named for its rich soil, then climb up Hustler Ridge and ride the undulating spine with its scenic vistas. As the route meanders along the ridge, it soon circles back to the south. After the next descent, you will pass through a village that was named after the mayor of Madison, who had suggested naming the town Janesville. In the next valley that you roll into, stop in a village named for its bear population. Coming full circle, you will pass through a village named for a Great Lakes steamer captain before you cross and then follow the Pine River. After passing a one-room schoolhouse museum, you will soon be back in Richland Center and ready to look at some of the buildings designed by Frank Lloyd Wright.

Start: Corner of Jefferson and Hazeltine Streets in Richland Center.
Length: 52 miles with a 23-mile option.
Terrain: Rolling with a couple major climbs. Most rural roads are paved if you want to customize the route.

Traffic and hazards: Use caution when riding on Highway 130 and when returning on Highway 14 in Richland Center.

Getting there: From Highway 14 turn east on Seminary Street into town. Go past the visitor center (the historic depot is on the corner of the block), then turn south on Jefferson Street, where you will find plentiful free parking.

This challenge starts at the seat of Richland County and travels through lush valleys and over forested ridges while visiting several communities along its path. Located in the center of the county on the Pine River, Richland Center was first settled in 1843 by trappers canoeing up from the Wisconsin River. By 1851 the village was surveyed and platted, and the town's population grew, along with the attendant churches, schools, and stores. In 1867 the world-renowned architect Frank Lloyd Wright was born here. After the ride, check out some of the buildings he designed fifty years later.

After leaving from the corner of Jefferson Street, ride through downtown past the visitors center at the historic depot. Just east of town you encounter your first climb. You will ride along at a 6 percent grade for the first mile, then all of a sudden you'll hit the wall of the ridge at a 13 percent grade. Take the high road at the top, turning left at the Sunset Orchard sign, and then roll along Hustler Ridge Road. For the next 10 miles you will meander around the coulees and ledges while enjoying the ridge's scenic splendor. Along this stretch you will pass roads to your right,

A Wisconsin round barn looms over a nearby farmhouse.

such as Buckta Hill and Coop Woods, that are paved and offer you shortcut options over to County Road NN. As you go around the horn from County Road DD to County Road NN, enjoy the aroma of alfalfa hay freshly cut from one of the ridgetop farm fields.

Soon you will start to descend the ridge, and for the next 6 miles the road follows Little Willow Creek down through the valley. As you coast through farmyards and along contoured fields, you might see a badger cross the road ahead of you. At County Road N those who prefer the 23-mile option should take a right and follow the road west back into Richland Center. The challenge continues south to Willow Creek Road, where you turn northeast and pedal through pasturelands until turning north on Highway 58 in Ithaca. This small rural hamlet was named after Ithaca, New York.

A quarter mile up the highway, turn east again and roll through another valley to Keysville. From 1855 to 1872 this community was centered around a church and known as St. Mary's. When a post office was established here, Judge E. W. Keyes, the mayor of Madison, suggested Janesville, but it was voted down, with most preferring using the mayor's name instead. Today the only thing left of the village is the church and a few residences.

After leaving the village on County Road N, you continue to roll southeast through the countryside for a couple more miles until reaching Highway 130. Turn south on the paved shoulder and ride down Four Springs Valley. At the 27-mile mark you are in Bear Valley, which received its name because of all the bear sightings there. The village has a few residence and a bar and grill if you need to stop, or continue 2 miles farther, after passing Four Springs Hollow, and stop at Bear Valley Park.

Even though the highway traffic is normally light here, use caution. There is no paved shoulder for the next 3 miles as you ride by flat farm fields with irrigated systems. After turning west on Highway 60, enjoy the lush green fields with a picturesque bluff border in the distance.

At the 38.4-mile mark, cross Highway 14 onto Highway 60 in Gotham, which was originally located next to the Wisconsin River and called Richland City. With the river banks eroding, around 1904 the town was moved its present site closer to the railroad tracks. The village was renamed for Captain M. W. Gotham, a friend of local storekeeper W. A. McNurlin. Gotham spent his winters with his family in Richland and enjoyed swapping tales with the men who worked the steamers on the Wisconsin River. In 1902 Captain Gotham perished in a storm on Lake Erie on the steamer he commanded. The village's corner store is a great place to stop if you need a snack.

After traveling east out of town, you will cross the Pine River Recreational Trail and then ride over the Pine River. Turn north after the bridge onto County Road TB and enjoy the scenery as the road follows the river. Just before reaching Indian Creek, you will pass the Akey School Museum on the right. This restored one-room school is open on weekends through the summer.

A couple miles farther north, on your left, you will likely see a hawk gracefully gliding on the air currents above as you pull into Twin Bluffs. With no school or church, and being close to the river, this settlement was originally known as Bug Town. In 1878, when the railroad came through and built a depot, the village was renamed for the two bluffs overlooking it.

If you prefer, and if you have wider tires for riding on gravel, you can pick up the Pine River Trail here. The challenge heads west up between the two bluffs. After a short 12 percent grade climb, the ride meanders to the northwest along County Road OO. For the next 4 miles enjoy riding over the rolling terrain. After passing a large dairy farm operation, it's only a mile farther to the trail again. The trail is paved 2 miles south from Richland Center, if you prefer to ride it back. Otherwise, the challenge uses the paved shoulder of Highway 14 to get back into the city on Jefferson Street.

Miles and Directions

0.0 From the corner of Jefferson Street, head east on West Seminary Street, crossing Main Street (Highway 14/Highway 80).

0.2 Take a right on Main Street.

0.3 Turn left on Hazeltine Street/County Road N.

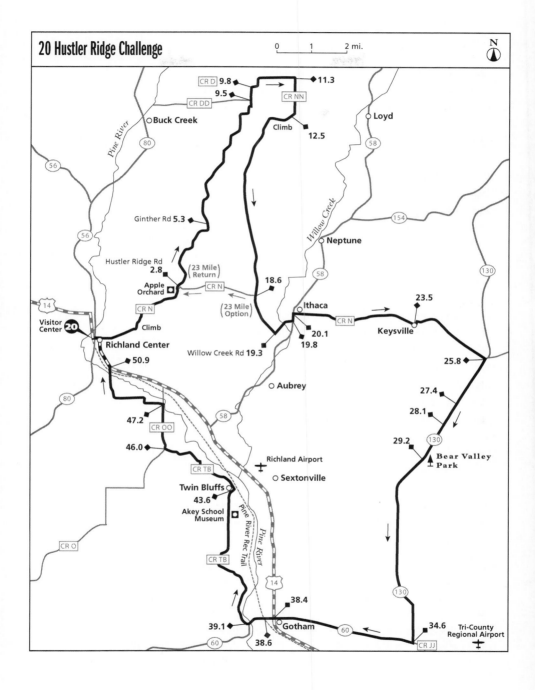

20 Hustler Ridge Challenge

0   1   2 mi.

N

CR D 9.8
11.3
9.5
CR DD
CR NN

Pine River

Buck Creek

Loyd

80

58

56

Ginther Rd 5.3

Willow Creek

154

Neptune

Hustler Ridge Rd
2.8
(23 Mile) Return

58

130

Apple Orchard
CR N

18.6

23.5

CR N
(23 Mile Option)

14

Ithaca
CR N
Keysville

Visitor Center 20

Climb
20.1
19.8

Richland Center
Willow Creek Rd 19.3

25.8

50.9

Aubrey

27.4

80
28.1

47.2
CR OO

58
29.2

130

46.0

Richland Airport

Bear Valley Park

CR TB

Sextonville

Twin Bluffs
43.6

Pine River Rec Trail

Akey School Museum

Pine River

CR O

CR TB

14

38.4

39.1
Gotham
34.6
Tri-County Regional Airport

38.6
60
60
CR JJ

2.8 Turn left on Hustler Ridge Road at the apple orchard. (Note: The 23-mile option returns here.)

5.3 Pass Ginther Road.

7.6 Pass Buckta Hill Road.

8.4 Pass Coop Woods Road.

9.5 Go straight ahead (right) onto County Road DD.

9.8 Take a right on County Road D.

11.3 Take a right on County Road NN.

12.5 Start to descend along Little Willow Creek.

18.6 Continue south on County Road N. (**Option:** Take a right on County Road N for the 23-mile option.)

19.3 Turn left on Willow Creek Road.

19.8 Turn left on Highway 58 in Ithaca.

20.1 Take a right on County Road N.

23.5 Pass Keysville.

25.8 Take a right on Highway 130 and ride down Four Springs Valley.

27.4 Pass Bear Valley.

28.1 Pass Four Springs Hollow.

29.2 Pass Bear Valley Park.

34.6 Take a right on County Road JJ (Highway 60).

38.4 Cross Highway 14 onto Highway 60 in Gotham.

38.6 Cross Pine River bike trail.

38.9 Cross Pine River.

39.1 Take a right on County Road TB.

43.6 County Road TB turns left in Twin Bluffs.

46.0 Take a right on County Road O.

47.2 Turn left on County Road OO.

50.3 Cross paved bike trail. **Option:** The Pine River Trail can be taken back to town (turn left onto the trail).

50.9 Turn left on Highway 14.

51.4 Take a right on Sheldon/Main Street.

51.8 Turn left on East Seminary Street and cross Highway 80.

52.0 Return to the corner of Jefferson Street.

Local Information

Richland Area Chamber of Commerce, 397 West Seminary Street, Richland Center; (800) 422-1318; www.richlandchamber.com.

Local Events/Attractions

Ocooch Mountain Fall Bike Tour; first Sunday in October; Richland Medical Center; (608) 647-6321; www.active.com.

Weggy Winery and Oak Ridge Vineyard, 30940 Oak Ridge Drive, Richland Center; (608) 647-6600; www.weggywinery.com.

Restaurants

Cafe Fiesta Fe, 130 South Main Street, Richland Center; (608) 647-4732.

Henning's Fish House, 1885 Allison Park Drive, Richland Center; (608) 647-6557.

PaPa's Donuts, 101 South Church Street, Richland Center; (608) 647-6090.

Accommodations

Ramada Inn, 1450 Veterans Drive, Richland Center; (608) 647-8869; www.whitehouse lodge.com.

Alana Springs Campground, 22628 Covered Bridge Road, Richland Center; (608) 647-2600; www.alanaspringscampground.com.

Bike Shops

Backroad Cycles, 340 West Court Street, Richland Center; (608) 647-4636.

Restrooms

Start/finish: Visitor center.
19.9: Ithaca Ballfield.
29.2: Bear Valley Park.
38.4: Gotham Park.
45.2: Ackley School Museum.

Maps

DeLorme: Wisconsin Atlas and Gazetteer: Page 33 B7.

Wisconsin State Bicycle Map (Mississippi River Section).

21 Round the River Cruise

Here, above the confluence of two great rivers, where Indian tribes once met to trade goods, this metric century offers you a scenic tour around the Lower Wisconsin River and back up the Mississippi. You leave from St. Feriole Island Park, riding through a historic prairie river town with a name taken from the French word for "dog." The route heads northeast and gradually makes its way along the ridge overlooking the Wisconsin River. You will pass the Kickapoo Indian Caverns, then turn southeast and cruise down the twisting road to a village named after an Indian chief. Now riding along the river's edge, you'll enjoy the scenery as the you ride up to Easter Rock. Cross the river—one of Wisconsin's main waterways—and roll into a town named for a settler who would sing, "Co Boss, co Bell!" As you follow the south bank of the Wisconsin River west, you will soon pass through a town named for all the early sawmills there. Now, before the two rivers converge, turn north and ride past several historic sites on your way back to Prairie du Chien.

Start: St. Feriole Island Park in Prairie du Chien.
Length: 63 miles with a 34-mile option.
Terrain: Rolling with a couple moderate climbs.

Traffic and hazards: Use caution when riding on Highways 27, 60, 133, and 35, as traffic can be fast.

Getting there: At the junction of Highway 27 East and Highway 35, turn west on Blackhawk Avenue, through the downtown district and over the bridge onto St. Feriole Island. Turn right on Water Street to the area next to the boat landing. Parking is free and plentiful.

Considered to be a neutral ground, many Indians tribes used this place to barter. The cruise starts in a prairie above the mouth of the Wisconsin River, where it flows into

Wauzeka Ridge offers 6 miles of rollers above the Wisconsin River.

the Mississippi River. The name Prairie du Chien comes from the Fox Indian chief who was known as Dog. Early French voyageurs called the place *Prairie du Chien,* or "Dog's Prairie."

In 1673 the area came under French rule, and then under British from 1763 through the Revolutionary War. The second-oldest settlement in Wisconsin, Fort Selby, was established here in 1814, but the British captured it. Then in 1816 the first Fort Crawford was built and witnessed the Red Bird Massacre. The second Fort Crawford was built in 1830, and this is where Chief Black Hawk surrendered. Having one of the best landing sites on the Mississippi gave this community a commanding commercial importance that led to its prosperity.

The cruise leaves from St. Feriole Island, at the corner of Bolvin and Water Streets, and heads north around the island. St. Feriole was a growing residential area until a record flood in 1965 moved the community to higher grounds. Today the island offers a glimpse of the city's early activities, with a cross-grid of streets that contain the Villa Louis and several other historic homes. Turn on Brisbois/East Washington Street in town, and ride up through the historic district. Just before you turn onto Wacouta Avenue, on your left is St. Gabriel's Church, home to the oldest Catholic parish in Wisconsin and still in operation today. Father Galteier, the first priest here and founder of St. Paul, is buried in the front of the church.

After you turn off Wacouta Avenue, head east on Blackhawk Avenue to where the road crosses Highway 35 and merges onto Highway 27. In 4 miles you will encounter a 7 percent climb while riding around the side of Mondell Hill. A couple miles farther you pass Irish Ridge Road. Soon you come up on Hazen Corners, a settlement of the past, where you turn right on County Road N and enjoy a gradual climb up to Wauzeka Ridge. For the next 6 miles the route twists and turns, overlooking Kickapoo Indian Caverns. On the descent the road snakes down to the bank of the Wisconsin River and the town of Wauzeka.

In the early 1800s an Indian chief named Wauzeka established a permanent camp here at the mouth of the Kickapoo River. The name of the chief and ridge means "wrinkled with pine," which is how the land looked before the logging boom. The first post office was established in 1848 and moved to the present location eight years later. At the 19.4-mile mark the route now travels east on the paved shoulder of Highway 60. Those who prefer the 34-mile option should take a right on Highway 60 back to Prairie du Chien. As you follow the Wisconsin River east, you will soon see it widen, creating Woodman Lake, and then pass through Boydtown. This village was named after Robert Boyd, who established the first settlement here in 1844.

After passing Christ Hollow, you will have another mile of riding along the scenic river before reaching Easter Rock. At Highway 61 take a right and cross the river into Boscobel, a charming little river town that was first settled in 1857. It is said that an early settler here had two cows, one named Boss and the other Bell. Each evening the farmer would call to the cows singing, "Co Boss, co Bell!" hence the town name. This is also the birthplace of the Gideon Bible, in room 19 of the Historic Boscobel Hotel. Consider having lunch at the Vale Inn Cafe at the corner of Wisconsin Avenue and Superior Street, across the street from the Boscobel Depot Museum.

After leaving to the south on Highway 61, you will soon turn southwest on Highway 133 along the Lower Wisconsin State Riverway. Even though the traffic is normally light here, use caution, as the road has no paved shoulder. Rolling through the river bottom terrain, you will soon pass through the village of Woodman. This town was named for Cyrus Woodman, who laid out the village lots and built a sawmill that provided work for the local residents. If you need to stop, there is a park and a tavern here.

A couple miles farther east, the road heads away from the river and you will pass Woodman Recreational Park. Turn west again onto County Road C, and for the next 3 miles enjoy riding the route's twisting and turning rollers. After passing the Baxter Lane Wildlife Area, you will pass the Russell Hill Wildlife Area at the top of a short 8 percent grade climb.

You then cruise down a twisting forested stretch and travel through Millville. The village's name originates from the number of sawmills that operated here in the early days. With bluffs on your left, you will then pass the Millville Bridal Nature Trail followed by the Lower Wisconsin River Boat Landing and Park. Before the confluence of the Wisconsin and Mississippi Rivers, take a right onto the paved shoulder of Highway 18, and cross back over the Wisconsin River through Bridgeport, which

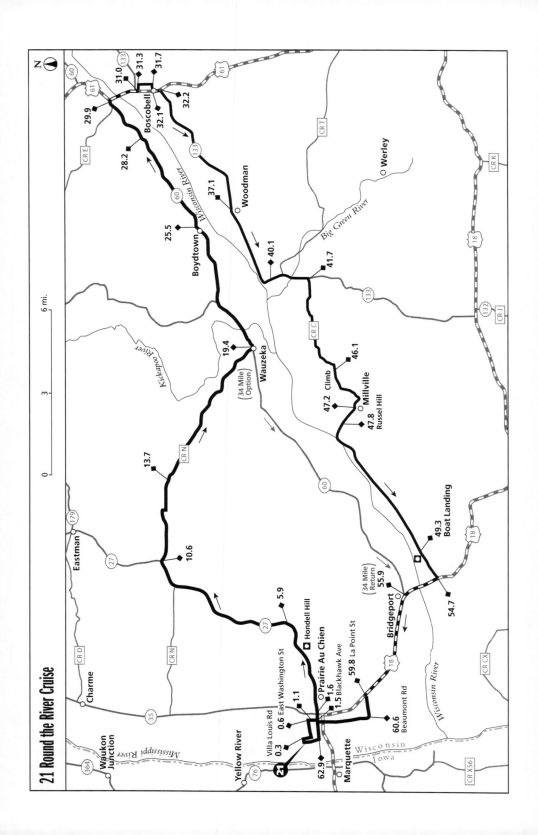

21 Round the River Cruise

was named for a covered toll bridge that once crossed the Mississippi River into Iowa near here. Today there are only a few retail establishments along the highway.

Back in Prairie du Chien, the route jogs to the west at the stoplight on Laporte Street and then follows Beaumont Road north. Along the lane you will pass the Fort Crawford Museum and the Prairie du Chien Historical Society, and farther along you will see the beautiful grounds of Wyalusing Academy and several other historic sites. At Blackhawk Avenue turn into the downtown area on North Water Street and cross back onto St. Feriole Island to the parking lot. After exploring the island, venture downtown for dinner and more historic sites.

Miles and Directions

0.0   From St. Feriole Island Park on the corner of Bolvin and Water Streets, ride north.

0.3   Take a right on north Villa Louis Street.

0.6   Turn left on Brisbois/East Washington Street.

1.1   Take a right on Wacouta Avenue.

1.5   Turn left on Blackhawk Avenue.

1.6   Cross Highway 35 onto Highway 27.

5.9   Pass Irish Ridge Road.

10.6 Take a right on County Road N at Hazen Corners.

13.7 Ride up Wauzeka Ridge.

19.4 Turn left on Highway 60 into Wauzeka. **Option:** Take a right on Highway 60 for the 34-mile option.

25.5 Pass through Boydtown.

28.2 Pass Christ Hollow.

29.9 At Easter Rock, take a right on Highway 61 and cross the Wisconsin River.

30.9 Enter Boscobel.

31.0 Turn left on Kansas Street.

31.3 Take a right on Wisconsin Avenue.

31.4 Pass Vale Inn Cafe at the corner of Wisconsin Avenue and Superior Street.

31.7 Take a right on Fremont Street.

32.1 Turn left on Highway 61.

32.2 Take a right on Highway 133.

37.1 Pass through Woodman.

40.1 Pass Woodman Recreational Park.

41.7 Take a right on County Road C.

46.1 Pass Baxter Lane Wildlife Area.

47.2 Pass through Millville.

47.8 Pass Russell Hill Wildlife Area

49.3 Pass Lower Wisconsin River Boat Landing and Park.

54.7 Take a right on Highway 18.

55.9 Pass through Bridgeport.

59.8 Turn left on LaPoint Street. (Note: The 34-mile option returns here.)

60.6 Take a right on Beaumont Road.

61.8 Pass Historic Fort Crawford Museum.

62.0 Pass Wyalusing Academy.

62.4 Turn left on Blackhawk Avenue.

62.9 Take a right on North Water Street.

63.0 Return to park.

Local Information

Prairie du Chien Area Chamber of Commerce and Tourism Council, 211 South Main Street, Prairie du Chien; (800) 732-1673; www.prairieduchien.org.

Local Events/Attractions

Fort Crawford Museum/Prairie du Chien Historical Society, 717 South Beaumont Road, Prairie du Chien; (608) 326-6960.
Kickapoo Indian Caverns, Scenic Highway 60, Wauzeka; (608) 875-7723; www.kickapoo indiancaverns.com.
Villa Louis Tours, 13 Water Street, St. Feriole Island; (608) 326-2721.

Restaurants

Hungry House Cafe, 531 North Marquette Road, Prairie du Chien; (608) 647-6557.
Vale Inn Cafe, 813 Wisconsin Avenue, Boscobel; (608) 375-4456.

Accommodations

AmericInn Lodge & Suites, 130 South Main Street, Prairie du Chien; (608) 326-7878; www.americinnprairieduchien.com.
Big River Camp Ground, 106 West Paquette Street, Prairie du Chien; (608) 326-2712.

Bike Shops

Backroad Cycles, 340 West Court Street, Richland Center; (608) 647-4636.

Restrooms

Start/finish: St. Feriole Island Park.
19.6: BP station in Wauzeka.
31.4: Boscobel Depot Museum.
37.9: Woodman City Park.
40.1: Woodman Recreational Park.

Maps

DeLorme: Wisconsin Atlas and Gazetteer: Page 32 D1.
Wisconsin State Bicycle Map (Mississippi River Section).

Southern Wisconsin

22 Beetown Challenge

As you ride through Grant County, you will soon discover how the early lead-mining rush influenced the growth of this area and today's road route options. This challenge offers both excitement and beauty. It leaves on Beetown Road in a community named after a Pennsylvania town and rolls south, passing a village named for a fierce storm that went through the area after the first settlers arrived. After rolling along toward the Mississippi River bluffs, use the next town, with a name that in Spanish means "lead," for a rest stop. Now, in your low gear, climb back up the bluff and turn back to the north. After crossing the Grant River, ride up the valley floor to a town named for an overturned tree with a beehive in its trunk and a large lead nugget at its roots. Soon you reach a thriving agriculture community that went through names faster than you can shift from granny to your high ring. As you return from the northwest, you may have to use that low gear one more time on the roller coaster cruise back to Lancaster.

Start: At the corner of Maple and Monroe Streets in downtown Lancaster.
Length: 55 miles with a 32-mile option.
Terrain: Rolling with several major climbs. Many secondary roads are paved, so you can customize your ride; pick up a county map with paved road designations.
Traffic and hazards: Traffic is normally light on all the roads, with the exception of Highway 35.

Getting there: On Highway 61 in Lancaster, turn east on Maple Street to Monroe Street. Free street parking is available east of the corner.

Centrally located in Grant County, this challenge leaves from downtown Lancaster. In 1828 Major G. M. Price settled here and proposed the name Ridgeway. A relative who emigrated from Lancaster, Pennsylvania, wished to retain a remembrance of the eastern town and induced Price to adopt this name instead. The ride heads to the west side of town following Highway 35 (Beetown Road) and the paved shoulder of Highway 35. You then turn southwest on County Road N and roll over the lush green countryside.

As you round the next turn and head straight south, the road climbs at an 8 percent grade over the next half mile. Just before the road veers to the west, you will see a round barn, and soon the road turns back to the south through Hurricane. At the time settlers were moving into the area, a strong storm blew down several trees here, hence the name. After riding another mile through rolling farm fields with bluffs in the background, turn left on County Road U. Those who prefer the 32-mile option will take a right here and head northwest to Beetown.

The challenge now turns southeast along the narrow valley floor. After passing Graham Hollow, you will be summoned to shift down for your next climb. You will have a steady 9 percent climb and enjoy a couple grand rollers before reaching Potosi. Until 1845 this town was called Snake Hollow because the valley winds blew between the bluffs to the river like a snake. Then in 1845 the name was changed to Potosi, which most agree was derived from the Spanish word meaning "lead." Willis St. John, the patriarch of the Potosi mines, discovered a cave in the bluffs that was rich in lead and is still known as St. John's Mine. The town is now home to the Potosi Brewery and is known as the "Catfish Capital of Wisconsin."

After you turn onto the Great River Road, you will cruise down the hill on the world's longest Main Street. Along the way you will pass St. John's Mine and Museum and several rest stop options. At the Mississippi River the challenge takes a right on the paved shoulder of Highway 133, at Potosi Station. After passing the mouth of the Grant River, you will find an uphill grade of rollers. At each dip the next hill gets a little higher. When you reach the top, the road meanders along the bluff and offers some great views of eagles soaring over the river.

You then turn north away from the river and pass through another historic village, Burton. This old mill town was built by Daniel R. Burt, on the Grant River, and was a nucleus in its early years, with a post office, general store, and blacksmith shop. Enjoy the rolling terrain as you leave the river and head back up to County Road U. Now turning west, the 32-mile option rejoins the challenge, which meanders up the valley floor to Beetown. In 1827 Cyrus Alexander found a trace of a mineral in the cavity made by bees in a tree. He dug a little further and found a nugget of lead weighing 425 pounds. The lode discovered was called "bee-lead" and thus originated the name of the town. You will find several rest stop options in this quaint little farming community.

The route continues on to the northwest, but those taking the 32-mile option should ride east on the paved shoulder of Highway 81 up Porter Bridge Road. The challenge continues straight north, merging on Highway 35 into Bloomington.

This village was called Lander when it was first settled in 1850. Then when Henry Taft built the first mill here, the name was changed to Tafton. A few years later the villagers were on the outs with Taft, who was having financial troubles. At the same time the Spencer Blacksmith Shop got a patent on a new device for sowing oats. This created a big boost for agriculture, and the townspeople expressed their elation by coming up with a new town name, Blooming. In 1867 the Wisconsin legislature approved the application to change the name to Bloomington. Today the town offers several options to those needing a rest stop.

On the south side of town, the route now turns onto County Road A and starts riding up the valley floor. A mile ahead you will be summoned to use that stored energy for one more major climb. At the junction of County Road J, as the route turns back toward the southeast, enjoy several miles of sinfully fun rollers through the gyrating prairie lands. At Bowen School Road, the 32-mile option rejoins the route as you cruise back into Lancaster.

Upon your return, if you are a train buff, travel 10 miles north to Fenimore and

22 Beetown Challenge

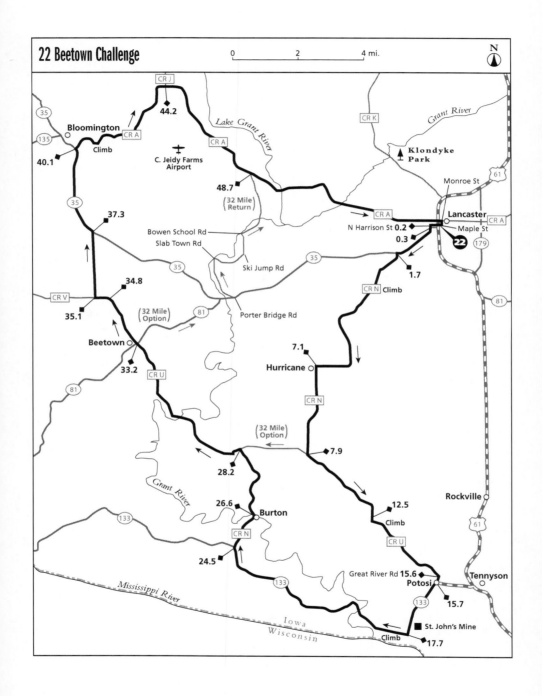

0   2   4 mi.

N

CR J

44.2

Lake Grant River

CR K

Grant River

35

Bloomington

135

CR A

Climb

CR A

40.1

C. Jeidy Farms Airport

Klondyke Park

Monroe St

61

48.7

(32 Mile Return)

CR A

Lancaster

CR A

35

N Harrison St **0.2**

Maple St

0.3

22

179

37.3

Bowen School Rd

Slab Town Rd

Ski Jump Rd

35

1.7

CR N Climb

81

CR V

34.8

35

7.1

Hurricane

35.1

(32 Mile) Option

81

Porter Bridge Rd

Beetown

CR N

33.2

CR U

(32 Mile) Option

7.9

Rockville

61

(32 Mile) Option

28.2

12.5

Climb

Grant River

CR U

26.6

Burton

133

CR N

24.5

Great River Rd **15.6**

Tennyson

Potosi

Mississippi River

133

15.7

Iowa

St. John's Mine

Wisconsin

Climb

17.7

visit the railroad museum. The highlight here is a steam engine affectionately known as "Dinky" that operated on narrow-gauge lines from 1878 to 1926.

Miles and Directions

0.0 Head east on Maple Street from the corner of Monroe Street.

0.2 Turn left on North Harrison Street.

0.3 Turn onto Highway 35.

1.7 Turn left on County Road N.

7.1 Pass through Hurricane.

7.9 Turn left on County Road U. **Option:** Take a right on County Road U for the 32-mile option.

12.5 Pass Graham Hollow.

15.6 Take a right on the Great River Road into Potosi.

15.7 Take a right on Highway 133.

17.7 Take a right at Potosi Station.

24.5 Take a right on County Road N.

26.6 Pass Burton.

28.2 Turn left on County Road U. (Note: The 32-mile option briefly returns here.)

33.2 Pass through Beetown. **Option:** The 32-mile option turns right on Highway 81, then right on Highway 35, left on Porter Bridge Road, right on Slab Town Road, left on Ski Jump Road, cross river, right on Bowen School Road, and right on County Road A.

34.8 Turn left on County Road V.

35.1 Take a right on County Road U.

37.3 Turn left on Highway 35.

40.1 Take a right on County Road A in Bloomington.

44.2 At County Road J, continue on County Road A.

48.7 Pass Bowen School Road. (Note: The 32-mile option returns here.)

54.1 Cross Highway 61 in Lancaster,

54.6 Take a right on Monroe Street.

55.0 Return to corner of Maple and Monroe Streets.

Local Information

Lancaster Area Chamber of Commerce, 206 South Madison Street, Lancaster; 338 North Iowa Street, Dodgeville; (608) 723-2820; www.lancasterwisconsin.com.

Grant County Tourism Council; (866) 472-6894; www.grantco.org.

Local Events/Attractions

St. John's Mine and Museum, 129 Main Street, Potosi; (608) 763-2121.

Fennimore Railroad Museum, 610 Lincoln Avenue, Fennimore; (608) 822-6144; www.fennimore.com/railroad.

Restaurants

Doolittle's Pub & Eatery, 135 South Jefferson Street, Lancaster; (608) 723-7676.

Happy Joe's Pizza & Ice Cream Parlor, 105 Alona Lane, Lancaster; (608) 723-4101.

Accommodations

Best Western Welcome Inn, 420 West Maple Street, Lancaster; (608) 723-4162.

Klondyke Secluded Acres, 6656 Pine Knob Road, Lancaster; (608) 723-2844.

Bike Shops

Momentum Bikes & Boards, 25 West Main Street, Platteville; (608) 348-6888; www.momentumbikes.com.
The Village Bikesmith, 220 West Adams Street, Platteville; (608) 348-3911.

Restrooms

Start/finish: Grant County Courthouse.

15.7: Hickory Hill Park in Potosi.
33.2: Corner Station in Beetown.
40.2: Bloomington Library.

Maps

DeLorme: Wisconsin Atlas and Gazetteer: Page 25 B5.
Wisconsin State Bicycle Map (Mississippi River Section).
Grant County Bicycle Map.

23 Pearl of Pecatonica Cruise

During the lead-mining boom of the early 1800s, this unglaciated region in the southwestern part of the state offered newcomers many opportunities; today it's a cycler's paradise. This cruise leaves from a town that once was known for producing pearl button blanks and takes you on an adventure over hills and through dales. As you ride north, you will soon visit a town where fresh cheese curds are available daily. You'll then head up around Yellowstone State Park before cruising south to a village named by a Scottish settler in honor of the Duke of Argyle. Following the East Branch of the Pecatonica River, you will pass a town that was originally the site of a fort built to protect settlers during the Black Hawk War. Farther south, you will come to a city on Wolf Creek that was named after a gentleman who came here for the lead but was instrumental in the treaties with Indians. Now circling back to the northeast, it's time to ponder the two decisions you will soon need to make back in Darlington: (1) what flavor ice cream, and (2) one scoop or two.

Start: In Darlington at the corner of Washington and Ann Streets, next to the park.
Length: 50 miles with a 32-mile option.
Terrain: Rolling with a few moderate hills.

Traffic and hazards: Traffic is normally light on the highways this route follows, though care should be taken, especially on Highway 78, where there is no shoulder.

Getting there: From Highway 23 (Main Street) in Darlington, turn west on Ann Street and go one block to the park. There is a parking lot on the left, and on-street parking is also available.

This cruise leaves from the park west of the Barber Shop Hotel and heads north on Main Street (Highway 23) through downtown Darlington. Originally named Willow Springs, the town was renamed for Joshua Darling, who furnished the money for the purchase of the land here. The town was also called the "Pearl of the Pecatonica" during the time when clams were harvested from the river to produce pearl button blanks. Ride out of town on Highway 23, turn left on County Road F near the Lafayette County Courthouse, and head north.

Now rolling northwest through the countryside, at Mount Pleasant Road take a sharp left up through Otter Creek Valley, where the pungent smell of clover fills the air. Soon you are passing the Bunklow Cheese Factory, where County Road G merges with F and enters the village of Fayette. If you are a connoisseur of Wisconsin's squeaky golden nuggets, you'll be pleased to know that cheese curds are made here daily. The village, whose name is a contraction of *LaFayette,* was originally settled in 1828, but the Black Hawk War slowed down growth for a number of years. Along with the cheese factory, the town has a tavern and the Yellow Lake Dairy Bar if you need to stop.

Another mile east of town, County Road F turns to the north again. If you prefer the 32-mile option, continue east on County Road G. Otherwise the cruise soon passes Lake Road, the entrance for Yellowstone State Park. After passing the park entrance, the road grade starts to climb, at a moderate 8 percent, into the lush farm fields at the top. At the 14.9-mile mark the route turns south and rolls down through the Yellowstone River valley.

At the turn east on County Road G, the 32-mile option briefly rejoins the cruise. In another half mile, those who have selected the shortcut option will take a right on Highway 81 and head back to Darlington. The cruise continues east for another quarter mile and arrives in Argyle. Established in 1844, the town was originally given the name Hazel Green for a settler's wife. When applying for a post office, they were informed that there was already a town with that name. Allen Wright, a Scottish settler, suggested Argyle in honor of the Duke of Argyle, whom he admired. After crossing the East Branch of the Pecatonica River, you will find several options for a rest stop. In the middle of town, at the junction of Highway 78, the cruise now turns south.

Ride with caution while leaving town, even though traffic is normally light, as there is no paved shoulder. Soon the grade of the road gradually rises for the next mile, then swaggers slightly to the southwest, following the East Branch of the Pecatonica River. Just before you pass Five Corners, you will cross over the river and then coast down to Wiota. Originally established as Fort Hamilton, when the town was platted in 1828, it took the name Wiota. The name came from a term used to define very deep, moderately well-drained soils formed by an alluvium. Because of this rich fertile ground, the prosperity of the town was greatly enhanced by farming. As you pass the Zimmerman Cheese Factory, there is a historic display on Fort Hamilton.

After leaving town on Highway 78 heading west, you will ride along the Pecatonica River before you reach Gratiot. This community was established in 1828 by Henry Gratiot, a friend of Colonel Hamilton, who came here to dig lead but then established Gratiot's Grove with a sawmill on Wolf Creek. Throughout the Black Hawk War era, the settlement was turned into a stockade, and Mr. Gratiot was instrumental in settling the dispute with the Indians. After the Indian uprising a

23 Pearl of Pecatonica Cruise

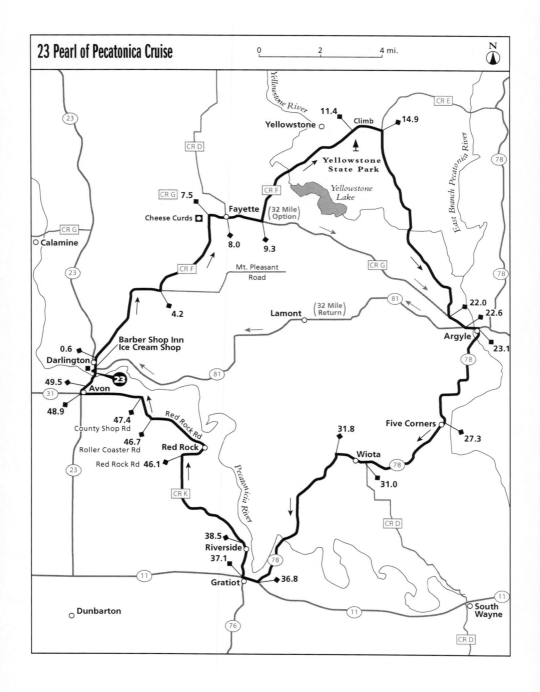

0   2   4 mi.

N

Yellowstone River

11.4   Climb   14.9

Yellowstone

CR E

78

CR D

Yellowstone State Park

Yellowstone Lake

East Branch Pecatonica River

CR G   7.5

CR F

Fayette   (32 Mile Option)

Cheese Curds

8.0   9.3

CR G

Calamine

23

CR G

CR F

Mt. Pleasant Road

4.2

Lamont   (32 Mile Return)

81

22.0
22.6

Argyle

78

23.1

Barber Shop Inn
Ice Cream Shop

0.6

Darlington

81

78

49.5

23

Avon

31

48.9

Five Corners

27.3

47.4

County Shop Rd

46.7

Roller Coaster Rd

Red Rock Rd

Red Rock

31.8   Wiota

78

31.0

Red Rock Rd   46.1

CR K

Pecatonica River

23

CR D

38.5

Riverside

37.1

11

76

78

36.8

Gratiot

11

11

South Wayne

Dunbarton

CR D

gristmill was built and the town flourished. If you haven't had lunch yet, consider Fuller's Nixon House.

After crossing over the Wolf Creek Bridge, the cruise turns north and travels to Riverside. Located at the mouth of Wolf Creek, where it empties into the Pecatonica River, this village was established in 1856. Continue northwest on County Road K, onto Red Rock Road, and then head up to the village of Red Rock, named for the red hematite "needle" ore found there. Turn north on Roller Coaster Road, then left onto County Shop Road, and with a right on Ames Road, you return back to Darlington.

Miles and Directions

0.0   Leave from Ann Street.

0.1   Turn left on Highway 23.

0.6   Take a right County Road F.

4.2   At Mount Pleasant Road, County Road F takes a sharp left up Otter Creek Valley.

7.5   Take a right on County Road G at the Bunklow Cheese Factory.

8.0   Pass through Fayette.

9.3   Turn left on County Road F. **Option:** Continue east on County Road G for the 32-mile option.

11.4   Pass Lake Road, the entrance for Yellowstone State Park.

14.9   Take a right County Road N.

22.0   Turn left on County Road G. (Note: The 32-mile option briefly returns here.)

22.6   Turn left on Highway 81. **Option:** The 32-mile option turns right on Highway 81.

23.1   Take a right on Highway 78 at Argyle. (Note: Rest stop options are a quarter mile into town.)

27.3   Pass Five Corners.

31.0   Pass through Wiota on Highway 78.

31.8   At County Road M, Highway 78 takes a sharp left.

36.8   Take a right on Highway 11 into Gratiot.

37.1   After crossing the bridge over Wolf Creek, take a right on County Road K.

38.5   Pass Riverside.

46.1   Take a right on Red Rock Road.

46.7   Take a right onto Roller Coaster Road.

47.4   Turn left on County Shop Road.

48.9   Take a right on Ames Road.

49.5   Take a right on the paved shoulder of Highway 23.

50.0   Return to parking lot.

Local Information

Darlington Chamber of Commerce, 439 Main Street; (888) 506-6553; www.darlingtonwi.org.
Visit Lafayette County; (866) 304-7229; www.lafayettecounty.org.

Local Events/Attractions

Depot Museum, Lafayette County Historical Society, South Washington Street; (608) 776-8340.

Restaurants

L & M Ice Cream & Bake Shoppe, 333 Main Street, Darlington; (608) 776-3853.
Riverwood Family Restaurant, 128 South Main Street, Darlington; (608) 776-8910.
Fuller's Nixon House, 132 Highway 11, Gratiot; (608) 922-6617.

Accommodations

The Barber Shop Hotel, 123 West Ann Street, Darlington; (608) 776-3138; www.barber shophotel.com.

Pecatonica River Trails Campground, 100 Harriet Street, Darlington; (608) 776-4970.

Bike Shops

Momentum Bikes & Boards, 25 West Main Street, Platteville; (608) 348-6888.

Restrooms

Start/finish: ATV Gasoline Alley next to the park.
11.9: Yellowstone State Park.
22.6: Argyle Park.
31.1: Wiota City Park.
37.5: Fuller's Nixon House in Gratiot.

Maps

DeLorme: Wisconsin Atlas and Gazetteer: Page 26 C3.
Wisconsin State Bicycle Map (Mississippi River Section).
Bicycle Lafayette County (www.co.lafayette.gov).

24 Mineral Challenge

In a county named after an Indian tribe whose hunting grounds once dominated the area, this ride leaves from a town named for Wisconsin's first governor. You will ride north and pass a state park that is also named after this governor, then climb up Pleasant Ridge. At the top enjoy several miles of scenic vistas before coasting down into the next valley, where you will find a photo opportunity at a historic gristmill. As the route follows the creek down the valley floor from the mill, you will soon turn onto a road that soldiers from Prairie du Chien built in 1835. The ride continues south through Long Valley and a town that has a restaurant with a bike on its roof. Now circling to the east, you arrive in a community named after the mining camp that went up here in the 1820s when prospectors were swarming the hills looking for lead. Turning to the north, enjoy the countryside as the challenge returns to Dodgeville.

Start: Centennial Park and Pool in Dodgeville.
Length: 72 miles with a 33- and 65-mile option.
Terrain: Rolling with several hills and one major climb.

Traffic and hazards: Traffic is normally light on this route's highways, though caution should be used, especially on Highway 39.

Getting there: From Iowa Street/Highway 23 in Dodgeville, turn east on Parry Street. The parking lot is 3 blocks ahead.

This challenge leaves from Dodgeville in the heart of Iowa County, named after the Iowa Indians, whose hunting grounds once dominated this area. The town was named for Henry Dodge, who came here to stake out a mining claim and built a smelter. He later became first governor of the Wisconsin Territory. After riding out of the parking lot at the Centennial Park and Pool, travel north through town on Union Street. This city-designated bike route is uniquely designed so you only have stop signs at the higher elevated cross-streets, allowing you to keep your speed and cadence for the next hill.

After crossing Highway 18 and Military Road, the route continues north on County Road Z, and soon you are crossing the Military Ridge State Trail. This 40-mile crushed limestone trail was built on the abandoned Chicago & Northwestern Railroad line and connects Iowa County to Madison. In another mile you pass a paved bike trail into Governor Dodge State Park, if you want to make a side trip. Rounding the next curve, you pass a campground as the road follows the border of the state park.

After passing Chimney Rock Road, the grade starts to climb, so get ready to visit granny and dance on those pedals. At the top you reach Pleasant Ridge. When settlers came to this area, they found the ridge above the valley breathtaking, and the wind currents on the bluff made the bug problem at that time less of a hassle. Today at the 9-mile mark, the Pleasant Ridge Store is a great place to stop for breakfast or lunch. They are open at 7:00 a.m. for breakfast and until 11:00 p.m., serving Ridge Top Burgers.

As you ride along the ridge you will soon see a silhouette of a lady on your left, waving to you just before you turn onto Far Look Road. Now heading east, follow the ridge past many beautiful hillside farms. Once on Erdman Road, the grade will soon start to drop as you coast down to the next valley. At the bottom take a right on Mill Road. Here you will pass a truck farm with some great-looking produce. In a short while the road rises slightly and follows the edge of the ridge around to Mill Creek, where the old Hyde Mill still stands. This is a great photo opportunity if you brought your camera. On the National Register of Historic Places, the old mill's waterwheel is still intact.

In 1850 William Hyde from Prince Edward Island came here and built a dam for the mill. The gristmill thrived, and he started a village along with the Hyde Store, which is a half mile west on County Road H. Surrounded by lush woodlands and prairie openings, the community grew with a blacksmith shop, cheese factory, and shoe shop. Today all the businesses are gone except for the store, which has been converted into a tavern. Here you can get a bottle of water or other beverage if you need to stop. Now riding south, with little effort, meander down the valley floor as Mill Creek runs along with you.

Soon you are cruising down Pleasant Valley, and at the 27.8-mile mark you cross the Military Ridge State Trail again. In another quarter mile the route turns east on County Road YZ, or Military Road. This road was built by soldiers from Fort Crawford in Prairie du Chien in 1835 to connect with Fort Howard in Green Bay. Those who prefer the 33-mile option will turn right here and head back to town.

The challenge continues south on the low-traffic, secondary Highway 191. Riding down through Banner Valley, then through Long Valley, watch for deer. At the 39.5-mile mark you reach Hollandale. In 1887 Bjorn Holland built a small shack here and put in a stock of goods to supply the construction crew working on the Illinois Central Railroad. A small farming community called Bennville soon grew around the general store, and after the completion of the railroad, the town took the name of the store's proprietor. If you are ready for lunch, watch for the cafe with a bike on the roof as you ride down State Street.

Now the route slips across Highway 39 onto County Road K and continues south. If you prefer a metric (65-mile) ride, turn west and ride the paved shoulder of Highway 39 to Mineral Point. After leaving town, the challenge encounters a 9 percent grade climb before reaching County Road DD. You will encounter another short climb as you head west and pass the Wind Ridge Farm. The farms over the next 10 miles practice contoured farming, and here you will enjoy some of Wisconsin's finest rollers. Passing County Road W, the terrain mellows as you ride along the Yellowstone River. Soon you will pass the Pleasant View Community Church, a unique stone block church built in 1914.

At the 57.3-mile mark you are in Mineral Point, one of the oldest communities in Wisconsin. It began in the 1820s with prospectors, or "badgers," swarming over the hills of southwestern Wisconsin looking for lead. After the soft bluish-gray metal was discovered here, a "mineral rush" began, and the mining camp that formed around the diggings eventually was called Mineral Point. Here you will find several more options for lunch. Your first choice is a few blocks north on Shakerag Road, near the Pendarvis Cornish Miners Colony Museum, where there is a cafe named after the street. The cafe offers a garden floral essence and songbirds serenading you from the surrounding trees.

After lunch cross the street and find out how Merry Christmas Mine got its name. It was one of the nation's few large zinc mines operating between 1906 and 1913, and is now part of a forty-three-acre educational park with walking trails that highlight early crevice mines, or "badger holes." The prairie trails begin at the edge of the Pendarvis Park parking lot on Shakerag Road.

You will find several more options for lunch as you ride along High Street. This is a unique cycling experience, as the shopping district stretches out over a half mile through town, with a steady 5 percent uphill grade. Here along the way you will find

Hyde Mill is on the National Register of Historic Places.

24 Mineral Challenge

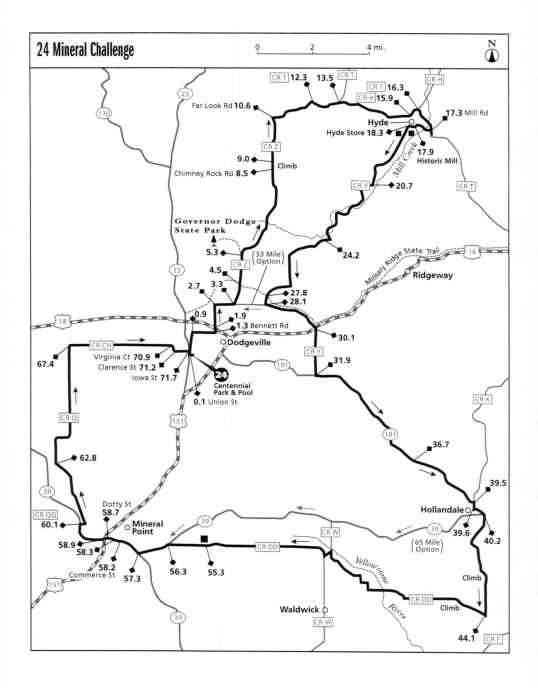

0   2   4 mi.

N

CR T **12.3**   **13.5**   CR T

CR T **16.3**

CR H

Far Look Rd **10.6**   CR H **15.9**

17.3 Mill Rd

CR Z

Hyde

Hyde Store **18.3**

17.9
Historic Mill

9.0   Climb

Chimney Rock Rd **8.5**

Mill Creek

CR Y   **20.7**

CR T

Governor Dodge
State Park

5.3

(33 Mile
Option)

CR Z

4.5

24.2

Military Ridge State Trail

18

Ridgeway

2.7   **3.3**

27.8
28.1

0.9

1.9

1.3 Bennett Rd

30.1

Dodgeville

CR Y

31.9

CR CH

67.4

Virginia Ct **70.9**

Clarence St **71.2**

Iowa St **71.7**

191

24
Centennial
Park & Pool

CR K

0.1 Union St

CR Q

191

36.7

151

39.5

62.8

Hollandale

39

Dotty St
58.7

CR QQ

60.1

Mineral
Point

39

CR W

39

39.6

40.2

(65 Mile
Option)

58.9

58.3

CR DD

Yellowstone

Climb

58.2

Commerce St

57.3

56.3   **55.3**

River

CR DD

Climb

151

39

Waldwick

CR W

44.1   CR F

23

130

23

18

39

the Red Rooster Cafe, famous for their miners' pasties, or enjoy a cool gelato next door at the Spotted Dog Gallery before leaving town.

At the top of Mineral Point, turn left on Ridge Street (Highway 39) and then take a right on Fountain Street (still Highway 39) and cross the new four-lane Highway 151 to County Road QQ. This quiet lane passes along a golf course and passes a couple homes with ornamental mixtures of flowers in their front yards. You then turn onto County Road Q and roll north through the open countryside back to Dodgeville. After returning to the park, take advantage of the city pool and showers before exploring the town.

Miles and Directions

0.0 Leave Centennial Park and Pool parking lot east on Parry Street.

0.1 Take a right on Union Street.

0.9 Take a right on North Street.

1.3 Turn left on Bennett Road.

1.9 Cross Highway 18.

2.7 Take a right on County Road YZ.

3.3 Turn left on County Road Z. (Note: The 33-mile option returns here.)

4.5 Cross Military Ridge State Trail.

5.3 Pass bike trail into Governor Dodge State Park.

8.5 Pass Chimney Rock Road.

9.0 Pass through Pleasant Ridge.

10.6 Take a right on Far Look Road.

12.3 Take a right on County Road T.

13.5 Merge onto Erdman Road.

15.9 Turn left on County Road H.

16.3 Take a right County Road T.

17.3 Take a right on Mill Road.

17.9 Pass Hyde Mill.

18.2 Turn left on County Road H.

18.3 Pass through Hyde.

20.7 Take a right on County Road Y.

24.2 Pass through Pleasant Valley.

27.8 Cross bike trail.

28.1 Turn left on County Road YZ. **Option:** Turn right on County Road YZ for the 33-mile option.

30.1 Cross Highway 18 onto County Road Y.

31.9 Turn left on Highway 191.

36.7 Pass through Banner Valley.

38.9 Pass through Long Valley.

39.5 Take a right on County Road K/Highway 191 into Hollandale.

39.6 Turn left on State Street.

40.2 Cross Highway 39 onto County Road K. **Option:** Turn west on Highway 39 for the 65-mile option.

44.1 Take a right on County Road DD.

55.3 Pass Pleasant View Community Church.

56.3 Turn left on Highway 39.

57.3 Turn right on Highway 23 into Mineral Point.

58.2 Turn left on Commerce Street.

58.3 Take a right on High Street.

58.7 Turn left on Dotty Street.

58.8 Turn left on Ridge Street.

58.9 Take a right on Highway 39.

60.1 Take a right on County Road QQ.

62.8 Turn right on County Road Q.

67.4 Take a right on County Road CH.

70.9 Back in Dodgeville, take a right on Virginia Court.

71.2 Turn left on Clarence Street.

71.7 Take a right on Iowa Street.

71.8 Take a left on Parry Street.

72.0 Return to parking lot.

Local Information

Dodgeville Area Chamber of Commerce, 338 North Iowa Street, Dodgeville; (877) 863-6341; www.dodgeville.com.

Local Events/Attractions

Dodge Mining Camp Cabin, 205 East Fountain Street, Dodgeville; (608) 935-5557.

Lands' End Visitors Center, 1 Lands' End Lane, Dodgeville; (608) 935-6207.

Pendarvis Cornish Miners Colony, Shakerag Road, Mineral Point; (608) 987-2122; www.wisconsinhistory.org/pendarvis.

Restaurants

Grace Cafe, 138 North Iowa Street, Dodgeville; (608) 935-2233.

Jimmy's Restaurant & Lounge, 237 North Iowa Street, Dodgeville; (608) 935-3663.

Quality Bakery, 154 North Iowa Street, Dodgeville; (608) 935-3812.

Accommodations

Don Q Inn, 3658 Highway 23 North, Dodgeville; (800) 666-7848; www.fantasuite.com.

Governor Dodge State Park, 4175 Highway 23, Dodgeville; www.dnr.state.wi.us.

Bike Shops

Open Air Bike Repair, 438 Jefferson Street, Oregon; (608) 835-2049.

Restrooms

Start/finish: Centennial Park and Pool.

5.8 Governor Dodge State Park.

9.0: Pleasant Ridge Store.

18.3 Hyde Store.

35.9: Hollandale Park.

58.4: Next to Pendarvis Park parking lot in Mineral Point.

Maps

DeLorme: Wisconsin Atlas and Gazetteer: Page 26 A3.

Wisconsin State Bicycle Map (Mississippi River Section).

Iowa County Bicycle Map.

25 Devil's Head Challenge

This tour visits an area with many geologic quartzite remnants that date back to pre-historic times and offers the cyclist the temptation of several scenic challenges. You leave from a town nestled along the river that was named after a French explorer. Riding counterclockwise, this metric century follows the river to the west and then coasts down to a town that is home to the Mid-Continental Railway Museum, where you can see a rare survivor of steam trains, the 1907 Chicago & Northwestern locomotive No. 1388. You will then circle back to the east, ride below the ridge, and travel along the southern cliffs of Devil's Lake State Park. Next you'll cruise south down to the Wisconsin River and enjoy free passage across it by ferry. On the other side, take a circle tour around Gibraltar Rock and then through a village the Indians named for its good fishing. After returning on the ferry, the challenge will demand your energy reserve as you climb up the ridge, passing a Scottish estate. Once at the summit, adjust your cadence and cruise back into Baraboo.

Start: Mary Roundtree-Evans Athletic Field in Baraboo.
Length: 61 miles with 26- and 41-mile options.
Terrain: Rolling with several major climbs.

Traffic and hazards: Caution should be used when riding on the paved shoulders of Highway 12 and 136 near Baraboo and Highways 78 and 188 out of Merrimac.

Getting there: From Interstate 90/94 travel south on Highway 12. At Highway 33 turn left; after passing Ochsner Park and Zoo, take a right on Park Street and follow it south several blocks to the park, where there is plentiful free parking.

Nestled in the beautiful bluffs, the Baraboo area is a fun place to explore. Though the first claim holder here was John de la Rond, who originally settled at Ft. Winnebago in 1828, the unique name for the river and town came from Captain Barabeauf. A French explorer with Morgan's Expedition, he is said to have bartered with the Indians while wintering at the river's mouth in the early 1700s. With an abundant water supply for both lumber and rich farm land, the settlement grew and in 1866 a charter election claimed it a village.

The challenge leaves from Mary Roundtree-Evans Athletic Field and heads west. After riding out of town along the Baraboo River, cross Highway 12 onto Hatchery Road. As the route shimmies up to Rock Hill Park, you can see the water hurriedly caressing the rocks in the river as the Baraboo flows back toward town. Riding on the paved shoulder of Highway 136, turn south on County Road PF and roll down to North Freedom.

In 1846 the first pioneers arrived here and called the settlement Hackett's Corner. Then, when the railroad came through, two plats were made, one called Bloom, after George W. Bloom, and the other North Freedom, because the village was in

A toll-free ferry takes riders across the Wisconsin River on the Devil's Head Challenge.

the north part of Freedom Township. Later, when iron ore was discovered, the name was changed to Bessemer in honor of Sir Henry Bessemer, who invented the process of turning pig iron into steel. In 1890 the town's name reverted back to North Freedom and was incorporated.

As you ride into town, you will pass North Freedom Park on Linn Street. Another block ahead is Carol's Railroad Inn Cafe, a great place to stop if you haven't had breakfast. At the stop sign here, the challenge turns south, but you have a side-trip option to consider that is worth the extra mile round-trip, especially if you are into railroad history: the Mid-Continental Railway Museum. Take a tour with a train ride or just view the magnificent iron horses in the museum as you learn about the history of the railroad here in Sauk County. A highlight of this museum is a rare survivor of smaller steam trains, the 1907 Chicago & Northwestern locomotive No. 1388.

As the challenge turns back to the east on County Road W, the road grade will require you to shift down to your lower cassette for your first climb. Soon you are traveling through Hoot Owl Valley and the forested foothills ahead grow larger. After jogging south on Highway 12's 4-foot paved shoulder, turn left on Ski High Road and ride east again. At the Devil's Lake State Park border, turn south on Shore Road. Those who prefer the 26-mile option will head north up to the state park entrance and then east.

For the next 5 miles through the state park, the challenge meanders east along the road at the bottom of the south-facing cliff. At Highway 113 jog to the south down to County Road DL, then east to Marsh Road. Those who prefer the 41-mile option will continue to ride east on County Road DL.

Now the challenge heads south and coasts down to Merrimac. One of the earliest settlers in this area was Chester Mattson, who started a ferry here in 1848, with the settlement known as Matt's Ferry. Within a year the village was granted a post office and was renamed Colomar after the postmaster general at the time, but farmers and stagecoach drivers continued to call it Matt's Ferry. J. G. Train is credited with having the name changed to Merrimac, which came from Merrimack, New Hampshire.

As you wait for the ferry, you can visit the public restrooms or snack bar. Enjoy the trip across the river, as there is no charge—your tax dollars have covered the tab. Run by the Wisconsin Department of Transportation, the ride takes about a half hour with loading and unloading time.

On the other side of the Wisconsin River, in Columbia County, follow the bike lane off the ferry and take a right on Highway 188 along the riverbank that travels around Goose Egg Hill. Turn east on County Road V and follow the rolling terrain to County Road JA, the next crossroad. Here the challenge gradually climbs up along Gibraltar Rock and then coasts down across the highway into Okee.

It is said that the Indians who accompanied Father Marquette and Louis Joleit named this site in June of 1763. Some think that in Algonquin the word means "good fishing ground." They may be right: As you ride through this lakeside community, it is evident that fishing is a mainstay here. After circling around on Ryan Road, the route loops to the west on Chrislaw Road and returns back to the ferry crossing.

After unloading back in Sauk County, turn left on Highway 78 in Merrimac, then right on Baraboo Road. Two-tenths of a mile ahead, where Marsh Road turns left, continue north on Bluff Road. At the 44.7-mile mark you are back on County Road DL, where the 41-mile option returns. Here at the corner you will find a restaurant and just to the north is the Devil's Head Resort if you are looking for a place to have lunch.

For the next 3 miles the route heads east along the bottom of the Baraboo Range, then starts to climb. At Durward-Glen Road turn north and continue the ascent. A mile up the road you will pass Durward's Glen. Named after the Duward family, this forty-acre parcel of land consisting of hills and a valley is a miniature canyon. In between steep walls flows a spring-fed brook called Prentice Creek. At one time the creek produced the power to operate a mill that manufactured wooden shingles. In 1845 William Durward and his wife settled here from England. A publisher and author, Mr. Durward produced the first book of poetry in Wisconsin and also published the first Catholic magazine in the Midwest. Today this peaceful wooded area veils a retreat and conference center.

At Hog Hollow you're at the top of the ridge, and it is time to start cruising down County Road W. When you hit Highway 113 (26-mile option returns here),

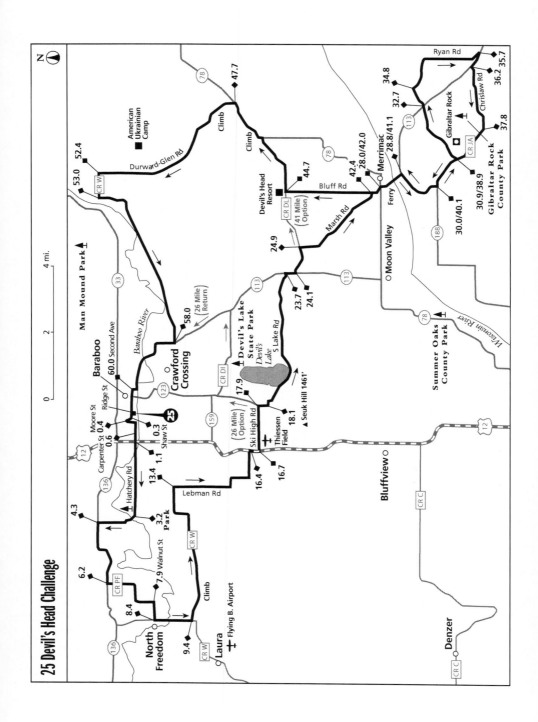

25 Devil's Head Challenge

N

American Ukrainian Camp

0   2   4 mi.

Man Mound Park

Baraboo River

Baraboo

Crawford Crossing

Devil's Lake State Park

Devil's Lake

Seuk Hill 1461'

Thiessen Field

Ski High Rd

26 Mile Option

North Freedom

Laura

Flying B. Airport

Bluffview

Denzer

Moon Valley

Merrimac

Ferry

Gibraltar Rock

Gibraltar Rock County Park

Ryan Rd

Chrislaw Rd

Summer Oaks County Park

Wisconsin River

Durward-Glen Rd

Devil's Head Resort

Bluff Rd

Marsh Rd

41 Mile Option

26 Mile Return

S Lake Rd

Lebman Rd

Walnut St

Ridge St
Moore St
Carpenter St
Shaw St
Second Ave
Hatchery Rd

Park

CR W
CR PF
CR DL
CR DI
CR JA
CR C

Climb

33
78
78
78
113
113
188
123
159
136
136
12
12

0.3
0.4
0.6
1.1
3.2
4.3
6.2
7.9
8.4
9.4
13.4
16.4
16.7
17.9
18.1
23.7
24.1
24.9
28.0/42.0
28.8/41.1
30.0/40.1
30.9/38.9
32.7
34.8
35.7
36.2
37.8
42.4
44.7
47.7
52.4
53.0
58.0
60.0

head north back into Baraboo. Follow the city streets along the river and past Circus World back to the park.

Miles and Directions

0.0 Leave Mary Roundtree-Evans Athletic Field on Ridge Street.

0.1 Turn left on Second Avenue.

0.3 Turn left on Shaw Street.

0.4 Turn left on Moore Street.

0.6 Take a right on Carpenter Street.

1.1 Cross Highway 12 onto Hatchery Road. (Note: Convenience stores are available here.)

3.2 Take a right at Rock Hill Park on the Baraboo River.

4.3 Turn left on Highway 136.

6.2 Take a left on County Road PF.

7.9 Take a right on Walnut Street into North Freedom.

8.2 Pass North Freedom Park on Linn Street.

8.4 Take a left on County Road PF at four-way stop. **Side-trip:** The Mid-Continental Railway Museum is 0.5 mile west.

9.4 Turn left on County Road W in Hoot Owl Valley.

13.4 Take a right on Lehman Road.

16.4 Take a right on Highway 12.

16.7 Turn left on Ski High Road.

17.9 Take a right on Shore Road. **Option:** The 26-mile option turns left here and travels 1.5 miles north past Devil's Lake State Park.

18.1 Take a left on South Lake Road.

23.7 Take a right on Highway 113.

24.1 Turn left on County Road DL.

24.9 Take a right on Marsh Road. **Option:** Continue east on County Road DL for the 41-mile option.

27.6 Take a right on Baraboo Road.

27.9 Turn left on Highway 78 into Merrimac.

28.0 Take a right on Highway 113.

28.2 Follow bike lane onto ferry.

28.7 Depart ferry and resume ride on Highway 113.

28.8 Take a right on Highway 188 around Goose Egg Hill.

30.0 Turn left on County Road V.

30.9 Turn left on County Road V at the junction of County Road JA.

32.1 Pass Gibraltar Rock.

32.7 Cross Highway 113.

32.9 Pass through Okee.

34.8 Take a right on Ryan Road (County Road V).

35.7 Take a right on Highway 113.

36.2 Turn left on Chrislaw Road.

37.8 Go right on County Road JA.

38.9 Take a right on County Road V.

40.1 Take a right on Highway 188 back to Merrimac.

41.1 Turn left on Highway 133 onto ferry.

42.0 Turn left on Highway 78.

42.2 Take a right on Baraboo Road.

42.4 Continue straight ahead on Bluff Road as Mash Road turns to the left.

44.7 Take a right on County Road DL; Devil's Head Resort is to the north. (Note: The 41-mile option returns here.)

47.7 Turn left on Durward-Glen Road.

48.6 Pass Durward's Glen.

52.4 Turn left on County Road W at Hog Hollow.

53.0 Take a right on County Road W.

58.0 Take a right Highway 113/Water Street into Baraboo. (Note: The 26-mile option returns here.)

58.7 Pass Circus World.

60.0 Turn left on Second Avenue.

60.4 Cross Highway 123.

60.9 Turn left on Park Street.

61.0 Return to park.

Local Information

Baraboo Area Chamber of Commerce, 600 West Chestnut Street, Baraboo; (800) 227-2266; www.baraboo.com.

Local Events/Attractions

Circus World Museum, 426 Water Street, Baraboo; (608) 356-0800; www.wisconsinhistory.org/circusworld.

International Crane Foundation, E-11376 Shady Lane Road, Baraboo; (608) 356-9462; www.savingcranes.org.

Mid-Continental Railway History Society, Museum Road, New Freedom; (800) 930-1385; www.midcontinental.org.

Baraboo Road Race–WCA; first week in June; www.wicycling.org.

Restaurants

Baker's Dozen, 424 Oak Street, Baraboo; (608) 356-2995.

Little Village Cafe, 146 Fourth Avenue, Baraboo; (608) 356-2800.

Carol's Railroad Inn Cafe, 104 East Walnut Street, North Freedom; (608) 522-4485.

Accommodations

Park Plaza Baraboo, 626 West Pine Street, Baraboo; (800) 814-7000.

Devil's Lake State Park, S5975 Park Road, Baraboo; (608) 356-8301; www.devilslakewisconsin.com.

Bike Shops

Baraboo River Bike Shop, 209 Granite Avenue, Reedsburg; (608) 524-0798.

Sandstone Bicycle Repair, 806 Washington Avenue, Wisconsin Dells; (608) 253-7781.

Restrooms

Start/finish: Mary Roundtree-Evans Athletic Field.

8.2 North Freedom Park.

20.9 Devil's Lake State Park.

28.0 Merrimac public restrooms.

32.1 Gibraltor Rock parking lot.

42.0 Merrimac public restrooms.

Maps
DeLorme: Wisconsin Atlas and Gazetteer: Page
35 A6.

Wisconsin State Bicycle Map (Southeast
Section).

26 Commuters Cruise

In a city with many miles of designated bike routes, this ride leaves from a park that
overlooks the picturesque Sugar River valley. The cruise travels counterclockwise to
the southwest, utilizing one of the city's commuter bike routes into the dale. After
crossing Military Ridge State Trail, you soon approach a town known as the "Troll
Capital of the World." An option is available in this Norwegian settlement for those
who prefer to ride the crushed limestone trail back. Otherwise the cruise turns
southeast down the valley floor, where you will soon be in a village named for
George Washington's home. You then circle back to the northeast and wind your way
up past Sugar Ridge on your way to a village once named Corners. Here, at the
crossroads of several roadways, the route safely maneuvers its way through town and
then veers off to the east. Turning north, the grade of the road gradually ascends on
another bike-designated roadway back into Madison.

Start: Eveler Park in Madison.
Length: 43 miles with a 19-mile bike trail
option.
Terrain: Rolling with a few moderate climbs.
Traffic and hazards: Caution should be used
when riding on the paved shoulder of Old
Highway 18 into Mount Horeb, the paved
shoulder of Highway 92 between Mount Horeb
and Mount Vernon, and County Road M out of
Verona.

Getting there: From the West Beltline Freeway in Madison, exit on Highway 12/14 south. At
the first stoplight turn right on the service road, then turn north along the freeway. Turn left at
Hammersley Road, then make a right on McKenna Boulevard. The park is on the left 1 block
north.

At the far southwest edge of a city situated between beautiful lakes formed in the
glacial period, the cruise begins at Eveler Park. The Winnebago Indians first had a
village here called *Dejop,* meaning "four lakes." Then in 1836, before any settlers
actually arrived, the site was selected as the capital of Wisconsin Territory.

With a village established and named in honor of President James Madison, settlers from many eastern states and Europe flocked in. Due to its designation as the
capital and known for its natural beauty, the city's growth was guaranteed as a center of state politics and education. By the time Madison became a chartered city in
1856, the community had grown to more than 9,000 residents. Before riding this
cruise, pick up a Madison Bicycling Resource Guide & Route Map so you can
enjoy more of this bike-friendly community.

After leaving Eveler Park in the southwest corner of Madison, the route turns south on McKenna Boulevard. Here you can follow the border of the park around to Gammon Road or take the trail through the park. From the south end of the park, ride west on Midtown Road. This is one of the bike-designated routes available for commuting in and out of Madison.

At the 3-mile mark you will need to prepare for your first hill. A moderate climb, it is set off by a series of Wisconsin rollers offering some spectacular views as you ride from one hilltop to the next. Now veering to the south on Timber Lane, the route soon jogs back to the west on Paulson Road. After you cross the Sugar River and the Military Ridge State Trail, shimmy up to County Road P. Just before Highway 18/151, turn west again on Ridge View Drive and maneuver through the turn-around that jets out onto Springdale/Old Highway 18 into Mount Horeb.

Settled by Norwegian immigrants in the 1870s, the town's Main Street is decorated with wooden troll carvings and is an excellent place to stop for a break. After crossing the Military Ridge State Trail, next to the trailhead in the downtown area, ride south and wind through the rolling city streets before merging onto the shoulder of Highway 92. Ride the paved shoulder of this secondary roadway for the next 5 miles to Mount Vernon.

Here you will find a flourishing little village in the Sugar River valley surrounded by grain farms. It is said that when settlers moved into this valley, they were reminded of the area around Mount Vernon, George Washington's estate in Virginia. You will find a park here with restrooms and the Gone Fishing Inn.

Two miles ahead on the highway, the cruise turns onto Spring Rose Road. As you ride the rolling terrain to the northeast, watch for deer in the valley's underbrush as the hawks soar above. Soon you will slide around the southern end of the ridge, cross the river, and turn on a road, all with *Sugar* in their names. In a few miles the cruise passes through the village of Verona.

For many years this settlement was known as Corners because it was at the crossing of a couple well-traveled roads. In 1848, at the suggestion of William Vroman, it was given the name Verona, which was the name of his native town in New York. Today, as two highways merge here, the route crosses over and then turns to the south, just before the Military Ridge State Trail. After slipping under Highway 18/151, meander through the south side of town and then ride east on County Road M, rolling out over the countryside once again.

Now turning onto Seminole Road, another designated bike route, the cruise circles back to the north up along the Beltline Freeway in Madison. After crossing the freeway, turn east on Hammersley Road and follow the Beltline for a mile, crossing over on the pedestrian bridge, and continue west back to the park.

Miles and Directions

0.0   From Eveler Park, go south on McKenna Boulevard, or take bike trial through the park to Gammon Road.

26 Commuters Cruise

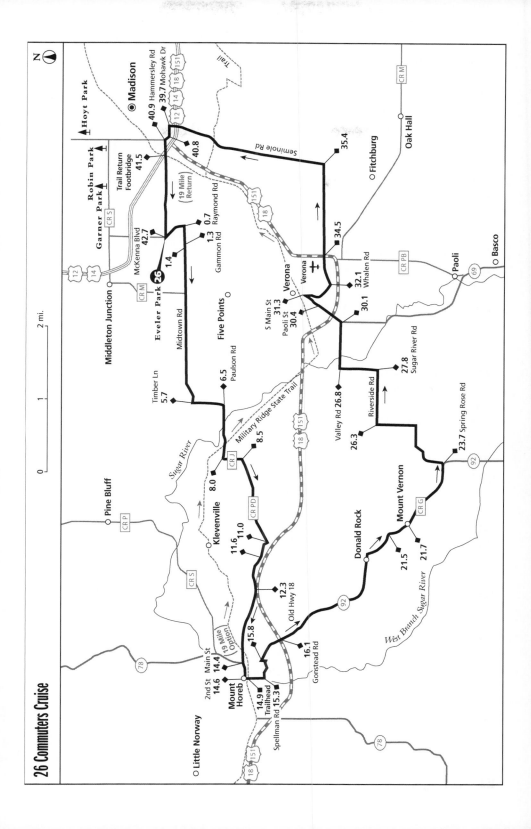

0.7   Take a right on Raymond Road.

1.3   Take a right on Gammon Road.

1.4   Turn left on Midtown Road.

5.7   Turn left on Timber Lane.

6.5   Take a right on Paulson Road.

7.7   Cross the Military Ridge State Trail.

8.0   Turn left on County Road J.

8.5   Take a right on County Road PD.

11.0   Take a right County Road P.

11.6   Turn left on Ridge View Drive.

12.3   At the turnaround, take a right onto Springdale/Old Highway 18.

14.0   Cross Military Ridge State Trail.

14.4   Turn left on Main Street in Mount Horeb.

14.6   Turn left on Second Street.

14.9   Cross Military Ridge State Trail. **Option:** This trail is a 19-mile option on crushed limestone.

15.3   Turn left on Spellman Road.

15.8   At the bottom of the hill, turn left on Vista Ridge Drive.

16.1   Turn left on Gonstead Road then right onto Highway 92, under Highway 18/151.

21.5   Pass County Road G.

21.7   Pass through Mount Vernon.

23.7   Turn left on Spring Rose Road.

26.3   Take a right on Riverside Road.

27.8   Turn left on Sugar River Road.

28.8   Take a right on Valley Road.

30.1   Turn left on Highway 69 into Verona. **Option:** Trail options available.

30.4   Cross under Highway 18/151 onto Paoli Street.

31.3   Take a right on South Main Street/County Road M.

32.1   Turn left on Whalen Road.

34.5   Cross Old Highway PB and then Highway 18/151.

35.4   Turn left on Seminole Road.

38.9   Cross over the Beltline Freeway.

39.7   Turn left on Mohawk Drive.

40.8   Turn left on Nakoma Road.

40.9   Cross Midville Boulevard onto Hammersley Road.

41.4   Cross over Beltline Freeway on pedestrian bridge.

41.5   Continue west on Hammersley Road. (Note: The 19-mile trail option returns here from Mount Horeb.)

42.7   Take a right on McKenna Boulevard.

43.0   Return to park.

Local Information

Greater Madison Convention & Visitors Bureau, 615 East Washington Avenue, Madison; (800) 373-4959; www.visitmadison.com.

Local Events/Attractions

Spoke Out to Keep Kids Safe Ride; third Saturday in May; (608) 256-3374; www.prevent childabusewi.org.

Tour de Cure; third Sunday in May; American Diabetes Association; (608) 833-1060; www.diabetes.org/tour.

Madison Critical Mass; last week in August; Wisconsin Sports Development; (608) 226-4780; www.ironmanwisconsin.com.

Harvest Ride–Multi-Day Tour; second week in September; (608) 836-7100; www.island wheat.com.

Cycling Group Fall Ride; third week in October; Bicycle Federation of Wisconsin; (608) 251-4456; www.bfw.org.

Restaurants

Gone Fishing Inn, 8646 Davis Street, Mount Vernon; (608) 832-6289.

Grumpy Troll Restaurant, 105 South Second Street, Mount Horeb; (608) 437-2739.

Tuscany Mediterranean Grill, 2969 Cahill Main, Madison; (608) 270-1684.

Accommodations

Quality Inn & Suites, 2969 Cahill Main, Madison; (608) 274-7200; www.qualitysuites madison.com.

Mendota County Park, 5130 County Road M, Madison; (608) 242-4576.

Bike Shops

Erik's Bike Shop, 680 South Whitney Way, Madison; (608) 278-9000.

Madison Bicycle Company, 4686 Cottage Grove Road, Madison; (608) 244-3027.

Recumbent Bicycles of Madison, 437 South Yellowstone Drive, Madison; (608) 271-0341.

Trek Bicycle Store, 8108 Mineral Point Road, Madison; (608) 833-8735.

Yellow Jersey Cycle Shop, 419 State Street, Madison; (608) 257-4818; www.yellow jersey.org.

For a complete list of bike shops in the Madison area, visit www.bfw.org.

Restrooms

Start/finish: Eveler Park.

14.4 Military Ridge trailhead.

21.6 Mount Vernon City Park.

Maps

DeLorme: Wisconsin Atlas and Gazetteer: Page 36 D1.

Wisconsin State Bicycle Map (Southeast Section).

Madison Bicycling Resource Guide & Route Map.

27 Sugar River Ramble

Leaving from a town called "America's Little Switzerland," this ramble makes a circle tour around both the Little Sugar and Sugar Rivers as it rolls through the countryside. After exploring the upper half of Green County, the route briefly slips up into northern Dane County and then returns to a community named after a city in Canada. Now back in Green County, as you cruise south the road twists and turns as it follows the Sugar River. Soon you will pass through a village named after a town in Ohio. Farther along enjoy the rolling terrain through grassy meadows where songbirds greet you as you ride by. Now turning to the west, stop for a snack and watch cheese being made the traditional way. After experiencing a couple Wisconsin rollers, you'll cruise into a town with a name that means "little mountain." The ramble comes full circle as you turn to the north, back to New Glarus for a "cow parade" and brewery tour.

Start: Sugar River trailhead in New Glarus.
Length: 32 miles.
Terrain: Rolling with a few moderate climbs.

Traffic and hazards: Caution should be used when riding on the paved shoulder of Highway 69 in New Glarus and in Belleville.

Getting there: From Highway 39/60 in New Glarus, turn west onto Fifth Avenue at the stoplight. Then cross the trail and turn left on North Railroad Street. Parking is free and plentiful 1 block north.

Nestled in the rolling hills of south-central Wisconsin, the ramble leaves from New Glarus. This village, situated on the Little Sugar River, was settled by Swiss immigrants in 1845. Forced to leave their home country by famine and unemployment, several families came to the United States to find a new home and create a settlement that mirrored their Swiss heritage. Finding the lush green hills here to their liking, the town was platted and named after the Canton Glarus in eastern Switzerland, where the settlers came from. New Glarus, with its many Swiss specialties, is a great place to start a ramble. Consider stopping at the village's authentic Swiss bakery for some rolls or crackers—you may need them later.

After leaving from North Railroad Street, the route crosses the Sugar River Bike Trail and jogs north on the highway's paved shoulder before traveling east on County Road W. As you pass the New Glarus Brewery (offering a great tour after your ride), you may want to drop into your granny gear to keep your cadence spinning up this moderate hill. Now rolling through the countryside in the valley, you will come to Ross Crossing. Here at the County Road CC crossroads, turn to the north and cross into Dane County on your way up to Belleville.

Located on the Sugar River, this village was founded by John Fredrick, who came to the area looking for a suitable water source for a gristmill. He selected this

27 Sugar River Ramble

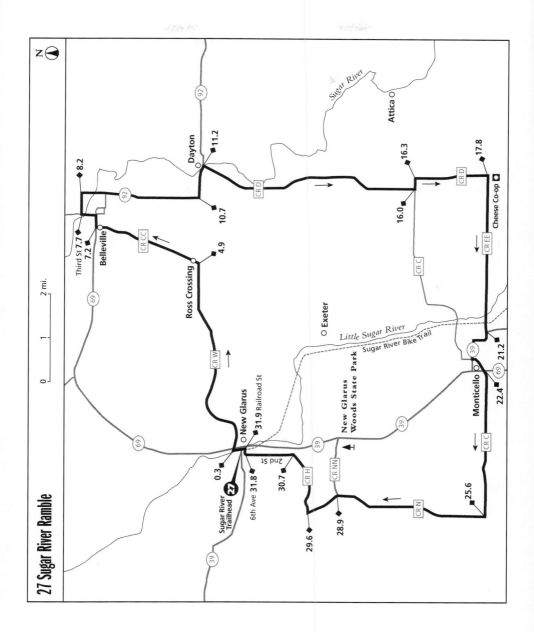

site and platted the village in 1842, naming it in honor of his native village of Belleville, Canada.

Here at the 7.4-mile mark, the city park has restrooms if you need to stop. Now turning back into Green County, the ramble continues rolling south, periodically crossing the Sugar River on its way down to Dayton.

Dr. Kirkpatrick and his family came here in 1852 and named the settlement after the Ohio town they had moved from. Today you will find only a few residences here as you pass through. Now turning on County Road D, continue traveling south, crossing the river one more time. At the 17.8-mile mark you will reach County Road EE and the Silver-Lewis Cheese Co-op. In this old-fashioned cheese plant, you can walk through the warehouse and see the workers making cheese in the next room. At the counter in the center of the packaging area, you can choose from a wide selection of cheeses and sausages that would go well with the bread you purchased earlier. Back on the road turning west, enjoy some great Wisconsin rollers. Soon you will cross the Sugar River Bike Trail and coast into Monticello.

Robert Witter built a sawmill here on the Little Sugar River and platted the village in 1843. With many businesses and the population swelling to a hundred, Foster Steadman became the postmaster in 1845. For his job he traveled a mail route from Monroe to Madison, the same route the stagecoach used, and on these journeys he noticed striking mounds bordering the long valley here. Needing a name for the post office, he called it Monticello, meaning "little mountain," in reference to the mounds, or bluffs, overlooking the village. This tranquil community next to Lake Montesian offers several options for lunch, or you might want to enjoy a picnic in the park with the fresh bread and cheese you have purchased along the way.

After crossing the highway, continue riding west over more lush country fields. You then turn to the north, where the ramble crosses several branches of Heft Creek before passing County Road NN to New Glarus Woods State Park. Now it's only a mile back to the community full of painted cows. Upon your return, if you have the energy, go on the New Glarus "cow parade." See if you can spot the colorful statues scattered throughout the business district before heading over to the brewery for a tour.

Miles and Directions

0.0 Leave from the trailhead on North Railroad Street.

0.1 Turn left on Sixth Avenue and cross the Sugar River Bike Trail.

0.2 Turn left on Highway 69.

0.3 Take a right on County Road W at the New Glarus Brewery.

4.9 Turn left on County Road CC at Ross Crossing.

7.2 Take a right onto Highway 69 in Belleville.

7.3 Turn left on Highway 69.

7.4 Pass city park in Belleville.

7.7	Take a right on Third Street.
8.2	Take a right on Remy Road/Highway 92.
10.7	Turn left on Highway 92.
11.2	Take a right on County Road D in Dayton.
16.0	Turn left onto County Road C.
16.3	Take a right on County Road D.
17.8	Take a right on County Road EE at the Silver-Lewis Cheese Co-op.
21.2	Continue west on Highway 39 into Monticello.
21.3	Take a right on County Road C.
22.4	Cross Highway 69.
25.6	Take a right on County Road N.
28.9	Pass County Road NN to New Glarus Woods State Park (located 1 mile east).
29.6	Take a right on County Road H.
30.7	Turn left on Second Street.
31.8	Take a right on Sixth Avenue in New Glarus.
31.9	Turn left on Railroad Street.
32.0	Return to trailhead.

Local Information

New Glarus Chamber of Commerce, Sugar River Trailhead, New Glarus; (800) 527-6838; www.swisstown.com.
Green County Tourism; (888) 222-9111; www.greencounty.org.

Local Events/Attractions

New Glarus Brewery Tours, Highway 69 and County Road W, New Glarus; (608) 527-5850; www.newglarusbrewing.com.
Swiss Historical Village, 612 Seventh Avenue, New Glarus; (608) 527-2317; www.swisshistoricalvillage.com.
Tour de Cheese; first Saturday in June; www.foruminc.com.
Pedal for Paws; first Saturday in July; Green County Humane Society; (608) 325-9600; www.greencountyhumane.org/pedal.

Restaurants

Glarner Stube, 518 First Street, New Glarus; (608) 527-2216.
New Glarus Bakery, 534 First Street, New Glarus; (608) 527-2916.

M & M Cafe, 126 North Main Street, Monticello; (608) 938-4890.

Accommodations

Swiss Aire Motel, 1200 Highway 69, New Glarus; (800) 798-4391.
New Glarus Woods State Park, Highway 69 and County Road NN, New Glarus; (608) 527-2335.

Bike Shops

Village Pedaler, 5511 Monona Drive, Monona; (608) 221-0311.

Restrooms

Start/finish: Sugar River trailhead and visitor center.
7.4: Belleville City Park.
21.4: Monticello City Park.

Maps

DeLorme: Wisconsin Atlas and Gazetteer: Page 27 B6.
Wisconsin State Bicycle Map (Southeast Section).

28 Five Arch Cruise

With hundreds of miles of bike-friendly roads, the options here are endless for exploring the cultural, historical, and natural attractions of southern Rock County. The cruise leaves from a city with a name that was coined from a French word meaning "handsome ground" and heads west. As you ride along a tree-lined lane, you will soon arrive at an 1860s water-powered gristmill open for tours most weekends. Farther west visit the site of a river town that met its demise after a railroad merger. Now rolling through farm fields up to Orfordville, the route soon circles east to a village named after a hymn sung at a town meeting. You then cross over the Rock River and pass through a stagecoach village on Turtle Creek. As you cross the creek you will see a remarkable railroad bridge, of European design, that was built in 1855 and is still in use today. You then circle back on the south bank of the creek and pass another village, given the French name for "limestone," before returning to Beloit.

Start: Riverside Park in Beloit.
Length: 62 miles with a 27-mile option.
Terrain: Flat to gently rolling.
Traffic and hazards: Use caution crossing

Highway 81 onto Portland Avenue in Beloit, after leaving Orfordville on Highway 213, again on County Road G, and when crossing the bridge on Lathers Road at mile 53.2.

Getting there: From Interstate 39/90 head west on Highway 81 to Beloit. At Riverside Drive, just before the Rock River, turn right; Riverside Park is a quarter mile north on the left.

This cruise leaves from a city called the "Gateway to Wisconsin," on the Rock River at the mouth of Turtle Creek. Originally this was the site of the Winnebago Indian village called *Ke-chunk-nee-shun-nuk-ra,* or "The Turtle." One of the earliest pioneers and merchants here, Caleb Blodgett, dubbed this place New Albany, but a citizen committee soon renamed it. Although the exact history remains disputed, it seems that the name Beloit was coined from the French word *balotte,* meaning "handsome ground"; the spelling was then fashioned after Detroit, which the community saw as a great symbol of trade and growth.

Before leaving on the cruise, stop at the visitor center for information on things to do and see after your ride in southern Rock County. From Riverside Park, cross the river after passing the visitor center. As you ride over the bridge, notice on your right one of the retrofitted old foundry building, now painted with a mural, that depicts the town's success.

After heading west on Portland Avenue, turn south past the Historic Hanchett Bartlett Homestead on Division Street. Here James Hanchett, a pioneer contractor and builder of dams, built this 1857 Victorian farmstead. He was well-known for building dams in Indiana, Illinois, and Wisconsin, including the first dam across the Rock River.

As you continue west for the next 5 miles, enjoy a slightly rolling and canopied lane. At South Smythe School Road the route jogs north and then west again on West Mill Pond Road to the Beckman Mill and Park. This restored mill, built in 1868, is on the National Register of Historic Places and is open for afternoon tours on weekends throughout the summer. Turn south on County Road H near the park and mill. For the 27-mile option, take a right on County Road H and head north.

At the 11.9-mile mark, as the cruise heads west again, you will pass Jan's K Market. After turning left on Brandherm Road, the route starts to jog northwest and follows the Sugar River until you reach the defunct settlement of Avon. The village was established in 1844 and took its name from the English river that was made famous by its connection with William Shakespeare. Besides waterpower, the town's brightest hope for growth was the prospect of the Sugar River Railroad building its main line through the town. With the promise of growth, the town's population exceeded 400 and a number of shops, a cheese factory, and a gristmill were established. But when the Sugar River Railroad merged with the Milwaukee Railroad, the plans for the line were abandoned.

If you have the time, ride through this sparsely populated village of platted streets and get a ghostly feel of this town and its loss. Riding north now, the store is gone, but the cruise travels on Avon Store Road. At the 21-mile mark cross Highway 81 and take a right on Skinner Road to the east. The cruise then turns north at Fussum Road and rolls up to Orfordville on County Road K.

This busy little farm community was settled in 1856 by two pioneers, both of whom wanted to have their last name used for the town. When the surveyor came to plot the village, he suggested the name Oxford, for a town in New Hampshire. It was later changed to its current name because Oxford was already in use. There are several options for lunch here at the 30-mile mark.

Now riding south on the paved shoulder of Highway 213, the route turns east again at Plymouth Church Road. About a half mile ahead you pass County Road H, where the 27-mile option briefly rejoins the route. At County Road D turn north and follow the road into Afton. Those who prefer the 27-mile option should turn right and head back to Beloit.

Afton was originally incorporated as Middledale, but in 1854 the postmaster requested a change because of the number of other villages with that name. It is said that at a town gathering to discuss a name, the meeting was opened with a prayer and the song "Flow Gentle Sweet Afton," and the name was overwhelmingly selected. There are a couple options for lunch here if you need to stop.

After leaving town, take a right on Happy Hollow Road, then cross over the Rock River and ride southeast onto ELT Townline Road and then onto East Creek Road. You will soon pass through Tiffany, which was settled in 1840 on the north bank of Turtle Creek. The settlement had a tavern that became a stagecoach stop, named after George Tiffany, who operated the stage line out of Milwaukee. Then

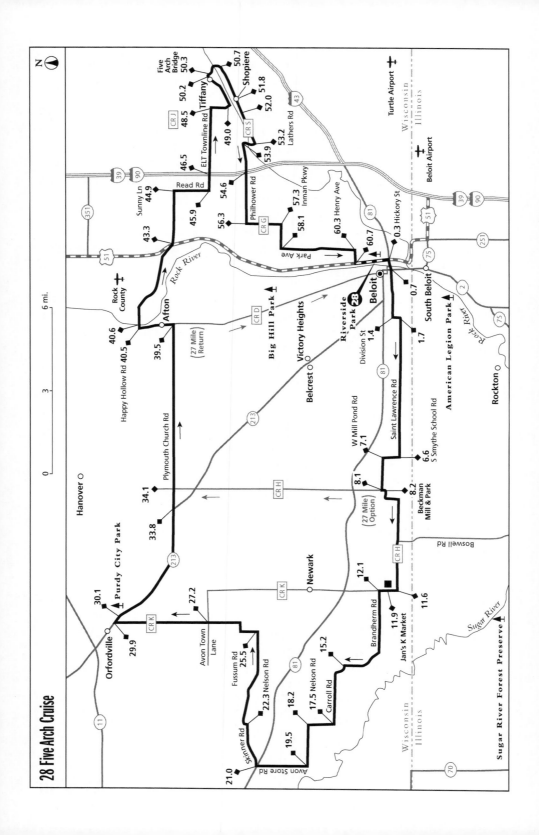

28 Five Arch Cruise

in 1855 the Chicago, St. Paul & Fond du Lac Railroad built tracks through here connecting Janesville with Gary, Illinois.

You will soon approach Turtle Creek as you head south. While crossing over the single-lane township bridge, off to your right you will see the beautiful, historic Five Arch Railway Bridge. This stone trestle is a remarkable monument to design and workmanship. Each stone for the foundation was especially selected from a quarry in Waupon and then cut and placed by hand. It was modeled after French rail bridges and is still in use today.

Now on the south bank, turn back to the west on County Road J and ride into the village of Shopiere. This village was first called Waterloo because of a battle between early settlers. The feud was settled, and the post office was given the French name *Shopiere,* meaning "limestone." Here you will find the Shopiere Bar & Grill if you need to stop.

Ride another mile west and then take a right on Lathers Road. When crossing the single-lane bridge back over Turtle Creek, use caution, as the steel grating can be slippery. At Creek Road turn west again. After crossing I–39/90, the route merges onto Philhower Road and soon turns south and returns to Riverside Park in Beloit.

Miles and Directions

0.0 From Riverside Park, ride south on Riverside Drive.

0.3 Take a right on Hickory Street and cross the Rock River.

0.7 Head straight onto Portland Avenue.

1.4 Turn left on Division Street, past the Hanchett Bartlett Homestead.

1.7 Take a right on Saint Lawrence Road.

6.6 Take a right on South Smythe School Road.

7.1 Turn left on West Mill Pond Road.

8.1 Turn left on County Road H. **Option:** Turn right on County Road H for the 27-mile option.

8.2 Pass Beckman Mill and Park.

11.6 Take a right on County Road K.

11.9 Pass Jan's K Market.

12.1 Turn left on Brandherm Road.

15.2 Turn left on Carroll Road.

17.5 Take a right on Nelson Road.

18.2 Turn left on Beloit-Newark Road.

19.5 Take a right on Avon Store Road.

20.9 Cross Highway 81.

21.0 Take a right on Skinner Road.

22.3 Jog to the left on Nelson Road, then right on Skinner.

25.5 Turn left on Fussum Road.

27.2 Turn north on County Road K.

29.9 Take a right on Highway 213 outside of Orfordville. (Note: Lunch options are a half mile north in town.)

33.8 Turn left on Plymouth Church Road.

34.1 Pass County Road H. (Note: The 27-mile option briefly returns here.)

39.5 Turn left onto County Road D. **Option:** The 27-mile option turns right on County Road D back to Beloit.

39.8 Pass through Afton.

40.5 Take a right on Happy Hollow Road.

40.6 Cross over the Rock River.

43.3 Take a right on Highway 51 and then a left onto Sunny Lane.

44.9 Take a right on Read Road.

45.9 Turn left on ELT Townline Road.

46.5 Cross over I–39/90.

48.5 Take a right on County Road J.

49.0 Turn left on East Creek Road.

49.9 Pass through Tiffany.

50.2 Take a right on Smith Road.

50.3 Cross Turtle Creek (view the Five Arch Bridge).

50.7 Take a right on County Road J.

51.8 Pass through Shopiere.

52.0 Pass County Road J and merge onto County Road S.

53.2 Take a right on Lathers Road, using caution on the bridge's steel tread surface.

53.9 Turn left on East Creek Road.

54.6 Cross back over I–39/90 onto Philhower Road.

56.3 Turn left on County Road G.

57.3 Take a right on Inman Parkway.

58.1 Turn left on Park Avenue.

60.3 Take a right on Henry Avenue.

60.7 Turn left on Riverside Drive.

62.0 Return to park.

Local Information

Beloit Convention & Visitors Bureau, 1003 Pleasant Street, Beloit; (800) 423-5648; www.visitbeloit.com.

Local Events/Attractions

Historic Beckman Mill, County Road H and Mill Pond Road, Beloit; (608) 365-1600.

Wisconsin Cycling Camp; second week in August; (262) 736-2553; www.pactour.com.

Restaurants

Fourth Street Cafe, 935 Fourth Street, Beloit; (608) 362-6657.

Villa Pizza & Family Restaurant, 217 West Beloit Street, Orfordville; (608) 879-3336.

Shopiere Bar & Grill, 5227 East County Road J, Shopiere; (608) 362-6349.

Accommodations

Fairfield Inn & Suites, 2784 Milwaukee Road, Beloit; (608) 365-2200.

Turtle Creek Campsites, I–39/90 and Shopiere Road, Beloit; (608) 362-7768.

Bike Shops

Beloit Sport Center, 557 East Grand Avenue, Beloit; (608) 365-6952.
Zucchini Bike Shop, 942 Wisconsin Avenue, Beloit; (608) 365-1161.

Restrooms

Start/finish: Riverside Park.

8.2: Beckman Mill and Park.
30.1: Purdy City Park.
51.8: Sweet Allen Memorial Park in Shopiere.

Maps

DeLorme: Wisconsin Atlas and Gazetteer: Page 29 D4.
Wisconsin State Bicycle Map (Southeast Section).

29 Round the Rock Cruise

You will find many points of interest along this cruise, beginning with a community with a rich history that spans from the Black Hawk War to automobile manufacturing. You will leave from a beautiful park setting and ride through the downtown historic district. Then following the west bank of the Rock River, you ride past the historic twenty-six-room Lincoln-Tallman House, where Abraham Lincoln visited. Circling up to the north you will then enter a small village that lost its dream of growth and prosperity when the railroad laid its tracks a couple miles to the north. Now jogging to the east, ride through a community where Indians once found it easy to cross the river. As you travel north again, visit the town where the railroad eventually passed through. You then ride southeast to a town that was instrumental in the development of the Underground Railroad. Now coming full circle, ride through some of the area's most productive farmland before you start the gentle descent back into Janesville.

Start: Palmer Park in Janesville.
Length: 42 miles with a 29-mile option.
Terrain: Rolling with a few moderate climbs.

Traffic and hazards: Caution should be used when riding on the paved shoulder of Highway 59 out of Edgerton and County Road M out of Milton.

Getting there: From Interstate 39/90 turn west into Janesville on Highway 11. After passing Mohawk Road, turn right on Palmer Pass. There is plentiful free parking around the visitor center.

You will experience the nostalgic feeling of yesteryear as this tour visits the northern half of Rock County. The rural towns and villages along this route are all steeped in history. You begin at a spot on the Rock River where the Winnebago Indian originally had a village named *E-nee-poro-poro,* meaning "round rock" or "outcropping rock from the river." When the early pioneers found this site during the Indian War of 1832, they named it Black Hawk. Then in the spring of 1937, Henry F. Janes, who operated a ferry service on the river, petitioned for a post office. With the Indian chief's name already in use, the postal office selected the name Janesville. It is said that the first post office was a cigar box nailed to a log.

The new town prospered, due in large part to the combination of available waterpower and rail lines, and manufacturers like Janesville Machine started to lead the nation in the production of agricultural equipment. By 1918 the company merged with General Motors, and SUVs are still made here today.

After leaving from Palmer Park, next to the visitor center, head east to the downtown historic district and cross the Rock River. Notice all the unique commercial architecture as you ride by. A historic walking tour brochure is available at the visitor center that will assist you with exploring after you return. As you ride along the river on Franklin Avenue, you will pass the Wisconsin Wagon Company, where the Janesville Coaster Wagon started production in the early 1900s.

After passing under the railroad trestle, turn onto Mineral Point Road. Those who prefer the 29-mile option should continue north on Franklin Avenue. The cruise then comes to the top of the hill, where you will find the historic Lincoln-Tallman House on your left. Continue west and, if you haven't had breakfast yet, stop at the Fat Frog Cafe at the 3.7-mile mark on your way out of town. Next enjoy rolling down the lane to where the cruise turns north. Soon you are crossing the highway in Leyden. When pioneers settled here they named the corner community after Leyden in the Netherlands, the refuge of the Pilgrims before they sailed to America.

After continuing north over rolling farm fields, you soon pass through the village of Fulton. Platted in 1843 by Herbert Fulton, this unique setting is on a peninsula projecting to the south and is nearly surrounded by the winding Yahara River. With the hope that the railroad would soon come through, business in the town expanded, but the tracks were laid farther north and the village slipped back to a small farm community. You have a couple options for a rest stop here: As you turn right, you can stop at Murwin's General Store, and a block farther north on the river, you'll find Murwin County Park.

Now traveling east on County Road M to Indianford, the cruise take a sharp left on High Street just before the dam. Indianford was so-named because the shallow riverbed here was used by the Winnebago Indians to cross the Rock River. After merging onto County Road F, the route heads north up to Edgerton.

Originally, when the Milwaukee & Waukesha Railroad laid tracks northeast of Fulton, the station was called Fulton Station. As the town grew, the citizens wanted the settlement to have its own identity. Benjamin Edgerton, the chief surveyor, laid out the original line for the track, and when he returned to survey the settlement, he was asked if the town could use his name. He jokingly replied, "Better wait until I'm dead. I might do something in the meantime to discredit the name." The town prospered with the rail line, and today you can find several options if you need to stop for lunch.

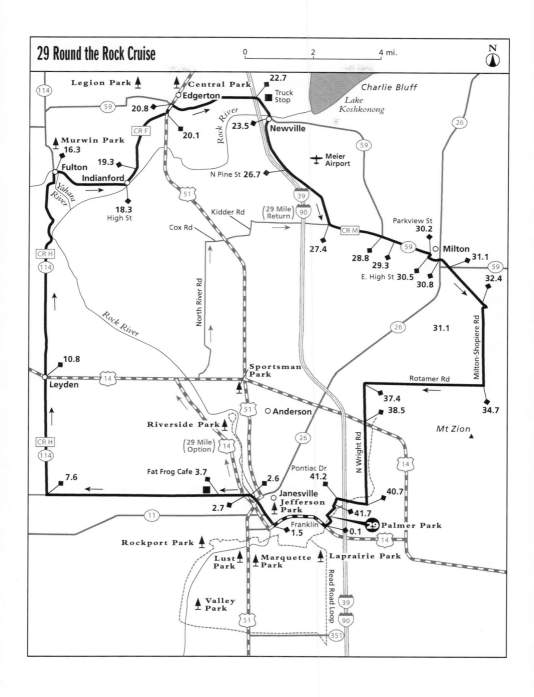

29 Round the Rock Cruise

0   2   4 mi.

N

Legion Park   Central Park   22.7

114

59

Edgerton   Truck Stop

20.8   Charlie Bluff

Lake Koshkonong

CR F   20.1   23.5   Newville

26

Rock River

Murwin Park   Meier Airport

16.3   19.3   59

Fulton   N Pine St 26.7

Indianford

Yahara River   51

18.3   Kidder Rd   39

High St   90

Cox Rd   (29 Mile Return)   Parkview St

CR H   CR M   30.2

114   27.4   59   Milton   31.1

28.8   29.3   59

E. High St 30.5   32.4

30.8

Rock River   26   31.1

North River Rd   Milton-Shopiere Rd

10.8   Rotamer Rd

14

Leyden   Sportsman Park   37.4   34.7

38.5

51   Anderson   Mt Zion

Riverside Park

CR H   (29 Mile Option)   26

114   14   N Wright Rd   14

7.6   Fat Frog Cafe 3.7   Pontiac Dr   40.7

2.6   41.2

Janesville   Jefferson Park   41.7

2.7   29 Palmer Park

11   Franklin   0.1

1.5   14

Rockport Park   Laprairie Park

Lust Park   Marquette Park

Read Road Loop

Valley Park   39

51   90

351

Continue east on the paved shoulder of Highway 59. After crossing I–39/90, the next village you visit is Newville. When Edgerton laid out the rail line, he named this station as well. Leaving Newville, travel south on North Pine Street down to County Road M, where the cruise heads east. Here the 29-mile option returns and the ride continues to Milton.

When settlers first came to this area, they found the intersection of two Indian trails. The land was covered in tall grass, so the settlers' first name for the village was Grainfield. But when a post office was applied for, Prairie du Lac was submitted because of the lakes in the area. Rejected due to the possible confusion with another town of the same name, Milton was selected in 1839. It is said that the name came from the author of the classic novels *Paradise Lost* and *Paradise Regained,* which were popular at the time. If you have the time and interest, stop at the Milton House. This National Historic Landmark, located at the junction of Highways 26 and 59, was constructed by the Underground Railroad conductor and Wisconsin pioneer Joseph Goodrich. Here you will also cross the Ice Age Trail.

After leaving town on County Road M, you soon veer south on Milton-Shopiere Road and then jog west on Rotamer Road before resuming the cruise to the south on North Wright Road. The road you ride back into town is one of Janesville's designated bike routes. After crossing Highway 14, the route offers a gentle descent over the next 3.5 miles back to the park.

Miles and Directions

0.0 Ride south on Mohawk Road from Palmer Park.

0.1 Take a right on the paved shoulder of Highway 14 through Janesville.

1.4 Cross the Rock River.

1.5 Take a right on Franklin Avenue.

2.6 Turn left on Mineral Point Road. **Option:** Continue north on Franklin Avenue for the 29-mile option. Go right on Washington Street, right on Highway 14, left on North River Road, right on Woodhue Drive, right on Juniper Drive, left on County Road F, right on Consolidated School Road, right on Cox Road, left on Kidder Road, right on County Road M, and take CR M to the main route.

2.7 Pass the Lincoln-Tallman House on your left.

3.7 Pass the Fat Frog Cafe.

7.6 Take a right on County Road H.

10.8 Cross Highway 14 at Leyden.

16.3 Take a right on County Road M at the Murwin Store in Fulton.

18.3 Turn left on High Street at the dam in Indianford.

19.3 Turn left (north) on County Road F.

20.1 Turn left on Highway 51 into Edgerton.

20.8 Take a right on Highway 59.

22.7 Cross I-39/90 into Newville.

23.5 Take a right on Newville Road after the bridge.

26.7 Turn left on North Pine Street.

27.4 Turn left on County Road M. (Note: The 29-mile option returns here.)

28.8 Merge onto Highway 59 into Milton.

30.2 Take a right on Parkview Street.

30.5 Turn left on East High Street.

30.8 Cross Highway 26.

31.1 Cross Highway 59 back onto County Road M.

32.4 Jog to the right on Milton-Shopiere Road then left on EMH Townline Road.

34.7 Take a right on Rotamer Road.

37.4 Turn left on North Wright Road.

38.5 Cross Highway 14 and continue down North Wright Road.

40.7 Take a right on Ruger Avenue.

41.2 Turn left on Pontiac Drive.

41.7 Turn left on Lexington Street.

41.8 Take a right on Mohawk Road.

42.0 Return to park.

Local Information

Janesville Area Convention & Visitors Bureau, 51 South Jackson Street, Janesville; (800) 487-2257; www.janesvillecvb.com.

Local Events/Attractions

Rotary International Botanical Gardens, 1455 Palmer Drive, Janesville; (608) 752-3885.

Rock 50/50 Bike Tour; fourth Sunday in May; (608) 756-7832; www.rockoutdoorevent.com.

Rotary Club Pie Ride; third Sunday in June; (608) 758-2988; www.janesvillemorning rotory.com.

Restaurants

Fat Frog Cafe, 15 North Arch Street, Janesville; (608) 752-9908.

Town Edge Restaurant, 1102 North Main Street, Edgerton; (608) 884-9866.

The Squeeze Inn, 105 Merchant Row, Milton; (608) 868-5966.

Accommodations

Microtel Inn, 3121 Wellington Place, Janesville; (608) 752-3121; www.microtelinn.com.

Turner Ernest Campgrounds, 208 Milton Avenue, Janesville; (608) 868-3985.

Bike Shops

Bike Works, 600 Center Avenue, Janesville; (608) 758-8158.

Cruz'n the Trail Inc., 932 Glen Street, Janesville; (608) 741-0390.

Michael's Cycles, 2716 North Pontiac Drive, Janesville; (608) 752-7676.

Restrooms

Start/finish: Palmer Park.

16.4: Murwin County Park.

22.9: I-39/90 truck stop.

29.3: Railroad Park in Milton.

Maps

DeLorme: Wisconsin Atlas and Gazetteer: Page 29 C5.

Wisconsin State Bicycle Map (Southeast Section).

30 Lance's Wisconsin Challenge

On this route you will explore some of the same Jefferson County roads that Lance Armstrong used to test his equipment before the Tour de France. The challenge departs from a town named after a general who put down the Black Hawk uprising, then travels northeast through the rolling countryside. Soon you will visit a town on the shores of Rock Lake, which is said to have sacrificial pyramids at its bottom. Farther north visit the town where TREK bikes are made. Now rolling east, the route crosses the Crawfish River at Old Plank Road. You then arrive in a community on the Rock River, where you should visit the fifty-seven-room Historic Octagon House. Now circling to the south, ride through the river-bottom flats and pass through a town that, at the turn of the twentieth century, became the dairy center of the state. Riding the final stage of the challenge, pass through the county seat with its Civil War era architecture. Now it's just a short jaunt back to Fort Atkinson.

Start: Jones Park in Fort Atkinson.
Length: 67 miles with a 37-mile option.
Terrain: Flat to semi-rolling.

Traffic and hazards: Use caution riding on Highways 18 and 19 and when crossing Highway 26, as traffic can move fast.

Getting there: From the junction of Highways 12 and 89 in Fort Atkinson, turn west on Third Street/Highway 12 and go to Janesville Park. Turn left here and head south; Jones Park is on the left, with plentiful free parking.

This challenge starts in Fort Atkinson in southeastern Wisconsin, on the Rock River. In 1832 the government sent troops under the command of Brigadier General Henry Atkinson to build a stockade here, Fort Coskong. With the help of future presidents Zachary Taylor, Abraham Lincoln, and Jefferson Davis, the uprising led by Chief Black Hawk was put down. When settlers moved into the area in 1836, the name was changed to honor General Atkinson, and five years later Congress approved the town's charter. Today, with its feet firmly rooted in America's early pioneer history, this community is a great place to establish headquarters while touring Jefferson County.

The ride begins in Jones Park, across from the city's paved bike trail, then crosses the Rock River and travels northwest on city streets. After leaving town on Bankers Road, you'll roll through the countryside, passing horse farms and apple orchards as you make your way north. Crossing the Glacial Drumlin Trail, you soon ride along the eastern shore of Rock Lake, through Lake Mills.

Legend has it that Rock Lake was originally named Lake Tyranena, meaning "sparkling waters," by Native Americans who lived here in 1066. Appealing to their gods for relief from a long drought, they built sacrificial pyramids, which are now at the bottom of the lake. Captain Joseph Keys settled here in 1837 and constructed a

The Historic Octagon House in Watertown has fifty-seven rooms.

sawmill by the stream next to the lake. A couple years later he built a gristmill using the same waterpower source. Becoming a true "mill town," when platted it took that name. A few years later the Winnebago Indians shared their knowledge of the "stone teepees" at the bottom of the lake.

You can learn more about the mounds at Aztalan State Park, indulge at one of the downtown eating establishment, or visit the lakeside park when passing through town on Ferry Drive. At Lake Street those who prefer the 37-mile option should turn right here. The challenge continues northwest past Interstate 94. At County Road O turn north and ride single-file if in a group, as traffic is heavier here. After passing Dr. J. S. Garmans Nature Preserve, you soon approach Waterloo.

When settler Bradford Hill arrived, the Indian name for this village was Maunesha. Finding the area picturesque, with the river running in a half-circle, Bradford platted a town here. A few years later, in 1859, the village took its name from the 1815 Battle of Waterloo. At the 24-mile mark, take a tour of the TREK plant and museum, which has some of Greg Lemond's and Lance Armstrong's road bikes from the Tour de France. Another option is Firemen Park, where the 1911 C. W. Parker Carousel still operates. Follow County Road G out of town and head east. As the road swings to the north, you will be riding along the Crawfish River to Hubbletown.

Originally known as Hubbleville, Hubbleton is on Old Plank Road/Highway 19. The town was established in 1852 by Levi Hubbell, who owned a plot here.

Centered between Waterloo and Watertown, it was a shipping center first on the plank road and then from the station for the Chicago, Milwaukee & St. Paul Railroad. Today there are only a few residences here and a tavern if you need to stop. Now crossing the river, take a right on Hubbleton Road and travel east to Watertown.

This was originally another Indian village called *Ka-Ka-ree,* which means "ox bow" and describes the double bend in the Rock River here. The first white settler was Timothy Johnson, who camped next to the river and in 1836 laid claim to a settlement he called Johnson Rapid. When the village was platted, it was renamed Watertown for a city in New York. With the completion of Plank Road, in addition to the two railroads that passed through, the town became a busy thoroughfare in southern Wisconsin.

With the north half of the town straddling Dodge County, you will find several options for lunch and many local attractions that are worth taking in. If you have the time, something worth doing is the Historic Walking Tour on Main Street and the Historic Breweries Tour. As you following the route through town, you will pass by the Historic Octagon House, built in 1854, on Sunset Avenue. Now traveling south on River Drive, you follow the Rock River. After crossing under I–94, you will pass a park on the way into Johnson Creek. At Milwaukee Street take a left into the village, where the 37-mile option returns from County Road B.

Originally established as a mill site in 1838 by Timothy Johnson, by the turn of the twentieth century Johnson Creek had become the butter, egg, cheese, and milk center of the state. You will find a few options here if you need to take a break. The route crosses Highway 26 as you leave town and continues south on County Road Y. At Jefferson Junction you will cross the Glacial Drumlin Trail before reaching the town of Jefferson.

Here at the fork of the Crawfish and Rock Rivers, the village was organized by the Territorial Legislature in 1839 and became the county seat. Both the village and the county took its name from early settlers who were from Jefferson County, New York. As you pass through the downtown area, you will find that many of the original buildings are still being used, giving the business district a unique appearance. As the route travels through the southeast corner, you will pass St. Coletta. Built in 1904, this beautiful campus is the oldest and largest Roman Catholic residential school for the mentally challenged in the United States.

Following County Road K south, you are soon back in Fort Atkinson to explore the city and enjoy dinner at Cafe Carp, in the downtown area along the river.

Miles and Directions

0.0   Take a right on Janesville Avenue from Jones Park.

0.5   Turn left on Roberts Street.

0.7   Cross the Rock River.

1.0   Cross Highway 12.

1.5   Turn left on Cramer Street.

30 Lance's Wisconsin Challenge

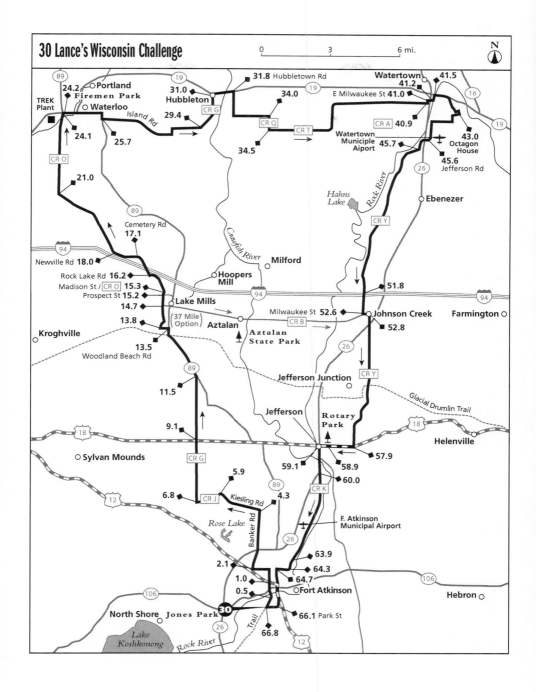

0   3   6 mi.

N

TREK Plant

89 — Portland
24.2 Firemen Park
31.0 Hubbleton
19
31.8 Hubbletown Rd

Watertown
41.5
41.2
E Milwaukee St **41.0**
16
19

Waterloo
Island Rd
29.4
CR G
34.0
CR Q
CR T
CR A **40.9**
Watertown Municiple Aiport **45.7**
43.0 Octagon House
45.6 Jefferson Rd

24.1
25.7
34.5
26

CR O
21.0
Hahns Lake
Rock River
CR Y
Ebenezer

89
Cemetery Rd
17.1
Crawfish River
Milford

94
Newville Rd **18.0**
Rock Lake Rd **16.2**
Madison St / CR O **15.3**
Prospect St **15.2**
14.7
Hoopers Mill
Lake Mills
94
51.8
94
Farmington

Kroghville
13.8
(37 Mile Option)
Aztalan
Milwaukee St **52.6**
CR B
Johnson Creek
52.8

13.5
Woodland Beach Rd
Aztalan State Park
26

89
11.5
Jefferson Junction
Glacial Drumlin Trail
CR Y

9.1
18
Jefferson
Rotary Park
18
Helenville

Sylvan Mounds
CR G
57.9

5.9
59.1
58.9
60.0

6.8
CR J
Kiesling Rd
4.3
CR K

12
Rose Lake
Banker Rd
89
26
F. Atkinson Municipal Airport

2.1
63.9
64.3
64.7
106

1.0
0.5
Fort Atkinson
Hebron

106
30
North Shore Jones Park
26
Trail
66.1 Park St

Lake Koshkonong
Rock River
66.8
12

2.1 Take a right on Banker Road.

4.3 Turn left on Kiesling Road.

5.9 Turn left on County Road J.

6.8 Take a right on County Road G.

9.1 Cross Highway 18.

11.5 Turn left on Highway 89.

13.5 Turn left on Woodland Beach Road in Lake Mills.

13.8 Take a right on Ferry Drive.

14.6 Pass Lakeside Park.

14.7 Pass Lake Street/County Road B. **Option:** Turn right on County Road B for the 37-mile option.

15.2 Turn right on Prospect Street.

15.3 Turn left on County Road B/Madison Street.

16.0 Pass under Interstate 94.

16.2 Take a right on Rock Lake Road.

17.1 Turn left on Cemetery Road.

18.0 Take a right on Newville Road.

21.0 Turn right on County Road O.

24.1 Take a right on Highway 19 into Waterloo.

24.2 Pass Firemen Park.

24.4 Take a right on Highway 89.

25.7 Turn left on Island Road.

29.4 Take a right on County Road G.

31.0 Take a right on Highway 19 at Hubbletown.

31.3 Cross the Crawfish River, along Old Plank Road.

31.8 Take a right on Hubbletown Road.

34.0 Take a right on County Road Q.

34.5 Turn left on County Road T.

40.9 Turn left on County Road A in Watertown.

41.0 Take a right on East Milwaukee Street.

41.2 Turn left on Water Street at the Riverside Market Center.

41.5 Take a right on Highway 19/Main Street.

42.1 Take a right on College Avenue.

42.5 Turn left on Western Avenue.

42.6 Take a right on Richards Avenue.

42.7 Turn left on Thomas Avenue.

42.9 Take a right on Charles Street.

43.0 Take a right on Sunset Avenue at the Octagon House.

43.3 Turn left on County Road X/12th Street.

43.5 Take a right on Mary Street.

45.2 Turn left on River Drive.

45.6 Take a right on Jefferson Road.

45.7 Cross Highway 26 onto County Road Y.

51.8 Pass under I–94 into Johnson Creek.

52.6 Turn left on Milwaukee Street/County Road B. (Note: The 37-mile option returns here.)

52.8 Take a right on Sunset Avenue/County Road Y.

53.1 Cross Highway 26 on County Road Y.

57.9 Take a right on Highway 18 into Jefferson.

59.1 Turn left on Main Street/Highway 26.

60.0 Turn left on County Road K.

63.9 Turn left on High Street in Fort Atkinson.

64.3 Take a right on Cramer Street.

64.7 Turn left on Main Street.

65.6 Cross the Rock River.

66.1 Take a right on Park Street.

66.8 Take a right on Janesville Avenue.

67.0 Return to park.

Local Information

Fort Atkinson Area Chamber of Commerce, 224 North Main Street, Fort Atkinson; (888) 733-3678; www.fortchamber.com.

Jefferson County Tourism Council, County Courthouse, Jefferson; www.jctourism.com.

Watertown Area Chamber of Commerce, 519 East Main Street, Watertown; (877) 733-9886; www.watertowntourism.com.

Local Events/Attractions

Hoard Historical Museum, Fort Atkinson Historical Society, 407 Merchants Avenue, Fort Atkinson; (920) 563-7769; www.hoard museum.org.

TREK Factory Bicycle Tours, 801 West Madison Street, Waterloo; Wednesdays and Fridays at 10:00 a.m.; (920) 476-2191; www.trek bikes.com.

Lake Tour Bike Trek; first week in June; American Lung Association; (800) 586-4872; www.lungwisconsin.org.

Tour de Fort Metric Century; third Sunday in August; (920) 563-5279; www.jcbc.info.

Tyranena Oktoberfest Ride; first Saturday in October; (920) 648-8699; www.tyranena.com.

Restaurants

Cafe Carp, 18 South Water Street, Fort Atkinson; (920) 563-9391; www.cafecarpe.com.

Upper Krust, 210 South Water Street, Watertown; (920) 206-9202.

Accommodations

La Grange B & B, 1050 East Street, Fort Aitkinson; (920) 563-1421.

The Lamp Post Inn, 408 South Main Street, Fort Atkinson; (920) 563-6561.

Aztalan State Park, 11235 Highway Q, Lake Mills; (920) 648-8774; www.wiparks.net.

Bike Shops

Cool Bikes, W3360 Beryl Drive, Watertown; (920) 885-9516.

Restrooms

Start/finish: Jones Park.

14.6: Lakeside Park in Lake Mills.

24.2: Firemen Park.

41.2: Riverside Market Center in Watertown.

52.4: Veterans Park in Johnson Creek.

58.9: Rotary Park.

Maps

DeLorme: Wisconsin Atlas and Gazetteer: Page 29 A5.

Wisconsin State Bicycle Map (Southeast Section).

Jefferson County Bicycle Map.

31 Southern Kettle Challenge

At the gateway to the beautiful Kettle Moraine State Forest, biking here is renowned. You leave from a town named for the silt at the river's bottom and ride east. Along the route experience the peacefulness of rolling hills as the challenge approaches a village named after an oasis city in the Syrian Desert. Riding the rolling ridge, you pass Ottawa Trail Park as the route turns southward. You then cruise down to a town named by a couple of surveyors who saw a large bald eagle rise up. Farther south you pass an open-air museum that showcases early pioneer living in Wisconsin. Rolling in and out of the kettled forest, you soon pass through another village that was once used as a stagecoach stop. Next you sidestep southwest and stop in a village named after a French general. Now circling to the west on Kettle Moraine Road, stop at a well dug in 1895 and fill your water bottles. You then come full circle back to the north and soon return to the lakefront park in Whitewater.

Start: Cravath Lakefront Park in Whitewater.
Length: 45 miles with a 29-mile option.
Terrain: Hilly with several climbs.
Traffic and hazards: Use caution merging onto Business Highway 12 and crossing onto East Main Street. Also be careful riding on the paved shoulder of Highway 67, as traffic can be fast.

Getting there: From downtown Whitewater, on Business Highway 12, go west on Whitewater Street for 1 block. The park is on the left and offers plenty of free parking.

This challenge departs from Cravath Lakefront Park in Whitewater, a community steeped in history and with an eye to the future regarding education. Before the first settlers arrived in 1836, the Potawatomi tribe lived here and named the river *Wau-be-gan-naw-pocat,* or "white water," which referred to the white clay and sand at the stream's bottom. Three years after a stone mill was built, the village started to grow. Then in 1852 the first rail line was laid across Wisconsin and came through here, spurring industrial growth. Looking to its future, the Whitewater Normal School was founded in 1868. This institution of higher education was the first in the state to grant four-year degrees and is now the University of Wisconsin, Whitewater.

The ride leaves from the park on the south side of the downtown district and follows Main Street east across the river. In a few blocks you pass the Historic Carlsen House, at 840 East Main Street. This home was built in the 1850s and is one of more than seventy historic sites you can see here if you are interested in early American architecture. Request a free copy of the Whitewater historical brochure at the chamber office.

Now crossing the railroad tracks, merge onto Bluff Road. For the next 4 miles the road is fairly flat as you ride east. After passing an irrigated sod farm, turn north on Big Spring Road. The route then crosses the railroad tracks, turns to the

31 Southern Kettle Challenge

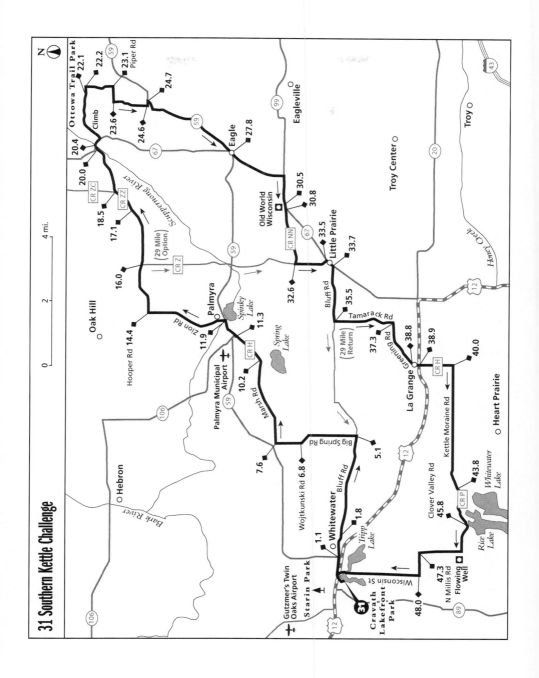

northeast into Jefferson County, and heads through the prairie grassland to the town of Palmyra.

This village was settled in 1842 by two brothers who were students of the Bible. They liked the looks of the area so much that they named the settlement after an oasis city in the Syrian Desert. There are a couple options here if you need to stop. Now riding out of town on the narrow paved shoulder of Highway 59, as you pass Spinky Lake, turn left on Zion Road.

The terrain offers a number of moderated rollers as you ride the ridge and follow the western side of the Southern Kettle Moraine. At County Road Z, those who prefer the 29-mile option should take a right. Otherwise, cross into Waukesha County, where many stretches of the lane are covered by canopies of trees that provide shade as you ride along County Road ZZ.

The challenge continues east, crossing the Scuppernong River. After a short jog south on Highway 67, you will be summoned to your first major climb. Now you are riding the rolling ridges to Ottawa Trail Park, a nature and historic park that makes a good rest stop. At the corner the route turns south on Waterville Road and follows the eastern side of the forest. Jogging to the west, the road rolls down Ulrickson Road and into the town of Eagle.

The village was originally named Eagle Prairie by a couple of surveyors who saw a large bald eagle rise up when they were platting this section of the county. In 1836, when a settlement was started here, it was called Eagleville. Later it was renamed Pittman for the man who recorded the plat, but then the railroad came through in 1850 and renamed the village Eagle Center. Lunch options here include the Coyote Canyon Saloon & Grill. After leaving on the paved shoulder of Highway 67 south, in a couple miles you pass Old World Wisconsin.

If you have explored the state and wondered how its early pioneers lived, stop at this historic site devoted to nineteenth-century immigrant life. Many buildings have been moved and restored here depicting the heritage and lifestyles of Wisconsin pioneers. Six different settlements have been created depicting the lives of African-American, Finnish, Danish, German, Norwegian, and Polish immigrants, all in an open-air setting. Now riding back into the rolling Kettle Moraine State Forest, you soon turn south on County Road Z. Here, those who selected the 29-mile option briefly return to the main route as it approaches Little Prairie.

Established in the 1860s as a stagecoach stop, the village was named for the small prairie that stretched through the forest here. Today there are a few homes but no rest stop options. Ride Highway 67's paved shoulder for a short distance, then veer off to the right on Bluff Road and head west. At Tamarack Road the challenge turns south, and those who have selected the 29-mile option continue riding west back to Whitewater. The challenge cruises along on the twisting, forested County Road H and soon arrives in the village of La Grange.

This small community is said to be named after General Lafayette's native town in France. You will find a rest stop option here, the La Grange General Store & Backyard Bike Shop. Along with retail and full-service bike repair, the store offers a top selection of deli sandwiches and beverages. After crossing Highway 12, a mile farther, turn right on Kettle Moraine Road and head west.

For the next 5 miles the route is scenic as it wraps around the fingers of Rice Lake through Kettle Moraine State Forest's Hickory Woods Group Campground. After turning north on Clover Valley Road, you soon pass Clover Creek. Here, at the edge of the stream, at the 45.8-mile mark, is a flowing artesian well dug by hand to a depth of 55 feet in 1895, where you can replenish your water supply.

In less than 4 miles, the challenge jogs to the west a couple times as it continues north, returning to the park in Whitewater.

Miles and Directions

0.0   From Cravath Lakefront Park, take a right on Whitewater Street.

0.3   Take a right on Main Street/Highway 12.

0.6   Turn left back on Main Street.

1.1   Head straight ahead on Main Street, at the Highway 59 junction.

1.8   Cross tracks onto Bluff Road.

5.1   Turn left on Big Spring Road. (Note: The 29-mile option returns here.)

6.8   Cross tracks onto Wojtkunski Road.

7.6   Take a right on Marsh Road.

10.2   Turn left on County Road H into Palmyra.

11.3   Head straight ahead on Highway 59.

11.9   Turn left on Zion Road.

14.4   Take a right on Hooper Road.

16.0   Cross County Road Z. **Option:** Turn right on County Road Z for the 29-mile option.

17.1   Turn left on County Road ZZ.

18.5   Pass County Road ZC.

20.0   Take a right on Highway 67.

20.4   Turn left on County Road ZZ.

22.1   Pass Ottowa Trail Park.

22.2   Take a right on Waterville Road.

23.1   Take a right on Piper Road.

23.6   Turn left Ulrickson Road.

24.6   Turn left on County Road X.

24.7   Take a right on Highway 59.

27.8   Turn left on Highway 67 in Eagle.

30.5   Pass Old World Wisconsin.

30.8   Take a right on County Road NN.

32.6   Turn left on County Road Z. (Note: The 29-mile option briefly returns here.)

33.5   Take a right on Highway 67 at Little Prairie.

33.7 Take a right on Bluff Road.

35.5 Turn left on Tamarack Road. **Option:** The 29-mile option continues west on Bluff Road.

37.3 Take a right on Greening Road.

38.8 Turn left on County Road H.

38.9 Cross Highway 12 at La Grange.

40.0 Take a right on Kettle Moraine Road.

43.8 Cross County Road P.

45.8 Take a right onto Clover Valley Road.

45.8 Turn right and pass Clover Creek. (Note: Well water is available here.)

47.3 Turn left on North Millis Road.

48.0 Take a right on South Wisconsin Street.

49.6 Take a right on Colburn Lane.

50.0 Return to park.

Local Information

Whitewater Chamber of Commerce, 171 West Main Street, Whitewater; (262) 473-4005; www.whitewaterchamber.com.

Walworth County Visitors Bureau, 9 West Walworth Street, Elkhorn; (800) 395-8687.

Local Events/Attractions

Whitewater Historical Society Museum, 1435 Whitewater Street, Whitewater; (262) 473-2966.

Whitewater Weekend; second weekend in June; (847) 707-6888; www.pedalacross wisconsin.com.

Best Dam Bike Tour; first weekend in August; (800) 242-3358; www.wisms.org.

Kettle Moraine Optimist Ride; second Saturday in October; www.edu/uwwoptimist/kmor.

Restaurants

Jessica's Family Restaurant, 140 West Main Street, Whitewater; (262) 473-9890.

Squidy's Bar and Grill, 102 South Second Street, Palmyra; (262) 495-2588.

Coyote Canyon Saloon & Grill, 100 South Road, Eagle; (262) 594-3220.

Accommodations

Amerihost Inn & Suites, 1355 West Main Street, Whitewater; (262) 472-9400.

Kettle Moraine State Forest, Whitewater Lake Campground, S91W39091 Highway 59, Eagle; (262) 594-6200; www.wiparks.net.

Bike Shops

BicycleWise, 1130 West Main Street, Whitewater; (262) 473-4730; www.bicyclewise.com.

La Grange General Store & Backyard Bike Shop, County Road H and Highway 12, La Grange; (262) 495-8600; www.backyard bikes.com.

Restrooms

Start/finish: Cravath Lakefront Park.

22.1: Ottowa Trail Park.

45.0: Hickory Woods Group Campground.

Maps

DeLorme: Wisconsin Atlas and Gazetteer: Page 29 B7.

Wisconsin State Bicycle Map (Southeast Section).

32 Chocolate Lovers Ramble

After the glacial period, the southern half of Walworth County was left with moraines of rolling hills, and several picturesque lake settings. The tour starts in a village known for its chocolate shops, next to the shore of Wisconsin's second-deepest lake, then heads north to a lake community developed to sell newspapers. You then cut west across an old moonshine-runners' route and pass through a village that the circus once used as its winter pasture grounds. Now circling to the northeast, visit a city that was named for a set of elk horns found in a tree. You then travel along a road where werewolves have been sighted. Soon the ramble crosses into Racine County and visits a city dubbed "Chocolate City U.S.A." With an essence of chocolate still on your breath, pivot southwest on Spring Valley Road, back to Lake Geneva.

Start: Corner of Ann and Broad Streets in Lake Geneva.
Length: 42 miles with a 30-mile option.
Terrain: Rolling with only a couple small hills.

Traffic and hazards: Use caution on County Road F as it feeds into Interstate 43 and on the paved shoulders of Highways 50, 11, and 36, as traffic can be fast.

Getting there: From Highway 12 in Lake Geneva, follow Highway 120 southwest into town and take a left on Ann Street. Street parking around RRB Trek Cycles is free and plentiful.

Spend some time in southeastern Wisconsin's most extraordinary lake resort community, Lake Geneva. The Potawatomi Indians first inhabited the area and named the lake after their chief, Muck-Suck, which means "big foot." The French who passed through called it Gros Pied. John Brink surveyed the area in 1835 and felt that the lake was too beautiful for such uncouth names. Reminded of Geneva on the shore of Seneca Lake in New York, he select the name for both the lake and village.

The ride leaves from the streets just north of the medley of interesting shops in the lakeside downtown. About a mile out of town, those who prefer the 30-mile option will take a right on County Road NN, then another right on Bowers Road, and head north. The ramble veers to the northwest and makes a left on Palmer Road in the town of Como. Located on the lake's north shore, this community was developed by the *Chicago Tribune* in the 1920s. To encourage subscriptions, the paper would give a platted lot to each new customer. The only problem with this premium offer was that it took fifteen lots to build a house.

The stretch of road you ride west from Como was a favorite route for moonshine runners back in the Prohibition era. Soon you turn onto the paved shoulder of Highway 50, which crosses Delavan Lake into the city of Lake Lawn. The village received its name because the circus used this area to winter their animals. In an area once heavily forested with oak stands, they found lush green meadows for grazing around the lake.

Now turning north on County Road F, ride single-file with caution for the next mile, as this stretch of road is a feeder route to I-43. After crossing under the freeway, the route turns right and meanders northeast into Elkhorn. As he traveled along an army trail, Colonel Samuel F. Phoenix came across an open stretch of prairie here. Resting under a burr oak, he noticed an elk's horn hanging in the tree and christened the prairie Elkhorn, which the village took for its name. Here, at about the 14-mile mark, you are in the downtown area of the Walworth County seat, and you will find several options for a rest stop.

Depart town riding east, and after crossing the freeway, turn onto Bray Road. After passing Hospital Road, watch for the Bray Road Beast. It is said that several people have witnessed this monster. Although it seems impossible that a mythical creature like a werewolf could stalk this resort area, a number of bizarre encounters in the late 1980s have many pondering this very idea. Don't fret: The sightings have been at night, and in less than 3 miles you will be taking a right on Highway 11 through the village of Bowers, founded by a family of that name.

Now riding east on the highway's paved shoulder, you soon pass through Spring Prairie. Originally called Franklin, in 1837, a Dr. Hemminway built a log tavern here that served as a church, town hall, and post office. His wife, Abigail, suggested the current name for the prairie and the springs that discharged into Spring Brook. Leave the village heading northeast on Spring Prairie Road. In the next 5 miles the terrain becomes more rolling, and as you veer back to the east, prepare for your first climb. After crossing into Racine County, take a right on Honey Creek Road and cruise into Burlington.

This settlement on the Fox and White Rivers was originally called Foxville. In 1844, E. D. Putman, who had settled here, recommended naming it after his boyhood home of Burlington, Vermont. Today, with Nestle Chocolate and Confection, the town has been dubbed "Chocolate City, U.S.A." You will find plenty of options for lunch when visiting here.

You finally come full circle traveling back to the southwest on a series of roads that wind over the rolling terrain into Lake Geneva.

Miles and Directions

0.0 From Ann Street, turn right on Broad Street.

0.1 Turn left on Marshall Street/County Road H.

2.1 Pass County Road NN. **Option:** Turn right on County Road NN for the 30-mile option, then turn right in another mile on Bowers Road.

3.2 Turn left on Palmer Road at Como.

8.0 Take a right on the paved shoulder of Highway 50.

8.9 Take a right on County Road F.

9.9 Cross under I-43.

10.1 Take a right on Marsh Road.

12.8 Cross tracks onto Devendorf Street in Elkhorn.

13.1 Take a right on Centalia Street.

13.5 Turn left on Church Street.

32 Chocolate Lovers Ramble

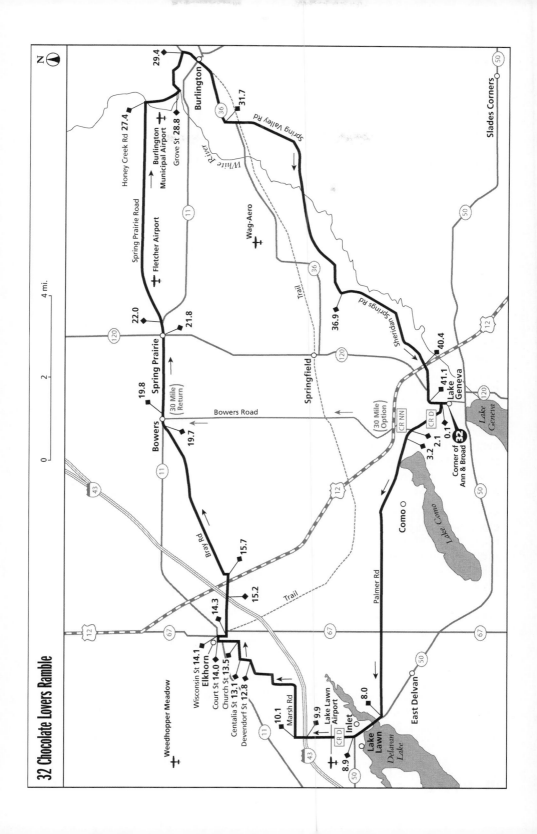

14.0 Take a right on Court Street.

14.1 Take a right on Wisconsin Street in downtown Elkhorn.

14.3 Turn left on Geneva Street/County Road H.

15.2 Cross I–43.

15.6 Cross Highway 12.

15.7 Turn left on Bray Road.

19.7 Take a right on Highway 11 in Bowers.

19.8 Pass Bowers Road. (Note: The 30-mile option returns here.)

21.8 Pass Highway 120 at Spring Prairie.

22.0 Turn left on Spring Prairie Road.

27.4 Take a right on Honey Creek Road into Burlington.

28.8 As the road curves left the name changes to Grove Street as it runs along Echo Lake.

29.4 Take a right on Highway 36/Milwaukee Avenue.

31.7 Turn left on Spring Valley Road.

36.9 Turn left on Sheridan Springs Road.

40.4 Cross Highway 12.

41.1 Turn left on Highway 120/Broad Street.

42.0 Return to Ann Street.

Local Information

Lake Geneva Convention & Visitors Bureau, 201 Wrigley Drive, Lake Geneva; (800) 345-1020; www.lakegenevawi.com.

Burlington Area Chamber of Commerce, 113 Chestnut Street, Burlington; (262) 763-6044.

Walworth County Visitors Bureau, 9 West Walworth Street, Elkhorn; (800) 395-8687.

Local Events/Attractions

Chocolate Festival; last weekend in May, Burlington; (262) 763-7794; www.chocolatefest.com.

Festival of Summer Bike Ride; first Saturday in August, Elkhorn; (262) 248-7741; www.whiterivercycleclub.com.

Flat Tire Memorial Tour; second Saturday in October; (262) 248-6646; www.fattirememorialtour.com.

Restaurants

Kilwin's Ice Cream & Chocolate Shoppe, 772 Main Street, Lake Geneva; (262) 248-4400.

Scuttlebutts Restaurant & Coffee Cafe, 831 Wrigley Drive, Lake Geneva; (414) 248-1111.

Vasili's Corner Cafe, 26 East Walsworth Street, Elkhorn; (262) 723-7100.

Charcoal Grill & Rotisserie, 580 Milwaukee Avenue, Burlington; (262) 432-3004.

Accommodations

The Cove of Lake Geneva, 111 Center Street, Lake Geneva; (800) 770-7107; www.cove-lake-geneva.com.

Big Foot Beach State Park, 17156 Highway 120, Lake Geneva; (262) 248-2528; www.wiparks.net.

Bike Shops

RRB Trek Cycles & Fitness, 629 Williams Street, Lake Geneva; (262) 248-2588.

Bob's Pedal Pusher, 466 South Pine Street, Burlington; (262) 763-7794.

Restrooms

Start/finish: RRB Trek Cycles.

14.2: Sunset Park in Elkhorn.

28.8: Echo Park in Burlington.

Maps

DeLorme: Wisconsin Atlas and Gazetteer: Page 29 D4.

Wisconsin State Bicycle Map (Southeast Section).

Bikes to Burlington (tri-county bike loops and trails).

Eastern
Wisconsin

33 Pickerel Cruise

A place of beauty, excitement, and fun, it's easy to lose yourself in the euphoria of riding options here. You leave from a community that means "pickerel," or "pike," in the Potawatomi language and ride along a scenic stretch of Lake Michigan. At Carol Beach, jet out to the west past Chwaukee Prairie Nature Preserve, then pass through a forgotten village named for three brothers surnamed Pike. After a brief dip past the Illinois state line, you'll enjoy more rollers once back in Wisconsin as the route meanders up around a set of beautiful lakes before passing the Dutch Gap Canal. You then cross the Des Plaines River and roll through an old village that started as a railroad station and was named for a family who owned and farmed the land there. Circling back to the east and riding along the flat grain fields, you will soon pass Dairyland Greyhound Park. After circling up along the airport, the route crosses Pike Creek a couple times and makes its way back into Kenosha passing the Washington Park Velodrome.

Start: Lake Front Park in Kenosha.
Length: 46 miles with a 21-mile option.
Terrain: Flat to rolling, with a few small hills.
Traffic and hazards: Use caution when riding on the paved shoulders of Highways 45 and 50. On County Road K and near the airport on County Road H, please ride single file as the paved shoulders are narrow.

Getting there: From Interstate 94 take exit 344 and turn east on Highway 50/Roosevelt Road into Kenosha. At Highway 32/Sheridan Road turn left, then at 57th Street take a right. You will find the park 3 blocks ahead on the left side.

Ideally located midway between Chicago and Milwaukee on the shore of Lake Michigan, the Kenosha area is a great place for a bicycle tour. Early explorers who reached the mouth of Pike Creek in 1835 found a Potawatomi Indian village here named *Kinoje,* or *Kenosha,* meaning "pickerel." The following year a village was established with a post office called Pike. A year later the name was changed to Southport because it was the southernmost part of the lake in Wisconsin. Then in 1850, when the village was finally incorporated, it took the original Indian name, Kenosha.

Today a place of beauty and fun, you will discover several additional bike-touring options after enjoying the Pickerel Cruise. Ride around town following the same routes the authentic Kenosha Transit Electric Streetcar uses to see the sights along Lake Michigan, or jump on the Pike Bike Trail and explore the shoreline. This section of trail, which you will cross on the cruise, connects Chicago to Milwaukee.

The cruise leaves from Lake Front Park at the corner of 57th Street and Third Avenue and travels south. As you ride along Eichelman Park and enter the historic district of Kenosha, you will pass the Kemper Center, which some say is haunted. Continuing along, look to your left at the sandy beaches along Lake Michigan, then

The beautiful town of Kenosha is located on Lake Michigan.

turn left on Second Avenue and ride past Southport Park. Veer to the west and ride around the marsh area before turning south again and continuing down Lake Shore Drive (First Avenue). As you cruise along this peaceful lane, amid the many beautiful landscaped homes, you will soon be at Carol Beach.

Here at the 6.1-mile mark the cruise turns away from the lake and heads west past the Chwaukee Prairie Nature Preserve. Now riding on 116th Street, you soon cross Highway 32 and in about another mile approach the old town of Tobin. This community was named for an early settler and had a station for the Chicago North Shore & Milwaukee Railroad. In another 0.2 mile you cross the interstate bike trail that starts in the north end of Chicago and stretches up to the south side of Milwaukee.

Upon reaching County Road ML, the route dips southwest down to Green Bay Road (Highway 31). Cross Highway 31 and travel northwest on Springbook Road up to County Road H. Those who prefer the 21-mile option should turn right here. The cruise turns left and heads west along the tree-lined country lane with picturesque hobby farms along the way. After crossing over I–94, turn left on West Service Road down to the state line. If you need a restroom stop, there is a gas station here. As you ride along the service road, if you look to your right you'll see the large tents that house elephants and other animals at the Renaissance Festival grounds.

Now riding west on County Road WG, follow the state line over slightly rolling terrain to Pikeville. Originally named Pikeville Corners, it was named for the three Pike brothers who settled around the one-room Pikeville School in the nineteenth century. The village is an unincorporated residential and agricultural community on the eastern shore of Mud Lake, with a tavern at the intersection, if you need to stop.

You'll ride along the state border for about a mile before the route dips down into Illinois and loops back up into Wisconsin on Deep Lake Road. As the ride meanders around Benet Lake, the terrain offers more rollers. Now circling back to the northeast, you pass several more hobby farms before reaching Highway 45. After a short stint south on the highway's paved shoulder, turn east on the wobbling County Road Q. You then pass Dutch Gap Canal, turn north, and cross the Des Plaines River. Now with a few small rollers, the route passes through Woodworth.

In the 1850s a station was built here for the railroad and a settlement was platted. The village was named for the Woodworth family, who owned and farmed the area surrounding it. Today the Woodworth Store is closed and there are only a few residences left. In another half mile the route jogs to the east on Highway 50's paved shoulder and then turns north again on County Road MB. After another mile turn east on County Road K, where you can enjoy another tree-lined corridor until crossing the interstate. On the east side of the freeway, you pass by the Dairyland Greyhound Park and then up through the new industrial park on County Road H. Here the 21-mile option returns.

As your cadence levels out along Kenosha Regional Airport, use caution, as the paved shoulder for the next mile is narrow. Turning east on County Road S, the road-

33 Pickerel Cruise

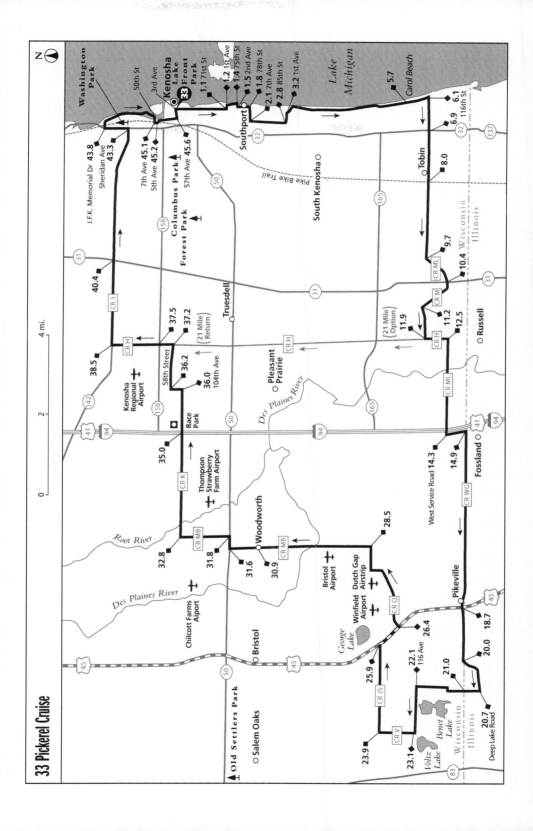

N

4 mi.

Washington Park

Lake Michigan

Kenosha

50th St
3rd Ave

71st St
1st Ave
1.1 75th St
1.2
1.4
1.5 2nd Ave
1.8 78th St
7th Ave
2.1
2.8 85th St
3.2 1st Ave

J.F.K. Memorial Dr 43.8
Sheridan Ave 43.3

7th Ave 45.1
5th Ave 45.2

57th Ave 45.6

Southport

5.7
Carol Beach

6.1
6.9 116th St

Columbus Park

Forest Park

Pike Bike Trail

South Kenosha

Tobin
8.0

40.4

Truesdell

9.7

10.4
CR ML

CR S

38.5

CR H

37.5
37.2

(21 Mile Return)

Pleasant Prairie

Des Plaines River

11.2
CR M

11.9

(21 Mile Option)

12.5
CR H

Russell

Wisconsin
Illinois

Kenosha Regional Airport

58th Street

36.2

36.0
104th Ave

Race Park

35.0

CR K

Thompson Strawberry Farm Airport

Root River

Des Plaines River

Des Plaines River

Woodworth

CR ML

West Service Road 14.3

14.9

Fossland

32.8

CR MB

31.8

31.6
30.9

CR MB

Bristol Airport

Dutch Gap Airstrip

28.5

CR WG

Pikeville

Chilcott Farms Airport

Bristol

Winfield Airport

George Lake

CR Q

26.4

18.7

Salem Oaks

Old Settlers Park

25.9

CR JS

22.1
116 Ave

21.0

20.0

20.7
Deep Lake Road

23.9

23.1

CR V

Voltz Lake

Benet Lake

Wisconsin
Illinois

way offers a wide paved shoulder for your return. You then cross Highway 31 and merge onto Washington Avenue back in Kenosha. In a little over 2 miles, you pass the Washington Park Velodrome—stop and watch, or participate if you have the energy.

Now circling south on J. F. Kennedy Memorial Drive into the downtown area, you soon are back at Lake Front Park. Pick up information about the Civil War Museum, the Rambler Legacy Gallery, and the Southport Lighthouse next to the History Center, or take a free tour at the Jelly Belly Center.

Miles and Directions

0.0 Go south on Third Avenue from Lake Front Park.

0.2 Pass Eichelman Park.

1.1 Turn left on 71st Street.

1.2 Take a right on First Avenue.

1.4 Take a right on 75th Street.

1.5 Turn left on Second Avenue and pass Southport Park.

1.8 Take a right on 78th Street.

2.1 Turn left on Seventh Avenue.

2.8 Turn left on 85th Street.

3.2 Take a right on First Avenue.

5.7 Pass Carol Beach.

6.1 Take a right on 116th Street.

6.9 Cross Highway 32.

7.8 Pass through Tobin.

8.0 Cross bike trail.

9.7 Turn left on County Road ML.

10.4 Cross Highway 31 (Green Bay Road) onto Springbrook Road (County Road ML).

11.2 Cross tracks onto 116th Street.

11.9 Turn left on County Road H. **Option:** Turn right on County Road H for the 21-mile option.

12.5 Take a right on County Road ML.

14.3 Cross over I-94 then take a left on West Service Road.

14.9 Take a right on County Road WG on the state line.

18.7 Cross Highway 45 at Pikeville.

20.0 Cross into Illinois.

20.7 Take a right on Deep Lake Road/VG7.

21.0 Cross back into Wisconsin on 210th Avenue.

22.1 Turn left on 116th Avenue.

23.1 Take a right on County Road V.

23.9 Take a right on County Road JS.

25.9 Turn right on Highway 45.

26.4 Take a right on County Road Q.

28.5 Turn left on County Road MB.

30.9	Pass through Woodworth.
31.6	Take a right on Highway 50.
31.8	Turn left on County Road MB.
32.8	Take a right on County Road K.
35.0	Cross under I-94.
36.0	Turn left on 104th Avenue.
36.2	Take a right on 58th Street.
37.2	Turn left on County Road H. (Note: The 21-mile option returns here.)
37.5	Cross Highway 158 by airport.
38.5	Take a right on County Road S.
40.4	Cross Highway 31 onto Washington Avenue.
42.8	Pass Washington Park Velodrome.
43.3	Turn left on Sheridan Avenue.
43.8	Take a right on J. F. Kennedy Memorial Drive through Pennoyer Park.
44.9	Take a right over the 50th Street Bridge from Simmons Island.
45.1	Turn left on Seventh Avenue.
45.2	Turn left on Fifth Avenue.
46.0	Turn left on 57th Street.
46.0	Return to park.

Local Information

Kenosha Area Convention & Visitors Bureau, 812 56th Street, Kenosha; (800) 654-7309; www.kenoshacvb.com.

Local Events/Attractions

Chase Food Folks & Spokes–Pro Am Bike Races; third Sunday in July; Kenosha YMCA; www.kenoshaymca.org.
ABR Track National; last weekend in July; (262) 654-6773; www.ambikerace.com.
Biking for Kids–Tour DeVour; second Sunday in August; (262) 637-7625; www.biking forkids.org.
Coffee Ride; third and fourth Saturdays in September; (800) 877-7025; www.southport-rigging.com.

Restaurants

Boat House Pub & Eatery, 4917 Seventh Avenue, Kenosha; (262) 654-9922.
Frank's Dinner, 508 58th Street, Kenosha; (262) 657-1017.
Grizzly's Saloon, 12711 Bristol Road, Pikeville; (262) 857-2682.

Accommodations

Best Western–Harborside Inn, 5125 Sixth Avenue, Kenosha; (262) 658-3281; www.bestwestern.com/harborsideinn.
Happy Acres KAMP Ground, 22230 45th Street, Bristol; (262) 857-7373.

Bike Shops

Ski & Sports Chalet, 5039 Sixth Avenue, Kenosha; (262) 658-8515.
Southport Schwinn, 7707 Sheridan Road, Kenosha; (262) 653-0204.
Total Cyclery, 2930 75th Street, Kenosha; (262) 652-2522.

Restrooms

Start/finish: Lake Front Park.
14.4: BP gas station along West Service Road.
42.8: Washington Park.

Maps

DeLorme: Wisconsin Atlas and Gazetteer: Page 31 D7.
Wisconsin State Bicycle Map (Eastern Section).

34 Beer Barrel Ramble

Heralded as the "City of Festivals," this metropolitan area is know for its rich ethnic heritage and breweries that grace the beautiful Lake Michigan shoreline. Visiting the oldest city in Wisconsin, the ramble makes a loop around the Milwaukee River, up to the northern end of the city, then circles back along the bluffs above the Lake Michigan shoreline. After starting at the Urban Ecology Center, you will be offered a medley of parks and old settlements (now suburbs) to ride through. Along the way visit a community first named for the sighting of an albino deer and another village named for the river and hills there. Closer to the bluffs enjoy cruising down Lake Drive past many large turn-of-the-twentieth-century homes. Next you pass an early settlement named for the whitefish that were frequently spotted in the bay. Coasting into the downtown area, enjoy the historic architecture and modern sculptures as you cross the river and circle back to the north. With a small climb up the hill, you ride next to the Beer Barrel Line Trail back to the start. Now that you have had a taste of Milwaukee, it's time to indulge.

Start: Urban Ecology Center, in Milwaukee's Riverside Park.
Length: 29 miles with a 24-mile option.
Terrain: Moderately sloping to the north with one hill to climb.

Traffic and hazards: Use caution, as the course uses many city streets, some with busy intersections as you twist and turn through the north side of Milwaukee.

Getting there: From Interstate 43 heading north in Milwaukee, get off at the Locust Street exit and head east. After crossing the Milwaukee River, take a right on Oakland Avenue and go 3 blocks. Take another right on Park Place and follow it to Newhall Lane. Street parking is free and plentiful.

Nestled along the magnificent bluffs overlooking Lake Michigan, this route enjoys a medley of communities that makes up the north side of Milwaukee, the largest city in Wisconsin. In the late 1600s Father Hennepin arrived at an Indian village here at the mouth of the river named *Millecki,* which means "good land." It was a meeting place, or council place, for several Indian tribes. Over the next hundred years, Indian tribes, explorers, traders, and then settlers disputed the pronunciation and spelling of the name of the city and river. Finally in 1844 it officially became Milwaukee, from an Indian word for "place by the river."

Before or after your ride, enjoy a wide array of attractions, events, and festivals, which the city is famous for. One of the attractions and a great way to tour the city is using a section of the 90-mile paved Oak Leaf Bike Trail system. Pick up a Milwaukee Bike Map, available at the visitor center, to assist you in riding safely through the city.

The waves roll into the shore of Lake Michigan while a rider rolls along the bluff.

The ramble starts at Riverside Park's Urban Ecology Center, another great attraction to check out. The center is in a retrofitted building and offers nature-based programs, including live exhibits and living green workshops. After leaving from the corner of Park Place and Newhall Lane, follow the streets around the south side and then turn left on Oakland Avenue. At the stoplight turn left again on Locust Street, cross the river, and follow the designated bike route west on Buleigh Street. After crossing over the freeway, you will notice some of this city's ethnic diversity as you pass by several retail shops.

For the next 1.5 miles after turning right on 14th Avenue, you ride through residential neighborhoods up to Cornell Street. Turn left and use caution, as traffic can be heavy riding west to Teutonia Avenue. Take a right here and after crossing the railroad tracks, take another right onto Hampton Avenue. In less than a mile heading east, you cross Green Bay Avenue and turn left onto the Milwaukee River Parkway. You will now ride north along the beautiful parkway system, running parallel to both the Milwaukee River and the Oak Leaf Bike Trail. You then cross Silver Springs Drive, where you can cut the ride short here by turning right. The ramble continues to the north, and you soon pass through Kletzsch Park.

Now turning east on Green Tree Road, enjoy the quiet tree-lined streets as you pass through the suburb of River Hills. Developed as a settlement in the 1920s, it took the name for the pleasant river and hills here. Except for the stretch crossing over I–43, you will find this community very tranquil.

Cross the freeway, turn onto North Yates Road and circle around to the northwest. Soon you will pass through another quiet neighborhood setting, the suburb of Fox Point. The village here was originally called Dutch Settlement because many of the settlers had come from Holland and wanted to be considered Dutch, but they had French surnames. Early surveyors called the land Fox Point, however, and the name stuck.

After turning left onto Santa Monica Road, another tree-lined boulevard, the route veers to the west on Indian Creek Parkway before traveling north again to the suburb of Brown Deer. When originally settled it was called White Deer by Dr. E. B. Walcott, who spied an albino deer while hunting in the area. It is said, however, that the conformists had their way: Because most deer are brown, the name was changed to Brown Deer in the early 1950s.

In another half mile you are at the upper end of Milwaukee's north side. Take a right on Fairy Chasm Road and then a second right onto Lake Drive in Bayside, a suburb with several subdivisions that was incorporated in 1953. After enjoying several miles of easy riding down the bike-friendly boulevard that skirts the bluff overlooking Lake Michigan, you enter the suburb of Whitefish Bay. Incorporated in 1892, this village was named for the numerous schools of whitefish that could be found in the beautiful bay, just a few miles north of downtown Milwaukee.

Lake Drive then passes Kensing Boulevard, and you enter the village of Shorewood. It is at this location, on the shores of the lake, that a Devonian rock deposit of alternating soft shale and limestone measuring 140 feet high was found, known as the Milwaukee formation. This city was originally platted as a village in 1836 and named Mechanicsville. Then in 1875 it was discovered that the limestone could be made into cement, and the village population grew. The name changed several times, finally to Shorewood in 1917.

As the ramble passes Lake Park, those who prefer to cut the ride short should turn right on Newberry Street. Otherwise, continue along the route overlooking Lake Michigan and then turn left on Farwell Avenue to the downtown area. As you ride on bike-friendly Kilbourn Avenue, notice the sculptures as you cross the river again. Now circling back to the north on Old World Third Street, you will pass the Milwaukee County Historical Society. As you make your way back across the river and up Commerce Street, you will experience the only major climb on this ramble. At the top turn on Humboldt Boulevard along the Beer Line Trail, and soon you will be back at the Urban Ecology Center.

Miles and Directions

0.0 From the Urban Ecology Center on Newhall Lane, travel east on Park Place.

0.1 Turn left on Barlett Avenue.

0.2 Turn right on Riverside Street.

0.3 Turn left on Oakland Avenue.

0.4 Turn left on Locust Street.

0.9 Take a right on Humbolt Boulevard.

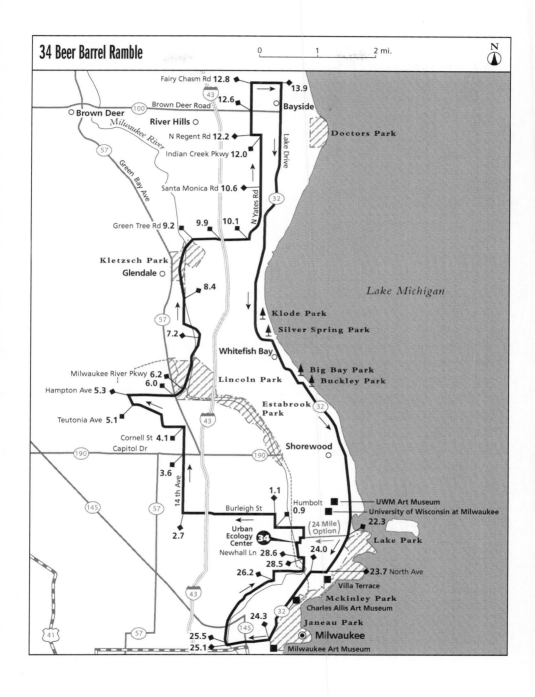

34 Beer Barrel Ramble

0   1   2 mi.

N

Fairy Chasm Rd **12.8** ◆   **13.9**

Brown Deer Road **12.6** ◆   (43)   ○ **Bayside**

○ **Brown Deer**   (100)

River Hills ○

Milwaukee River

N Regent Rd **12.2** ◆   **Doctors Park**

Indian Creek Pkwy **12.0** ◆

(57)

Santa Monica Rd **10.6** ◆

Green Bay Ave

Lake Drive

N Yates Rd

(32)

Green Tree Rd **9.2** ■   **9.9**   **10.1**

Kletzsch Park
Glendale ○

8.4 ◆

Lake Michigan

(57)

7.2 ◆

▲ **Klode Park**

▲ **Silver Spring Park**

Whitefish Bay ○

Milwaukee River Pkwy **6.2** ◆

6.0 ◆

▲ **Big Bay Park**
▲ **Buckley Park**

Hampton Ave **5.3** ◆

Lincoln Park

Teutonia Ave **5.1** ■

Estabrook Park

(32)

Cornell St **4.1** ■

Capitol Dr

Shorewood ○

(190)   (190)

3.6 ■

14 th Ave

1.1 ◆

Humbolt

0.9

UWM Art Museum

(57)

Burleigh St

University of Wisconsin at Milwaukee

22.3

(145)

(24 Mile Option)

Lake Park

2.7

Urban Ecology Center

34

24.0

Newhall Ln **28.6**

28.5

26.2

23.7 North Ave

Villa Terrace

(43)

Mckinley Park
Charles Allis Art Museum

24.3

(32)

Janeau Park

(41)

(57)

25.5

(145)

◉ **Milwaukee**

25.1

Milwaukee Art Museum

1.1 Turn left on Burleigh Street.

2.7 Take a right on 14th Avenue.

3.6 Cross Capitol Drive/Highway 190.

4.1 Turn left on Cornell Street.

5.1 Take a right on Teutonia Avenue.

5.3 Take a right on Hampton Avenue.

6.0 Cross Green Bay Avenue/Highway 57.

6.2 Turn left on Milwaukee River Parkway.

7.2 Cross Silver Springs Drive.

8.4 Cross Bender Road.

8.9 Pass Kletzsch Park.

9.2 Take a right on Green Tree Road.

9.9 Cross over I–43.

10.1 Turn left on North Yates Road.

10.6 Turn left on Santa Monica Road.

12.0 Turn left on Indian Creek Parkway.

12.2 Take a right on North Regent Road.

12.6 Cross Brown Deer Road/Highway 100.

12.8 Take a right on Fairy Chasm Road.

13.9 Take a right on Lake Drive/Highway 32.

22.3 Pass Newberry Street. **Option:** Turn right for the 24-mile shortcut option.

23.7 Make a right on North Avenue.

24.0 Turn left on Farwell Avenue.

24.3 Take a right on Kilbourn Avenue.

25.1 Turn right on Third Street.

25.5 Take a right on Commerce Street.

26.2 Turn left on Humbolt Boulevard.

27.5 Take a right on North Street.

28.3 Turn left on Oakland Avenue.

28.5 Turn left on Bradford Avenue.

28.6 Take a right on Newhall Lane.

29.0 Return to park.

Local Information

Visit Milwaukee, 648 North Plankinton Avenue, Suite 425, Milwaukee; (800) 231-0903; www.visitmilwaukee.org.

Local Events/Attractions

Milwaukee County Historical Society, 910 North Old World Third Street, Milwaukee; (414) 273-8288; www.milwaukeecountyhistsoc.org.

Urban Ecology Center, 1500 East Park Place, Milwaukee; (414) 964-8505; www.urban ecologycenter.org.

Tour de Cure; third week in May; American Diabetes Association; (888) 342-2383; www.diabetes.org/tour.

Tour de PA; first week in July; (414) 383-8274; www.publicallies.org/milwaukee/com.

Restaurants

Kilbourn Cafe, 139 East Kilbourn Avenue, Milwaukee; (414) 276-4793.

Pandi's In Bayside, 8825 North Lake Drive, Milwaukee; (414) 352-7300.

Accommodations

Park East Hotel, 916 East State Street, Milwaukee; (800) 328-7275; www.parkeast hotel.com.

Bike Shops

Adventure Bicycle, 6207 North 101st Street, Milwaukee; (414) 760-1493.

Ben's Cycle and Fitness, 1018 West Lincoln Avenue, Milwaukee; (414) 384-2236.

Benz Cyclery, 311 West Sliver Spring Drive, Milwaukee; (414) 962-0911.

Bikesmiths, 2865 North Murray Avenue, Milwaukee; (414) 332-1330.

Cory The Bike Fixer, 2410 North Murray Avenue, Milwaukee; (414) 967-9446.

East Side Cycle & Hobby, 2031 North Farwell Avenue, Milwaukee; (414) 276-9848.

Milwaukee Bike & Skate Rental, Mckinley Marina, Milwaukee; (414) 273-1343.

Wheel & Sprocket, 6940 North Santa Monica Boulvard, Milwaukee; (414) 247-8100.

Your Family Store, 827 West Burleigh Street, Milwaukee; (414) 264-0505.

Restrooms

Start/finish: Urban Ecology Center.
8.9: Kletzsch Park.
13.9: Lake Park.
25.2: Milwaukee County Historical Society.

Maps

DeLorme: Wisconsin Atlas and Gazetteer: Pages 31 A6 and 39 D6.

Wisconsin State Bicycle Map (Eastern Section).

Milwaukee Bike Map.

35 Covered Bridge Ramble

Visiting this area is like journeying back 150 years in time. The ramble begins in a village where cream-colored brick buildings dominate the historic downtown landscape, and continues through countryside where many aspects have remained unchanged for more than a century. Leaving west through the tree-lined streets, you will follow Evergreen Boulevard up along Cedar Creek. Soon the route turns to the north and takes you through an old settlement where the stone tavern is the only sign of its legacy. As you make a loop up and around Paradise Road, one of the state's "Rustic Roads," the route cruises east into a village named after an Indian tribe, where two major trails once intersected. Following the Milwaukee River back to the southwest, the ramble comes full circle and crosses Cedar Creek on the historic toll bridge that this ride is named for. Soon you are passing through a village named for its multiple road intersections. After crossing Highway 60, you return to historic Cedarburg.

Start: Cedarburg Community Center.
Length: 28 miles with a 20-mile option.
Terrain: Rolling.

Traffic and hazards: Use caution riding on the main county roads and when crossing highways.

Getting there: From Interstate 43 turn west on Highway C/Pioneer Road into Cedarburg. Turn north on Washington Avenue through the downtown area. The Cedarburg Community Center parking lot is on the left.

As you stroll around this town on Cedar Creek, you will notice that landmark preservation has become a point of pride for the community. Settled in 1845, German and Irish pioneers used the creek by harnessing the power of dams to run five mills. Cedarburg means "Village of Cedars" and probably came from a tale of a castlelike doctor's house that sat on a hill surrounded by cedars. The first settlers here lived in log shanties, and Washington Avenue was just a dirt road then. When the railroad came through in 1870, the town's growth was accelerated. Today Washington Avenue offers many historic buildings, including the Washington House Inn, which is listed on the National Register of Historic Places. Several of these historic structures offer restaurants and specialty food shops for your enjoyment before or after the ride.

You begin by leaving town on Evergreen Boulevard and turning west on Bridge Street. The route then turns north on Horns Corner Road and runs parallel to Kaehler's Mill Trail. A mile after crossing Highway 60, turn left on Cedar Creek Road, passing Creek Side Park, and follow the stream for another mile before turning north up to Decker Corner. In 1856 Carl Ludwig Deeche (pronounced *decker*) purchased the land here and started a general store. Soon after a tavern, blacksmith shop, and cheese-processing center were established. Today the only reminder of the community's past is the stone building that once housed the tavern, located across from the landscape nursery.

For the next 2 miles, pedal northwest along fairly flat terrain on the narrow paved shoulder of County Road NN. Then veering to the north on County Road M, ride over the undulating roadbed to Paradise Road. Turn east and enjoy this peaceful forested lane as you make your way down County Road Y to Cedar Sauk Road. From here it is 0.7 mile to Horns Corner Road at the Cedarburg Bog Nature Center. Those who prefer the 20-mile option should turn right here, but be sure to watch your mileage because the street sign is missing. In another mile heading east, the ramble passes Covered Bridge Road. Soon the route jogs to the north again for 1 mile, then follows Hillcrest Road east into Saukville.

For hundreds of years through the 1830s, the Menominee, Sauk, and Potawtomi Indian tribes all lived here near the meeting point of two major trails. After a government treaty was signed, these two paths became Dekorra Road and Green Bay Road, and the town was settled by Europeans in 1848. Five small milling settlements were merged, and the town took the name of the Sauk village that was here. If you stop at the park where the two trails crossed, take five and reflect as you sit on the bench next to the turn-of-the-twentieth-century bandstand shell. In Saukville you will also find a few options for lunch.

Now heading southwest along the Milwaukee River, you pass Riverside Park as you leave Saukville. Turn onto Cedar Sauk Road again in about a mile, where the

Riders stop to check out the historic covered bridge over Cedar Creek.

route jogs west, then south, then west again on Pleasant Valley Road. You will pass Pleasant Valley Nature Park at the 22.1-mile mark, if you need to stop.

At the intersection of Covered Bridge Road, at Kohn Park and Canoe Landing, turn south again. About a mile along another peaceful rolling road, you will come to the Historic Covered Bridge and Park at Cedar Creek. This is believed to be the last standing covered bridge dating from Wisconsin's pioneer days. The toll bridge was built in 1876 from pine logs cut and milled in Baraboo and fitted together using 2-inch hardwood pins and 3-inch plank flooring. A great photo opportunity, the bridge crosses Cedar Creek in a picturesque park setting.

Another mile south, cross Highway 60 onto County Road NN at Five Corners, which was settled by Patrick Halpin in 1884. Located at the junction of several roads, this village served the area with a blacksmith shop, saloon, school, stable, and the Five Corners Creamery. The settlement was originally known as Kennedy's Corners, after John Kennedy, who ran a saloon there. As you pass through town, if your sweet tooth is ready for some ice cream, check out Wayne's, a unique drive-in restaurant on the corner.

Now cruising back into Cedarburg on Washington Avenue, you will soon be back at the community center's parking lot. Take a stroll around town and see the five-story Cedarburg Mill, which was built in 1855 out of large blocks of gray limestone and could process up to 120 barrels of flour a day.

35 Covered Bridge Ramble

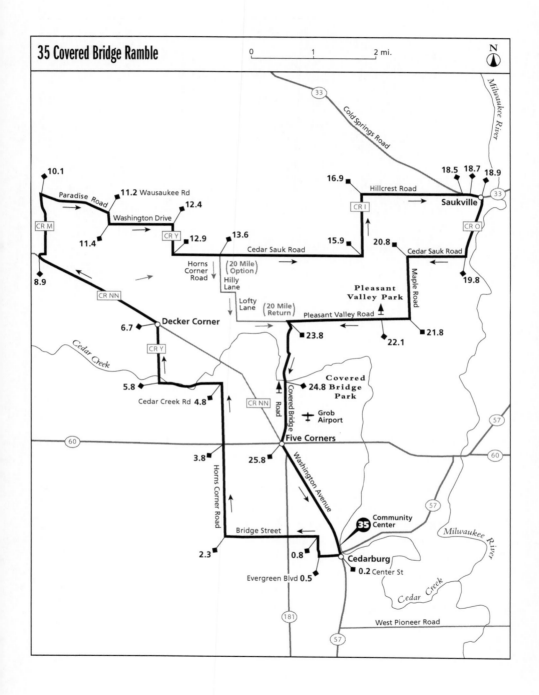

0   1   2 mi.

N

Miles and Directions

0.0 From the Cedarburg Community Center parking lot, take a right on Hanover Street.

0.2 Take a right on Center Street.

0.5 Take a right on Evergreen Boulevard.

0.8 Turn left on Bridge Street.

2.3 Take a right Horns Corner Road.

3.8 Cross Highway 60.

4.8 Turn left on Cedar Creek Road.

5.8 Take a right on County Road Y.

6.7 Turn left on County Road NN at Decker Corner.

8.9 Take a right on County Road M.

10.1 Take a right on Paradise Road.

11.2 Take a right on Wausaukee Road.

11.4 Turn left on Washington Drive.

12.4 Take a right on County Road Y.

12.9 Turn left on Cedar Sauk Road.

13.6 Pass Horns Corner Road at the Cedarburg Bog Nature Center. **Option:** Turn right on Horns Corner Road for the 20-mile option.

14.6 Pass Covered Bridge Road.

15.9 Turn left on County Road I.

16.9 Take a right on Hillcrest Road.

18.5 Take a right on Highway 33/Dakota Street into Saukville.

18.7 Pass Riverside Park.

18.9 Take a right on County Road O.

19.8 Take a right on Cedar Sauk Road.

20.8 Turn left on Maple Road.

21.8 Take a right on Pleasant Valley Road.

22.1 Pass Pleasant Valley Nature Park.

23.8 Turn left on Covered Bridge Road at Kohn Park and Canoe Landing. (Note: The 20-mile option returns here.)

24.8 Pass the Historic Covered Bridge and Park at Cedar Creek.

25.8 Cross Highway 60 onto County Road NN/Washington Avenue at Five Corners.

28.0 Take a right into the parking lot.

Local Information

Cedarburg Visitors Center, 480 Washington Avenue, Cedarburg; (800) 237-2874; www.cedarburg.org.

Local Events/Attractions

Cedarburg General Store Museum, W61 N480 Washington Avenue, Cedarburg; (262) 377-9620.

Cedarburg Cycling Classic; third Tuesday in July; www.cedarburgfestivals.org.
Bike for Wisconsin; third Sunday in September; (608) 251-4456; www.bfw.org.

Restaurants

Dancing Goat Espresso Bar & Cafe, W62 N605 Washington Avenue, Cedarburg; (262) 376-1366.
Parkview Grill Pub & Restaurant, 100 South Main Street, Saukville; (262) 284-1700.
Wayne's Drive-in, 1331 Covered Bridge Road, Five Corners; (262) 375-9999.

Accommodations

The Washington House, W62 N573 Washington Avenue, Cedarburg; (800) 554-4717; www.washingtonhouseinn.com.

Camp Will-O-Rill, 2039 East Hawthorne Drive, Saukville; (262) 692-2582.

Bike Shops

Grafton Ski & Cyclery, 1208 12th Avenue, Grafton; (414) 377-5220.

Restrooms

Start/finish: Cedarburg Community Center.
18.7: Riverside Park.
22.1: Pleasant Valley Nature Park.
24.8: Historic Covered Bridge Park.

Maps

DeLorme: Wisconsin Atlas and Gazetteer: Page 39 B6.
Wisconsin State Bicycle Map (Eastern Section).
Cedarburg Bike Trail/Road Map.

36 Northern Kettle Challenge

Welcome to the Northern Unit of the Kettle Moraine State Forest. If you have already experienced some of the Kettle's challenging topography in the Southern Kettle region, you will appreciate the similarities here in the Northern Kettle. This challenge starts in a town named after a local Indian chief, crosses the river, and follows its bank up to the kettled forest. Passing through a village named for a city in New York where many "Yankees" were from, the route jogs east up along the lush green farmlands that border the moraine. Turning north you pass through a settlement named after an Irish statesman. Farther north encounter a steady but modest incline as the route meanders around the irregular kettle pockets, scattered over the forested floor, to a town named by the founder's wife. After visiting the historic stagecoach inn and park, the fun really begins when cruising down the twisting Kettle Moraine Scenic Drive. At the far end of Long Lake, visit a community with a working mill, named after a town in Scotland. Now turning south, past the Ice Age Trail Center, it's an easy cruise along the Milwaukee River back to Kewaskum.

Start: Eisenbahn trailhead in Kewaskum.
Length: 50 miles with a 24-mile option.
Terrain: Rolling with a few major climbs.

Traffic and hazards: Use caution when riding on Highways 28 and 67, as traffic can be fast.

Getting there: At Highway 45 in Kewaskum, turn east on Highway 28. Cross the trail and turn left on Railroad Street. The trailhead parking lot is 1 block north.

Old stone churches such as this dot the rural Wisconsin landscape.

The challenge departs from the town of Kewaskum, on the west side of the northern unit of the Kettle Moraine State Forest. When the first European settlers arrived here in 1844 and started the community on a sharp bend in the Milwaukee River, it was named North Bend. This name, however, was too similar to West Bend, so in 1849 the name was changed to its current one, in honor of the Potawatomi Indian chief who lived and died here about the same time the township was organized. The chief's name means "a man able to turn fate whichever way he pleases." With the arrival of the railroad in the late 1840s, the town started to prosper.

You leave from Railroad Street at the Eisenbahn trailhead parking lot, where you will find several options to prepare you for the ride. This recently opened rail-to-trail spans from north West Bend up through Kewaskum to the county line. After riding east on Main Street/Highway 28, cross the river and follow the route up Riverview Drive. You will cross into Fond du Lac County, where you follow the route along the edge of the forest until you reach County Road S. Veering to the east, you are soon in the thick of the moraine as you pass through the village of New Fane.

A mill and settlement sprung up and merged with another settlement around 1859 to create this community along the East Branch of the Milwaukee River. New Fane was named after a town in New York from which the Yankee settlers had come from. Two miles farther west, turn onto Kettle Moraine Scenic Drive/County Road GGG, which offers a few challenging climbs as you make your way north.

As you ride along a forest lane, you will soon pass Mauthe Lake Recreation Area. After climbing a small hill, at the 8.2-mile mark is the Parkview General Store if you need to stop. Another mile up the road, the route jogs east and then back north along the eastern edges of the moraine before reaching County Road F. Those who prefer the 24-mile option should turn left here and rejoin the route at the 38.9-mile mark. The challenge zigzags to the east, then north, then east again into the village of Parnell.

This hamlet was named after Charles Stewart Parnell, an Irish statesman who claimed the lush green, rolling hills reminded him of Ireland. Now following County Road A, pass the state forest at the Parnell Trail Area and Tower as you skirt back into the northern section of the Kettle Moraine. At the 21-mile mark you will need to ride the shoulder of Highway 67 for a short distance before continuing north. Many of the pioneer farmsteads along this stretch have gone back to nature, but there are a few that are still being maintained. After passing County Road Z the route starts to meander around many natural landmarks on its way to Greenbush.

In 1844 Sylvanus Wade, his wife Betsy, and their nine children came to this area, where all they could see were trees and bushes. "See all the flora!" Betsy exclaimed. "We will have to name this place Greenbush, just like the town we came from in Massachusetts." In Greenbush visit the Wisconsin Historical Society Museum at Old Wade House State Park. The park showcases a complex of mid-nineteenth-century buildings that includes the Wade House, a stagecoach inn; a working water-powered sawmill; and many historic carriages. There are a couple lunch options up on Highway 23.

You then leave town on Cemetery Lane and cruise down the scenic Kettle Moraine Drive, twisting and turning as you roll through the forest around the kettles. In less than 2 miles you pass Greenbush Campground. At Highway 67 turn east onto the paved shoulder and then veer off on Forest Road for another mile of fun. After turning onto County Road U, the route travels south again and then merges onto Highway 67 for another short stint. Soon you are back riding the scenic country lanes down to Long Lake Recreation Area. As the route veers to the right on County Road F, those who selected the 24-mile option return to the challenge.

Back on the highway again, cruise east into Dundee, which was platted in 1856 by E. M. Macintosh, who built a mill here, then a hotel and saloon. The name came from his ancestral homeland in Scotland. You have a couple options for lunch here, and a chance to visit a working mill at the Dundee Mill Pond Park and Museum.

After riding out of town on the shoulder of Highway 67, in a half mile turn left on County Road G. Before turning, consider riding up the road to the Henry S. Reuss Ice Age Trail Center to learn more about the Kettle Moraine State Forest. Now riding south, along the Milwaukee River, enjoy a slight decline in the roadbed, making it easy to cruise back to Kewaskum.

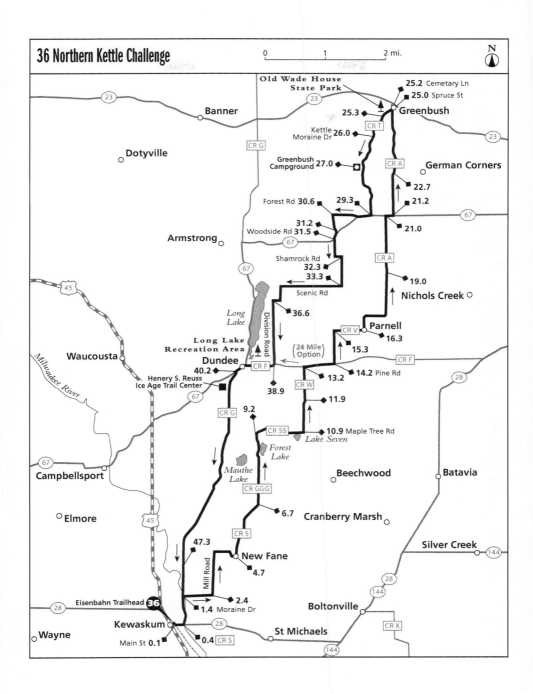

36 Northern Kettle Challenge

0   1   2 mi.

N

Old Wade House State Park

25.2 Cemetary Ln
25.0 Spruce St
Greenbush
25.3
CR T

Banner

Dotyville

CR G

Kettle Moraine Dr 26.0

German Corners
CR A

Greenbush Campground 27.0

22.7

21.2

21.0

67

Forest Rd 30.6   29.3

31.2
Woodside Rd 31.5

Armstrong

67

Shamrock Rd
32.3
33.3

CR A

19.0

67

Scenic Rd

Nichols Creek

Long Lake

36.6

CR V
Parnell
16.3

Long Lake Recreation Area

15.3

CR F

Dundee 40.2

(24 Mile Option)

13.2   14.2 Pine Rd

28

Waucousta

Henery S. Reuss Ice Age Trail Center

CR F

CR W

Milwaukee River

38.9

67

11.9

CR G

9.2

67

CR SS

10.9 Maple Tree Rd
Lake Seven

Campbellsport

Forest Lake

Mauthe Lake

Beechwood

Batavia

67

CR GGG

45

Elmore

6.7   Cranberry Marsh

Silver Creek

CR S

144

47.3

28

144

New Fane
4.7

Mill Road

Eisenbahn Trailhead 36

2.4
1.4 Moraine Dr

Boltonville

CR X

28

Kewaskum   28   St Michaels

Wayne

Main St 0.1   0.4 CR S

144

Miles and Directions

0.0 Turn south on Railroad Street from the Eisenbahn trailhead.

0.1 Take a right on Main Street/Highway 28.

0.3 Cross the Milwaukee River.

0.4 Turn left on Riverview Drive/County Road S.

1.4 Take a right on Moraine Drive.

2.4 Turn left on Mill Road.

4.7 Turn left on County Road S into New Fane.

6.7 Turn left on County Road GGG.

8.1 Pass Mauthe Lake Recreation Area.

8.2 Pass the Parkview General Store.

9.2 Take a right on County Road SS.

10.9 Turn left on Maple Tree Road.

11.9 Turn right onto County Road W.

13.2 Take a right on County Road F. **Option:** Turn left on County Road F for the 24-mile option.

14.2 Turn left on Pine Road.

15.3 Take a right on County Road V.

16.3 Turn left on County Road A.

19.0 Cross County Road U.

21.0 Take a right on Highway 67.

21.2 Turn left on County Road A.

22.7 Pass County Road U.

25.0 Turn left on Spruce Street in Greenbush.

25.2 Turn left on Cemetery Lane.

25.3 Take a right on County Road T.

26.0 Take a right on Kettle Moraine Drive.

27.0 Pass Greenbush Campground.

29.3 Take a right on Highway 67.

29.7 Take a right on Forest Road.

30.6 Forest Road (County Road U) turns left.

31.2 Take a right on Highway 67.

31.5 Turn left on Woodside Road (County Road U).

32.3 Take a right on Shamrock Road.

33.3 Take a right on Scenic Road.

35.5 Pass Kettle Moraine State Forest.

36.6 Turn left on Division Road.

37.8 Pass Long Lake Recreation Area.

38.9 Take a right on County Road F. (Note: The 24-mile option returns here.)

39.8 Turn left on Highway 67 into Dundee.

40.2 Turn left on County Road G.

47.3 County Road G turns into County Road S at the county line.

49.4 Take a right onto Highway 28 back into Kewaskum.

49.8 Take a right on Railroad Street.

50.0 Return to trailhead.

Local Information

Kewaskum Area Chamber of Commerce, P.O. Box 300, Kewaskum, WI 53040; (262) 626-3336; www.kewaskum.org.

Local Events/Attractions

Henry S. Reuss Ice Age Trail Center, N1765 Highway G, Campbellsport; (920) 533-8322; www.iceagetrail.org.

Old Wade House State Park, Wisconsin Historical Society, 135 Cemetery Lane, Greenbush; (920) 526-3271; www.wisconsinhistory.org/wadehouse.

Kettle Moraine Tour; second week in July; (414) 964-5822; www.edenexcursions.com.

North Kettle Moraine Tour; first week in October; (414) 671-4560; www.wisconsinbicycletours.com.

Restaurants

Gate Way Cafe, 1041 Fond du Lac Avenue, Kewaskum; (262) 626-2144.

Greenbush Inn, W7751 Plank Road, Greenbush; (920) 526-3444.

The Roadhouse, N3086 Highway 67, Dundee; (920) 533-8359.

Accommodations

Bonne Belle Motel, 900 Prospect Drive, Kewaskum; (262) 626-8414.

Mauthe Lake Campground, N1765 Highway G, Campbellsport; (262) 626-4305; www.dnr.wi.us/org/land/parks/specific/kmn.

Bike Shops

Pedal Moraine Cycle and Fitness, 1421 South Main Street, West Bend; (262) 338-2453.

Restrooms

Start/finish: City hall/library across from trailhead.

8.1: Mauthe Lake Recreation Area.

25.0: Old Wade House State Park.

27.0: Greenbush Campground.

37.8: Long Lake Recreation Area.

40.2: Henry S. Reuss Ice Age Trail Center.

Maps

DeLorme: Wisconsin Atlas and Gazetteer: Page 46 D4.

Wisconsin State Bicycle Map (Eastern Section).

37 Wanikamiu Cruise

At the southern tip of Lake Winnebago, enjoy a route that begins in a bike-friendly town with a French geographic description that means "bottom of the lake." After leaving town the cruise gradually mounts the scenic ridge, where you will enjoy the views looking out over Deneveu Lake before clicking into your high ring and cruising down the south side, passing a dairy operation with a statue of a cow on the corner. Now turning to the west, visit a town named after the Garden of Eden. Next the route jogs southwest to a village named after a poet, with a cheese plant the only thing there today. As River Road snakes to the west, you soon turn north on Mill Pond Road to a town named for the limestone quarries, where upon leaving you pass a large heard of elk. After crossing the highway, visit a town named after another poet and historian who sprang into popularity during the French Revolution. A couple miles farther north, the route turns to the east over semiflat farm fields. As you return to Fond du Lac, enjoy the bike-designated city streets that allow you to ride safely back to the park.

Start: Aquatic Park Center in Fond du Lac.
Length: 42 miles with a 28-mile option.
Terrain: Rolling with a few moderate hills.

Traffic and hazards: Ride-single file on County Roads T and B and on Esterbrook Road, as traffic can be heavy at times.

Getting there: From Highway 41 in Fond du Lac, travel north on Highway 175/Main Street to Pioneer Road. Turn right and follow Pioneer east to Martin Avenue, where you turn left. The park and fairgrounds are a half mile north on the right side, with plentiful free parking.

Before European explorers roamed this land, the Menominee Indians had a village here named *Wanikamiu,* which means "end of lake." When those first explorers arrived, they used the same waterways as the Indians, starting in Green Bay on the Fox River and down to Lake Winnebago. They set up a trading post here in 1836 and named it *Fond du Lac,* French for "bottom (foot) of the lake."

As you prepare for your ride, you will find many options to make your visit here pleasant. You leave from the Aquatic Park Center, next to the fairgrounds, and jog north and then east out of town. After crossing Highway 151, ride single-file for the next 2 miles on County Road T, using caution since there is no paved shoulder and traffic can get busy at times. You then turn south on Grand View Road, where you will encounter a 7 percent grade incline up the ridge. Before the ascent look off to your right at the great views of the countryside toward Deneveu Lake.

At the crest enjoy the hilltop rollers for another mile until jogging to the east on County Road H. As you head south, enjoy some more rollers through Wisconsin's

Modern dairies such as this are why Wisconsin
is known as America's Dairyland.

dairy land. Jogging to the east again on Sunny Road, you pass a large dairy operation with a statue of a cow in front. You then ride south on Winter Road and soon
reach Highway 45, where you turn west on the paved shoulder into Eden.

Adam Holiday founded this settlement in 1845. At a gathering to choose a name,
he stated, "Since it is recorded that Adam dwelt in the Garden of Eden, I know no
better name for our town than Eden." He then commented on its beauty, richness
of soil, fertility, and great abundance of fruit by the hand of God. There are a couple of options here if you need to stop.

After departing Eden, ride west on the narrow paved shoulder of County Road B.
Use caution here over the next 2 miles, as this is a local shortcut to Highway 41 and
traffic can be fast. After turning south onto County K, the route turns peaceful again.
In another mile it jogs to the west, and then south down to County Road F. As you
turn here you will see two wind turbines as you ride to the west. After passing under
Highway 41 and then crossing Highway 175, the road rolls over farm fields to the old
town of Byron. Settled in 1889, it is said to be named after the poet Lord Byron.

Take a right on Hickory Road at the Byron Cheese Plant and head north. In
another mile and a half turn left on Prairie Road. Those who prefer the 28-mile
option should continue to the right here. Soon the main cruise merges onto River
Road and dips back to the south following Campground Creek. At Mill Pond Road
the route starts it trek back to the north. Jogging to the west, you approach the city
limits of Oakfield.

This town was settled in 1840 and originally named Avaco. A few years later the
township was divided and the village was renamed Lime, for the extensive limestone
quarries here. The following year, however, the name was changed again to the present one because there were large stands of oak trees with open vistas in between. You
will find a couple options if you need to stop. As you ride north out of town, look to
your right and you will see a large herd of elk grazing in the pasture. Farther north the
terrain is fairly level as you make your way up to the town of Lamartine.

Originally this town, located on a stream that crossed Old Military Road, was
named Seven Mills Creek. It was later renamed for Alphonse de Lamartine, the
French poet and historian, who sprang into popularity during the French revolution
of 1848. There is a bar and grill here if you need to stop.

As you continue on Hillcrest Road, the county lane undulates under your bike
for the next 3 miles. At Forest Avenue Road circle to the east for a couple miles.
Approaching the city limits, the route follows some of the town's well-designated
bike routes to get you back to the park in Fond du Lac.

After returning, take a little trip down to the Galloway House and Village if you
are interested. This Midwestern version of an Italianate villa of Victorian elegance
was built in 1847 and then purchased by Edwin H. Gallow and remodeled to what
you see today. It was later donated to the Fond du Lac Historical Society, which has
added many buildings—including a gristmill and an early railroad depot with
caboose—to the grounds around this classic beauty.

37 Wanikamiu Cruise

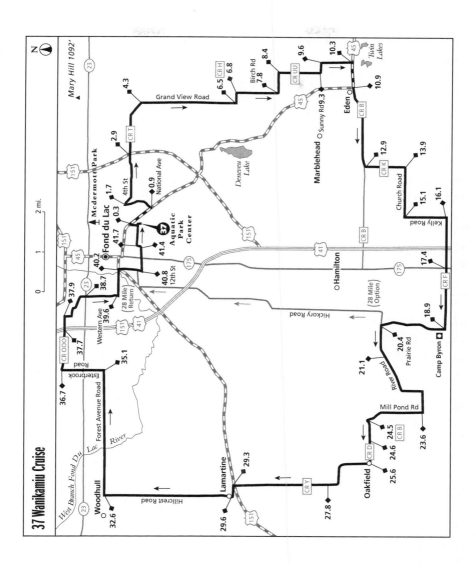

Miles and Directions

0.0 Take a right on Martin Avenue from Aquatic Park Center.

0.3 Take a right on Fond du Lac Avenue.

0.9 Turn left on National Avenue.

1.7 Take a right on Fourth Street/County Road T.

2.9 Cross Highway 151.

4.3 Take a right on Grand View Road.

6.5 Turn left on County Road H.

6.8 Take a right back on Grand View Road.

7.8 Turn left on Birch Road.

8.4 Take a right on County Road UU.

9.3 Turn left on Sunny Road.

9.6 Take a right on Winter Road.

10.3 Take a right on Highway 45 into Eden.

10.9 Turn left on County Road B.

12.9 Turn left on County Road K.

13.9 Take a right on Church Road.

15.1 Turn left on Kelly Road.

16.1 Take a right on County Road F.

16.8 Pass under Highway 41.

17.4 Cross Highway 175.

18.9 Take a right on Hickory Road at the Byron Cheese Plant.

20.4 Turn left on Prairie Road. **Option:** The 28-mile option turns right and continues north up Hickory Road. Entering Fond du Lac turn right on Dixie Street and then left on Morris and then right on 12th Street.

21.1 Turn left on River Road.

23.6 Take a right on Mill Pond Road.

24.5 Turn left on County Road B.

24.6 Turn left on County Road D into Oakfield.

25.6 Take a right on Main Street/County Road Y.

27.8 Pass elk farm.

29.3 Cross Highway 151 and turn left into Lamartine.

29.6 Take a right on Hillcrest Road.

32.6 Take a right on Forest Avenue Road.

35.1 Turn left on Esterbrook Road.

36.2 Cross Highway 23.

36.7 Take a right on County Road OOO.

37.7 Cross over Highway 141 onto Scott Street, back into Fond du Lac.

37.9 Take a right on Pearl Lane.

38.1 Turn left on Security Drive.

38.3 Take a right on North Peters Avenue.

38.4 Turn left on West Arndt Street.

38.6 Take a right on Seymour Street.

38.7 Cross Johnson Street/Highway 23.

39.6 Turn left on Western Avenue.

40.2 Cross Highway 151 and take a right on Morris Street.

40.8 Turn left on 12th Street. (Note: The 28-mile option returns here.)

41.1 Cross Highway 175.

41.4 Turn left on Ellis Avenue.

41.7 Take a right on Boyd Street.

42.0 Return to park.

Local Information

Fond du Lac Area Convention and Visitors Bureau, 171 South Pioneer Road, Fond du Lac; (800) 937-9123; www.fdl.com.

Local Events/Attractions

Galloway House and Village, Fond du Lac Historical Society, 336 Old Pioneer Road, Fond du Lac; (920) 922-1655; www.fdl.com/history.

Restaurants

Schreiner's Restaurant, Highways 41 and 23, Fond du Lac; (920) 922-0590; www.fdl chowder.com.

Village Pub & Grill, 210 North Main Street, Oakfield; (920) 583-3534.

Lori's Bar & Grill, W8147 County Road Y, Lamartine; (920) 929-4041.

Accommodations

Country Inn & Suites, 121 Merwin Way, Fond du Lac; (920) 924-8800.

Fond du Lac County Fairgrounds, Martin and Fond du Lac Avenues, Fond du Lac; (920) 929-3169.

Bike Shops

Attitude Sports, 223 North Seymour Street, Fond du Lac; (920) 923-2323.

Hank's Bike Shop, 315 West Division Street, Fond du Lac; (920) 922-0463.

Fond du Lac Cyclery, 209 South Main Street, Fond du Lac; (920) 923-3211.

Restrooms

Start/finish: Aquatic Park Center.

10.5: Eden Park.

24.6: Oakfield Park.

Maps

DeLorme: Wisconsin Atlas and Gazetteer: Page 46 B2.

Wisconsin State Bicycle Map (Southeast Section).

Fond du Lac Bike Map.

38 Two Lakes Cruise

This cruise leaves from a true harbor landmark destination, and each community you will explore has its own unique mark on the landscape. After leaving from a city on the bay named by the Potawatomi Indians, the route meanders along several rivers until reaching the edge of the Kettle Moraine hills. The first city you pass through was named after a faucet manufacturer, and the next town was named for the falls of the river that flows through it. You turn north next and visit a community a settler named after a city in Massachusetts where his early love lived and died. Farther north you'll circle around a lake and then through the town of the same name, where an Indian legend lives on today. Coming full circle, you travel through a town where a company made brats a household name. Now, gradually stepping down from one secondary road to the next, the route brings you back to Sheboygan.

Start: Kiwanis Park in Sheboygan.
Length: 48 miles with a 31-mile option.
Terrain: Wisconsin rollers with a few moderate climbs.

Traffic and hazards: Use caution when riding on the main county roads and when crossing highways, as traffic can be fast.

Getting there: From Interstate 43 head east into Sheboygan on Highway 23/Kohler Drive. At Erie Avenue take a right, then turn left on Service Road. At the next block take a right on 18th Street for 1 block, then a left on Niagara Avenue for another block. Turn right again on 17th Street; the park entrance is at the bottom of the hill with plenty of free parking.

The cruise starts in a beautiful harbor city with the Sheboygan River gracefully flowing through it, and you will find many landmark attractions to visit here before and after your ride. The Potawatomi Indians named the river, which means "waterway between two lakes." When the county was established it took the name of the river, but when the village was settled by German, Irish, and Dutch immigrants, it was originally named Morgan. The community grew, and in 1849 it changed its name to that of the county and river. Today you will find a renovated harbor next to the downtown area, with shops and cafes. A city bike trail leads out from this landmark harbor area and takes you to Kiwanis Park, where the cruise begins.

After you leave from the park grounds on the Sheboygan River, your leg muscles will encounter a bit of warmth as you climb the short 8 percent grade to Niagara Avenue. You'll then follow the route that parallels the Sheboygan Urban Recreational Trail, and will soon be cruising down Plank Road and crossing under I–43 through the trail tunnel. On the other side of the freeway, follow Twin Oaks Road around the Kohler plant in Kohler.

A farmer first platted the land here and named it Riverside, since it overlooked the Sheboygan River. In 1912 the Kohler Manufacturing Company, producers of

38 Two Lakes Cruise

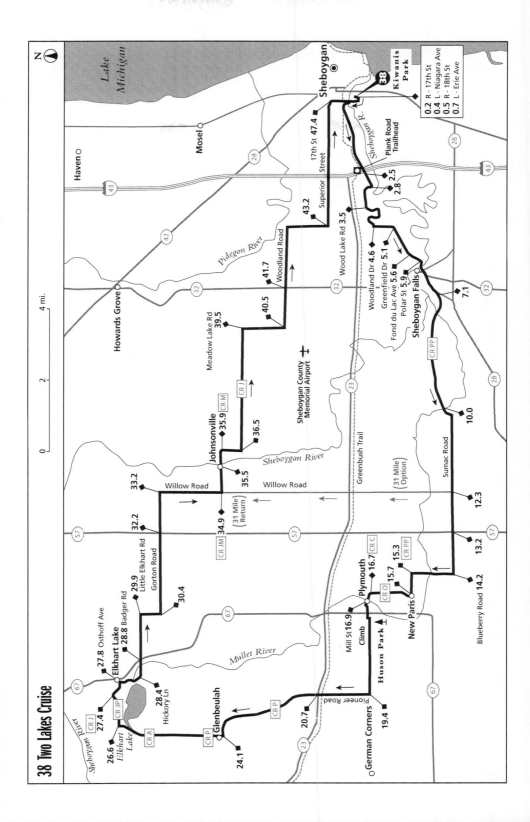

N

Lake Michigan

Haven ○

Mosel ○

Howards Grove ●

Sheboygan ●

Kiwanis Park

0.2   R - 17th St
0.4   L - Niagara Ave
0.5   R - 18th St
0.7   L - Erie Ave

17th St **47.4**

Superior Street

Plank Road Trailhead

Pidgeon River

2.5
2.8

Woodland Road **43.2**

Wood Lake Rd **3.5**

Woodland Dr **4.6**
Greenfield Dr **5.1**
Fond du Lac Ave **5.6**
Polar St **5.9**

Sheboygan Falls ○

41.7

40.5

7.1

Meadow Lake Rd **39.5**

CR J

CR M

Johnsonville ○ **35.9**

36.5

Sheboygan County Memorial Airport

Sheboygan River

CR PP

10.0

Willow Road   Willow Road

33.2   **35.5**

Greenbush Trail

(31 Mile Option)

Sumac Road

(31 Mile Return)

CR JM **34.9**

12.3

Little Elkhart Rd **32.2**

Badger Rd

29.9

Gorton Road

30.4

Osthoff Ave **27.8**

Elkhart Lake ○ **28.8**

CR C **16.7**
CR PP **15.3**

CR O **15.7**

Plymouth ○

Mill St **16.9**

Climb

Blueberry Road **14.2**

13.2

New Paris ●

Huson Park

CR JP **27.4**

26.6

Elkhart Lake

Hickory Ln **28.4**

Mullet River

CR A

CR P

Glenbeulah ○

24.1

Pioneer Road

German Corners ○ **19.4**

20.7

Sheboygan River

Lake Michigan

0   2   4 mi.

enamel plumbing fixtures, moved its plant here and the village was renamed Kohler. As you cross Highland Drive onto Wood Lake Road, you will pass through a new upscale community with shops. You then follow the river on Greenfield Drive and soon coast into Sheboygan Falls.

The village was named Rochester when platted in 1847, but it was later discovered that there was already a Rochester in Wisconsin, so the name was changed for the falls on the Sheboygan River. This quaint residential community, with its historic downtown area, offers visitors many points of interest if you have time to explore.

After leaving town, the terrain along the route begins rolling through agricultural croplands. As you pass Willow Road, those who prefer the 31-mile option should take a right here. Farther along, as you approach the Mullet River, the road winds back and forth over more traditional Wisconsin rollers until you reach New Paris.

This community was started in the 1840s when William Schwartz built a flour mill here. The mill changed hands several times, and in 1869 it was platted as a village by Vollier Wattier. Since he was French, he named it New Paris, and shortly after, a cider mill was added. Today New Paris is a part of Plymouth, which you will soon see as you turn north on Eastern Avenue.

Henry P. Davidson established Plymouth in 1845. He first called the settlement Springfield, but later his son Thomas named it Plymouth in honor of Plymouth, Massachusetts, where his early love lived and died. Plymouth offers several parks and a traditional downtown area, so enjoy—you will need some extra energy to get out of town.

Before leaving town, cross the Mullet River and follow Fond du Lac Avenue for the next mile up the hill. Now climbing, you will soon need to find your granny gears, as the grade hits 13 percent at one point. At the top, shift back to your high ring and cruise all the way down to Pioneer Road. You will soon cross the Old Plank Road Bicycle Trail as you ride north, at the 20.7-mile mark. This paved trail stretches from Greenbush, a few miles farther west, to Sheboygan. Now the cruise crosses Highway 23 and enjoys another set of rollers that take you up to the town of Glenbeulah.

This laid-back village was first named Clark's Mill for Hazel P. Clark, who set up a sawmill here in 1850. Three years later Edward Appleton was contracted to build a railroad and acquire a tract of land to plat as a village. He coined the name by combining the word *glen,* for the beautiful Kettle Moraine hills, which described the location, with *Beulah,* the name of his mother. Beulah, by the way, is a scriptural name that means "beautiful land" or "land of flower." The town offers a few establishments if you need a rest stop; otherwise, take a right and continue riding up toward Broughton Sheboygan Marsh Park and Wildlife Area. Two miles farther north, the road circles around Elkhart Lake, named by the Potawatomi Indian tribe that once inhabited the area.

When this village on the edge of the lake was first settled by German immigrants, it was called Rhine. Popular belief at that time was that the shape of the lake resembled the heart of an elk. According to an Indian legend, a young Indian maiden loved Wapita, who loved another of the chief's daughters. Scorned, the maiden told her troubles to a wise old tribeswomen, who told her, "Weep not! He loves another because her eyes are softer and hair is more silky then yours. Drink the blood from an elk's heart and you will become more beautiful. However, you will cease to love Wapita."

Soon after a storm, the young maiden went down to the lake just as an elk came bounding from the woods. After shooting it with an arrow, she removing its heart and drank its blood. Her eyes immediately became as dark as the dead elk's, and her hair soft and silky. When she returned to the camp and saw Wapita, his heart was smitten with love, but hers was hard and cold. Now in vain he strove for her favor, but she just laughed at him. As despair and grief filled Wapita, in madness he threw himself into the lake, which became his grave.

Today you can stroll through this prestigious resort community and visit the historic depot and Cottage Wood, a restored feed mill offering all the necessities you need to picnic in the park. There are several restaurant options for lunch as well. Continuing east, the terrain mellows with a few small rollers as you ride around Little Elkhart Lake. At the corner of Lake Elm Park Farms, turn onto County Road JM. Those who selected the 31-mile option will return and join you on your way to Johnsonville.

After crossing the Sheboygan River, you reach this town that has received national acclaim for its brats. It was originally called Schnappsville, but when the post office was established, the name was deemed inappropriate so it was changed to honor Andrew Johnson, the seventeenth president of the United States. You will continue riding east as you pass through this industrial area.

After 5 miles turn onto Woodland Road and follow the route southeast, past the airport and through town, back to the park. When you return, pick up the Sheboygan's History Walking Guide and explore.

Miles and Directions

0.0 Leave the park on Kiwanis Park Road.

0.2 Take a right on 17th Street.

0.4 Turn left on Niagara Avenue.

0.5 Take a right on 18th Street.

0.7 Turn left on Erie Avenue.

0.8 Turn left on the service road along Highway 23.

2.4 Cross under I-43 through the Plank Road Trail tunnel.

2.5 Turn left on the trail and resume on Erie Avenue.

2.8 Take a right on Twin Oaks Road around the Kohler plant.

3.5 Cross Highland Drive onto Wood Lake Road.

4.6 Turn left on Woodland Drive.

5.1 Turn right on Greenfield Drive.

5.6 Merge onto Fond du Lac Avenue.

5.9 Turn left on Polar Street.

6.2 Take a right on Monroe Street/County Road PP into Sheboygan Falls.

7.1 Take a right on County Road PP.

10.0 Turn left on Sumac Road.

12.3 Pass Willow Road. **Option:** Turn right on Willow Road for the 31-mile option.

13.2 Cross Highway 57.

14.2 Take a right on Blueberry Road.

15.3 Turn left on County Road PP.

15.7 Take a right on County Road O through New Paris.

16.7 Turn left on Eastern Avenue/County Road C into Plymouth.

16.8 Cross the Mullet River onto Mill Street.

16.9 Cross Highway 67 onto Fond du Lac Avenue/County Road Z.

19.4 Take a right on Pioneer Road.

20.7 Cross bike trail and Highway 23 onto County Road P.

24.1 Take a right on County Road A in Glenbeulah.

24.6 Continue straight on County Road P as County Road A turns right here.

26.6 Take a right on County Road JP.

27.4 Turn right on Gottfreid Street/County Road J in Elkhart Lake.

27.8 Take a right on Osthoff Avenue.

28.4 Turn left on Hickory Lane.

28.8 Cross Highway 67 onto Badger Road.

29.9 Take a right on Little Elkhart Road.

30.4 Turn left on Gorton Road.

32.2 Cross Highway 57.

33.2 Take a right Willow Road.

34.9 Turn left on County Road JM after passing Elm Park Farms. (Note: The 31-mile option returns here.)

35.5 Cross the Sheboygan River into Johnsonville.

35.9 Take a right on County Road M.

36.3 Turn left on County Road J.

39.5 Take a right on Meadow Lake Road.

40.5 Turn left on Woodland Road.

41.7 Cross Highway 32.

43.2 Turn left on Superior Street.

45.4 Cross under I-43.

47.4 Take a right on 17th Street.

47.7 Cross Highway 23.

49.7 Turn left on Kiwanis Park Road.

48.0 Return to park.

Local Information

City of Sheboygan Tourism, 807 Center Avenue, Sheboygan; (800) 689-0290; www.visitsheboygan.com.
Sheboygan County Convention & Visitors Bureau, 712 Riverfront Drive, Sheboygan; (920) 457-9495; www.sheboygan.org.

Local Events/Attractions

Sheboygan Historical Society and Museum, 3110 Erie Avenue, Sheboygan; (920) 458-1103.
Elkhart Lake Triathlon; second Sunday in June; (877) 262-8248; www.trifind .com/wi.html.
Superweek Road Race; third week in July; www.internationalcycling.com.

Restaurants

Arabella's Family Restaurant, 725 Indiana Avenue, Sheboygan; (920) 803-0300.
Park View Family Restaurant, 813 Monroe Street, Sheboygan Falls; (920) 467-1454.
Wilderness Roadside Inn, N5575 Highway 57, Plymouth; (920) 892-4544.
Lake Street Cafe, 21 Lake Street, Elkhart Lake; (920) 876-2142.

Accommodations

The Sheboygan Hotel, 723 Center Avenue, Sheboygan; (920) 458-1400.
Kohlar Andrea State Park, 1020 Beach Park Lane, Sheboygan; (920) 451-4080; www.wiparks.net.

Bike Shops

Bike N' Ski Warehouse, 1202 North Eighth Street, Sheboygan; (920) 457-2453.
Johnnie's Bike Shop, 1001 Michigan Avenue, Sheboygan; (920) 452-0934.
Wolf Schwinn Cycle & Fitness, 1702 South 12th Street, Sheboygan; (920) 457-0664.
Back Door Bike Shop, 828 Eastern Avenue, Plymouth; (920) 893-9786.

Restrooms

Start/finish: Kiwanis Park.
7.3: Riverside Park.
18.8: Huson Park.
27.6: Fisher Park.

Maps

DeLorme: Wisconsin Atlas and Gazetteer: Page 47 C7.
Wisconsin State Bicycle Map (Eastern Section).
Trails of Sheboygan County Bike Map.

39 Manitowoc Challenge

This metric century starts at a park along Lake Michigan's shoreline, in a town rich in maritime history, and tours parts of a county with the same name as the river and city. You will roll along the sandy dunes, pass through a Polish settlement, and then ride down to a village named after President Grover Cleveland. Now climbing away from the lake, the route rolls west to a village with a stagecoach inn and historic polling station. You will twist and turn along a couple rivers and follow the shore of a small lake before crossing over the third river, where the rocks in the water inspired a village's name. Now rolling to the north, you visit an old town that was named after a settler who built a stone tavern here. You then head east over undulating terrain and pass through a hillside town with a magnificent church. Soon you visit another community where the town name has been forgotten, but you can still buy an ice-cream cone for a quarter. Circling back along the south shore of Hartlaub Lake, you will soon be back in Manitowoc to explore its maritime attractions.

Start: Silver Creek Park in Manitowoc.
Length: 63 miles with a 35-mile option.
Terrain: Rolling with a few small hills.

Traffic and hazards: Use caution when crossing the highways and riding the main county roads, as traffic can be fast.

Getting there: From Interstate 43 turn onto Highway 151 and head east into Manitowoc. Turn right on Dewey Street and follow it to County Road LS, where you turn right. Silver Creek Park is a quarter mile south on your left. On the park road, turn left at the T and go to parking area next to the pavilion.

Harbored on the scenic shores of Lake Michigan, Silver Creek Park in Manitowoc is the departure point for this ride. When the first Europeans came to this place where whitefish were being speared at the mouth of the river, they thought they heard the Indians call it *Muneowk,* meaning "spirit land" or "mysterious influence." Around 1839 white settlers started arriving and the phonetic name changed to its current spelling. The town had one of the best natural ports on Lake Michigan, and when the first schooner was built here in 1847, Manitowoc's maritime tradition was born.

Today this beautiful port city has many options for you to discover before or after your ride. After leaving from the park on the south side of the town, enjoy the shoreline along Lake Michigan as you ride along the lakeshore, passing several berry farms on your way to Northeim.

This Polish farming and fishing village was established in the early 1860s. As you pass through you will see remnants of old log homes that are partially remodeled to help keep the past alive. Continue south past Fisher Creek Conservation Area, where you will find Fisher Creek Park and Beach on the other side of the creek. If you

39 Manitowoc Challenge

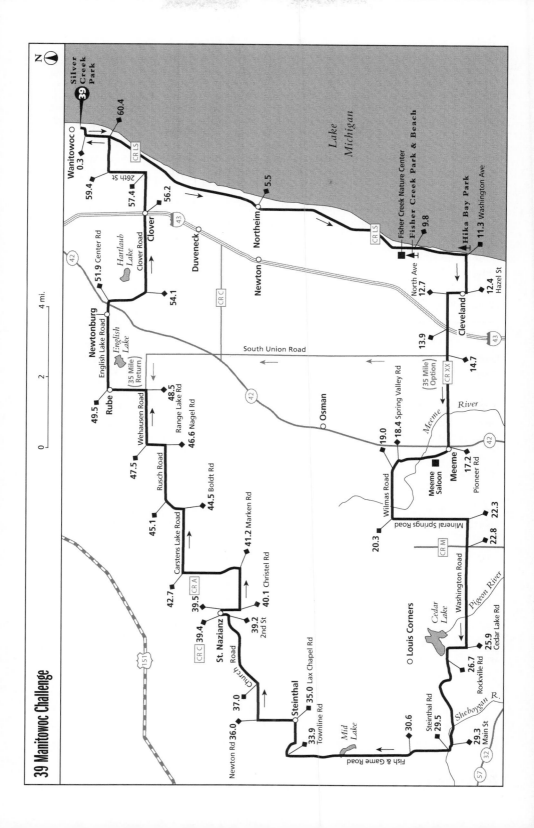

need to stop, there is another option a mile farther down the road, Hika Bay Park. As you ride from the lake you will also find a couple establishments in the village of Cleveland.

This village was originally known as Centerville Station when the railroad came through in 1873. When the post office was established twelve years later, the town was renamed in honor of the new president of the United States, Grover Cleveland. At the 12.4-mile mark take a right on Hazel Street and enjoy your first climb. Though a moderate hill, it should limber up your legs for the Wisconsin rollers ahead.

Now following the route out of town, ride over undulating farmlands and past stately old brick homes and farmsteads as you pass South Union Road. Those who prefer shortening the ride to 35 miles should turn right here. The challenge continues west and soon crosses Highway 42, onto Pioneer Road, to visit the village of Meeme.

The name of this town means "pigeon" in the Chippewa language. There is a potential rest stop here, the Meeme Inn, which was originally a stagecoach inn and is now a tavern. The little building next door served as the town's polling place into the nineteenth century. In 1847 German immigrants exercised their democratic right to vote in this simple wooden structure. Today it is only open to visitors on special occasions.

Now riding north, you soon pass through Spring Valley, or "German Meeme," as it was frequently called. Here once stood St. Fidelis Catholic Church and School next to the cemetery. It is now a ghost parish. After crossing the Meeme River and turning left on Williams Road, the terrain opens up as you pass several modern-day farms. Veer to the northwest and turn onto Cedar Lake Road, where you will enjoy meandering along the rolling lane with a shaded canopy that will cool you down on a hot day. At the 29.3-mile mark turn north on Main Street in Rockville.

This village sits on the south bank of the Sheboygan River. When first settled around 1860, the river ran shallow over the rocks, hence the name. Today a dam holds the water, creating a picturesque reservoir for you to stop and enjoy. There is a tavern here if you need a rest stop. Otherwise, enjoy more rollers as the road curves and rolls past several old farmsteads. When you reach Lax Chapel Road, turn east to another village of the past, Steinthal.

This community was named after a gentleman who built a stone tavern and store here. You will find a few homes in Steinthal as you make your turn across the Cedar River. Enjoy some more backcountry rollers on your way up to Church Road. For the next 2 miles the route travels northeast and you soon pass a goat farm. From here you can see a stunning church steeple off in the distance back to the east. At about the 39-mile mark, you are in St. Nazianz.

A pamphlet published in 1867 tells the story of this community, beginning in the Black Forest of Baden, Germany. Father Ambrose Oschwald organized his parishioners to leave Germany and form a Catholic village in America, where they could worship without being persecuted. After studying medicine for two years, Father Oschwald led his colony here, and he purchased 3,840 acres. Upon their arrival, they built two blockhouses and a church, which they named in honor of St. Gregory Nazianz.

Today this small village demonstrates a simpler time in history. Cruise down Second Street and you can see the well-maintained row houses, as the residents here enjoy their country lifestyle. As you continue on, you soon jog to the east, toward English Lake. Upon reaching Range Line Road, turn left and roll up to Rube, a village well known for its dairy.

It is said that this village was named after J. Fredrick Rube, a farmer who came with his family from Pommeran, Germany, in 1855 to claim land here. A few years later Joseph Thalhammer set up a store and saloon at the crossroads, and by 1884, he established a post office in his store, putting Rube on the map with two creameries. This once-thriving community has slipped away, except for the Pine River Dairy and a few residences. You can stop at the dairy and enjoy a 25-cent ice-cream cone or some of their Havarti cheese. Roll east out of Rube on English Lake Road to the next community you visit, Newtonburg.

While many pioneers strove to clear enough land to grub out an existence, it is said that the people of this new town, established in the mid-1800s, were always singing. Nicknamed "the land of song," the town was named in honor of Sergeant John Newton, a Revolutionary War hero from South Carolina. As you cross Highway 42, you will find that the village is mainly a residential hamlet. After crossing the highway, the road curves south around the shore of Hartlaub Lake then east again on Clover Road. After crossing under the interstate, you pass through the town of Clover.

Freidrich Sachse found a small meadow of clover here among the white pine forests and settled this village. Today locals know the corner as Wayer's Corner. In another mile heading east, turn north on 26th Street and follow the road up through a field of trees being groomed for somebody's front yard. Jogging to the north one more time, the route soon brings you back so you can explore Manitowoc.

Miles and Directions

0.0   Leave Silver Creek Park via the park road.

0.3   Turn left on 10th Street/County Road LS.

0.9   Pass Silver Creek Road.

5.5   Pass through Northeim.

9.7   Pass Fisher Creek Conservation Area.

9.8   Pass Fisher Creek Park and Beach.

11.3   Pass Hika Bay Park and take a right on Washington Avenue.

12.4   Take a right on Hazel Street in Cleveland.

12.7   Turn left on North Avenue.

13.1 Cross Dairyland Drive.

13.9 Cross under I-43 and continue on County Road XX.

14.7 Pass South Union Road. **Option:** Turn right on South Union Road for the 35-mile option.

17.2 Cross Highway 42 onto Pioneer Road.

17.7 Pass the Meeme Saloon and Historic Polling Center.

18.4 Turn left onto Spring Valley Road and ride through Spring Valley.

19.0 Turn left on Williams Road.

20.3 Turn left on Mineral Springs Road.

22.3 Take a right on Washington Road.

22.8 Pass County Road M.

25.9 Take a right on Cedar Lake Road.

26.7 Turn left on Rockville Road.

29.3 Take a right on Main Street in Rockville.

29.5 Take a right on Stienthal Road and cross the Sheboygan River and Dam.

30.6 Jog to the left on Fish and Game Road.

33.9 Take a right on Townline Road in Steinthal.

35.0 Turn left on Lax Chapel Road.

36.0 Take a right on Newton Road.

37.0 Turn left on Church Road.

39.2 Turn left on Second Street in St. Nazianz.

39.4 Take a right on County Road C.

39.5 Take a right on County Road A.

40.1 Turn left on Christel Road.

41.2 Turn left on Marken Road.

42.7 Take a right on Carstens Lake Road.

44.5 Turn left on Boldt Road.

45.1 Take a right on Rusch Road.

46.6 Turn left on Nagel Road.

47.5 Take a right on Wehausen Road.

48.5 Turn left on Range Lake Road. (Note: The 35-mile option returns here.)

49.5 Take a right on English Lake Road at the corner with the Pine River Diary in Rube.

51.5 Pass through Newtonburg.

51.9 Cross Highway 42 onto Center Road.

54.1 Turn left on Clover Road.

56.2 Cross I-43 into Clover.

57.4 Turn left on 26th Street.

59.4 Take a right on Silver Creek Road.

60.4 Turn left on County Road LS.

62.3 Take a right on Silver Creek Park Road.

63.0 Return to park.

Local Information

Manitowoc/Two Rivers Area Chamber of Commerce, 1515 Memorial Drive, Manitowoc; (800) 627-4896; www.manitowoc.info.

Local Events/Attractions

Pinecrest Historical Village, Manitowoc County Historical Society, 1701 Michigan Avenue, Manitowoc; (920) 684-5110; www.mchist soc.org.

Pine River Dairy, 10115 English Lake Road, Rube; (920) 758-2233; www.pineriverdairy .com.

Superweek Road Race; second week in July; www.internationalcycling.com.

Encore Bike Tour; third weekend in July; (414) 671-4560; www.wisconsinbicycletours.com.

Restaurants

Warren's Restaurant, 905 Washington Street, Manitowoc; (920) 682-2533.

Sessler's Meeme House, 14302 Pioneer Road, Meeme; (920) 693-8155.

Das Settlement's Opera Haus, 204 South Fourth Avenue, St. Nazianz; (920) 773-2803.

Accommodations

Holiday Inn, 4601 Calumet Avenue, Manitowoc; (920) 682-6000.

Manitowoc County Fairgrounds and Campsites, 4921 Expo Drive, Manitowoc; (920) 683-4378; www.manitowoccountyexpo.com.

Bike Shops

The Bicycle & Fitness Company, 301 North Eighth Street, Manitowoc; (920) 682-1944.

Nor-Door Cyclery, 4007 Highway 42, Fish Creek; (920) 868-2275.

Restrooms

Start/finish: Silver Creek Park.
9.8: Fisher Creek Park and Beach.
11.3: Hika Bay Park.
26.4: Cedar Lake Park.

Maps

DeLorme: Wisconsin Atlas and Gazetteer: Page 56 D3.

Wisconsin State Bicycle Map (Eastern Section).

Manitowoc County Bicycle Touring Guide.

40 Door County Classic

Praised by visitors from around the world as "Wisconsin's Cape Cod," this ride explores hundreds of coves offering culinary delights, state parks, and lighthouses. The route departs from a pioneer community that began with a couple sawmills and today is a maritime port city. As you follow along the Green Bay shoreline, visit a village named after a nest of duck eggs. Then climb the ridge and visit a town, originally a Menominee Indian village, with a name that means "trout fishing." At the gates of Peninsula State Park, enjoy miles of scenic park roads with a lighthouse to visit along the way. After reaching a town with a name chosen from the Bible, meaning "doubly fruitful," circle to the south to Lake Michigan's side of the peninsula. Along this shoreline visit a community named after the captain who discovered this bay. After jogging out into the countryside, you return to the shore to a village named after a battle in France that affected the Revolutionary War. You then pass a few tree farms and roll back into Sturgeon Bay to sample a few Scandinavian traditions: the Door County fish boil topped off with a slice of the county's cherry pie.

Start: Martin Park in Sturgeon Bay.
Length: 79 miles with 25-mile and 43-mile options.
Terrain: Rolling with several climbs.

Traffic and hazards: Use caution when crossing from County Road F onto Highway 42 in Fish Creek, riding through Peninsula State Park, and on Highway 57 between Valmy and Institute, as traffic can be busy and/or fast.

Getting there: From Highways 42/57 turn west on Michigan Street/County Road TT into Sturgeon Bay. At Third Avenue turn left and follow the road east to the park on Pennsylvania Avenue. Take a right and look for available street parking.

Situated at the midpoint of the nearly 90-mile-long Door County peninsula, Sturgeon Bay was named Graham when the first Euro-American settlement was established here in 1850. A few years later Mr. Stevens, an assemblyman, got a bill passed to change the name to Ottumba. It was later changed back to Graham, and in 1860 a petition was submitted to the county board to change the name to Sturgeon Bay, for the long fish-shaped bay and the sturgeon that were once plentiful here. Twenty years later, with the canal linking Sturgeon Bay to Lake Michigan completed, shipbuilding and traffic turned the village into a maritime port city.

This community makes a great place to start a ride. Turn left on Third Avenue leaving Martin Park, and then head down the hill on Michigan Street to First Avenue, just before the lift bridge. As you follow along the bay, notice the large boats being manufactured. Go up a small incline, turn onto Third Avenue/County Road B, and ride out of town. Across from the shipyards you will pass the Colonial Garden Bed

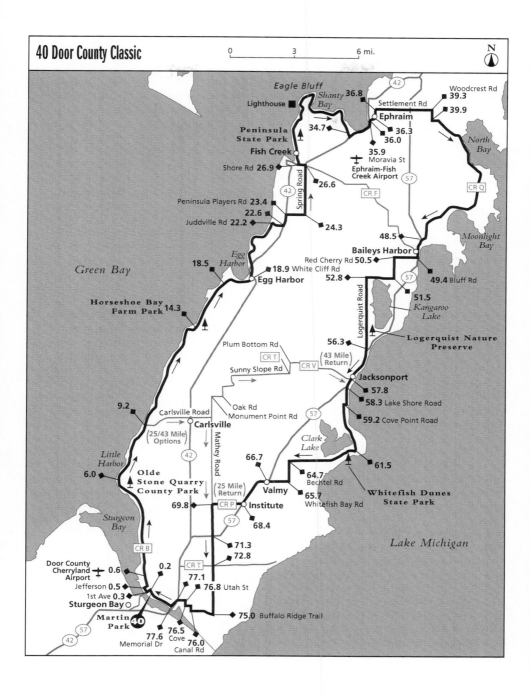

40 Door County Classic

0   3   6 mi.

N

Eagle Bluff

Lighthouse ■   *Shanty Bay* 36.8

Settlement Rd   Woodcrest Rd 39.3

Ephraim ○   39.9

34.7   36.3
36.0

Peninsula State Park   35.9
Moravia St
Fish Creek ○   Ephraim-Fish Creek Airport   *North Bay*

Shore Rd 26.9   26.6   CR F   57

26.9   CR Q

Peninsula Players Rd 23.4   24.3
22.6 ■
Juddville Rd 22.2 ◆   48.5 ■   *Moonlight Bay*

Green Bay   18.5 ■   *Egg Harbor*   **Baileys Harbor** ○
Red Cherry Rd 50.5
18.9 White Cliff Rd   49.4 Bluff Rd
Egg Harbor ○   52.8 ◆   57

Horseshoe Bay Farm Park 14.3   51.5
Kangaroo Lake

Plum Bottom Rd   56.3   **Logerquist Nature Preserve**

9.2   Sunny Slope Rd   (43 Mile Return)
Carlsville Road   CR T   CR V
Carlsville ○   **Jacksonport** ○   57.8
(25/43 Mile Options)   Oak Rd   58.3 Lake Shore Road
42   Monument Point Rd   57   59.2 Cove Point Road

Little Harbor   *Clark Lake*
6.0 ◆   66.7   61.5
Olde Stone Quarry County Park   64.7 Bechtel Rd
(25 Mile Return)   **Valmy** ○   **Whitefish Dunes State Park**
69.8 ◆   CR P   **Institute** ○   65.7 Whitefish Bay Rd
Sturgeon Bay   57   68.4   *Lake Michigan*
CR B
71.3
72.8
Door County Cherryland Airport 0.6   0.2   CR T
Jefferson 0.5   77.1
1st Ave 0.3   76.8 Utah St
Sturgeon Bay ○   75.0 Buffalo Ridge Trail
Martin Park ④⓪
57   77.6   76.5 Cove
42   Memorial Dr   76.0 Canal Rd

& Breakfast and the Red Oak Winery. This 1877 B&B was originally the residence of Thomas Henry Smith, a prominent businessman when the city received its charter. He was influential in establishing shipbuilding, quarrying, and markets for retail coal here.

Over the next 5 miles, County Road B gradually climbs at a 4 percent grade with one short 7 percent hike. At the 6-mile mark, you pass Olde Stone Quarry County Park on the bayside of Door County. Here is where much of the stone needed to build the town was quarried. Soon you pass Carlsville Road, and those who prefer the 25- or 43-mile options should turn here. If you choose either of these options, you will pass through Carlsville, which was settled in the 1890s and named for Carl Schuster, Carl Wolzien, and Carl Krueger, who all attended the German Lutheran Church in Valmy.

Continuing north on the classic, the route passes Horseshoe Bay Farm Park at the 14.3-mile mark, and if you need to stop, you will find a beach, picnic area, and restrooms here. Farther north pass South Trail/County Road T and continue north along the rolling shoreline course. After taking a left on Highway 42, you are soon in Egg Harbor.

The town was originally called *Che-bah-ye-sho-da-ning* by the Potawatomi Indians, meaning "ghost door." It was renamed Egg Harbor by Increase Claflin, who named most of the places here on the peninsula. In the process of retrieving a horseshoe out of the harbor, Clafin found a nest full of duck's eggs. You will find several options for a rest stop here.

Now turning onto White Cliff Road, your legs muscles will summon your body for an adrenaline boost for your first major climb. After jogging to the north again on the paved shoulder of Highway 42, turn up the ridge on Peninsula Players Road. In less than a mile, turn left onto Spring Road and continue climbing up another block. Ride the ridge for a couple miles to the intersection of County Road F and Highway 42, then coast down the hill into Fish Creek.

Formerly an old Menominee Indian site called *Ma-go-she-kah-ning,* meaning "trout fishing," it was Asa Thorp who is credited with promoting this settlement. In 1844 he left the Erie Canal with a caravan of fortune hunters bound for the west. In Buffalo, New York, he transferred to a steamer headed for Milwaukee and walked north into the wilderness. Having learned as a boy the trade of making woodenware, he paid his way by stopping at settlers' cabins to make wooden items for them. As luck would have it, a stranger noticed Thorp making butter firkins and said he should come up to Rock Island and make fish barrels.

While Thorp was on board a lake steamer to Washington Harbor, the captain pointed to Fish Creek as they passed and said, "A fella could make a lot of money if he built a pier there." Because of the rugged shoreline, the steamers had a hard time finding dry fuel between Greenbay and Washington Harbor. Arriving in port, Thorp made a claim to all the land on either side of Fish Creek. Then in 1853 he built a pier and hired men to cut wood for the steamers. Here at about the 27-mile mark, turn on Shore Road into Peninsula State Park. You will find several rest stop options and a bike shop before entering the park.

For the next 8 miles enjoy the state park setting as you follow Shore Road. Soon you pass the Eagle Bluff lighthouse and then Welcker's Point as you ride around Nicolet Bay. At the junction of Skyline Road, turn left toward Eagle Bluff on Shore Road. Riding through the park on a bicycle is free, but the roads are narrow and can be heavy with traffic, especially on weekends. Ride with caution and single-file when in a group, as there are some steep downgrades with tight corners and intersections. Now leaving the park, turn left back on Highway 42 and ride into Ephraim.

This village's name means "doubly fruitful" and was chosen from the Bible by Pastor Iverson of the Church of Brotherhood (Moravian Church). Under his leadership, in 1853 the first twenty-six settlers came by water from the Tank Colony at Fort Howard, in Green Bay, to make a beachhead near the hills in northern Door County. You will find the village gracefully nestled amid a stunning natural backdrop overlooking Eagle Harbor and the state park.

Leaving the highway as you turn onto Moravia Street, veer to the right and start climbing up the ridge again. Halfway up the hill, take a sharp right on County Road Q and continue climbing at a 10 percent grade. Now jogging first to the left and then to the right, roll across many natural prairie meadows on Settlement Road as you pedal east.

Soon you will be looking out over Lake Michigan as the classic cruises down the lake side of Door County. You first pass through North Bay and then ride along Moonlight Bay. A little farther you reach the paved shoulder of Highway 57 for a scenic cruise into Baileys Harbor, where you will find a few rest stop options.

This was the first settlement on the Door County peninsula. One day in 1848 Captain Bailey was returning from Buffalo with passengers bound for the west. As he headed his ship down Lake Michigan toward Milwaukee, a storm came up. Afraid the vessel was in danger of sinking, the captain looked for a bay to protect it from the wind. Soon he saw a large safe-looking inlet that was broad, deep, and easy for the ship to maneuver into. Staying there for several days, the captain explored the shores and found large stands of timber and a ledge of building stone. He shared this information with his employer upon his return, and they acquired the land around the harbor and set up a village to ship timber and stone back to Milwaukee.

After taking a right on Bluff Road, follow the route down County Road E and ride west along the catwalk between Upper and Lower Kangaroo Lakes. Then at Logerquist Road, turn south again. About 2 miles along the rolling meadow, you will pass Logerquist Nature Preserve and Trail on your way to the village of Jacksonport.

This was another old Potawatomi Indian village, originally called *Medemoya-Seebem,* meaning "old women's creek." In 1869 the town was platted and adopted its name in honor of President Andrew Jackson. The 43-mile option returns here from County Road V, and there are a few choices if you need to stop. Now jutting to the left, ride the forested road down to Cove Point. After taking a right on Clark Lake Road, cruise along Whitefish Dunes State Park on your way to Valmy.

It is said that after the town was established in 1899, the first postmaster, Ella Simon, named the town after the 1892 Battle of Valmy in France. In this conflict, the Prussian army withdrew from the French army, an action that prevented the Prussians from advancing on Paris to put down the French Revolution. You will find a general store in this residential hamlet if you need to stop. Leaving Valmy, for the next couple miles you ride on the paved shoulder of Highway 57, then take a right on County Road P into the village of Institute.

In 1892 this community was started as the St. Aloysius Institute by Benedictine sisters from New Jersey. Its original mission was to offer children in the Door County Catholic community an education. As the town emerged around the school, people started referring to the new community as Institute. Sister Clementon Braun Roth was the village's first postmaster, but a few years later a new postmaster wanted to change the name to his surname. The Post Office Department declined the request but did allow him to move the office from the Catholic school to Wester's Saloon, which still stands on the highway.

Now riding east, you soon turn left on Mathey Road, where those who selected 25-mile option rejoin the classic. As you travel south across the highway on Mathey Road, you will pass farm fields planted with pine tree seedlings. At Buffalo Ridge Trail follow the route back into Sturgeon Bay, and enjoy some of the treats Door County has to offer.

Miles and Directions

0.0 Turn left on Third Avenue from Martin Park
0.2 Turn left on Michigan Street.
0.3 Take a right on First Avenue.
0.5 Take a right on Jefferson Street.
0.6 Turn left on Third Avenue/County Road B.
0.7 Pass Colonial Garden Bed & Breakfast.
6.0 Pass Olde Stone Quarry County Park.
9.2 Pass Carlsville Road. **Option:** Turn right on Carlsville Road for the 25- or 43-mile options.
14.3 Pass Horseshoe Bay Farm Park.
18.5 Pass South Trail/County Road T.
18.6 Turn left on Highway 42 in Egg Harbor.
18.9 Turn left on White Cliff Road.
22.2 Take a right on Juddville Road.
22.6 Turn left on Highway 42.
23.4 Take a right on Peninsula Players Road.
24.3 Turn left on Spring Road.

26.6 Turn left on County Road F, then left on Highway 42, in Fish Creek.

26.9 Take a right on Shore Road in Peninsula State Park.

29.2 Stay to the left on Shore Road at the Bluff Road intersection.

31.1 Pass Eagle Bluff.

34.7 Leave park and turn left on Highway 42.

35.9 Take a right on Moravia Street in Ephraim

36.0 Take a right on County Road Q.

36.3 Turn left on Norway Street.

36.8 Take a right on Settlement Road.

38.3 Cross Highway 57.

39.3 Take a right on Woodcrest Road.

39.9 Turn left on County Road Q.

46.0 Pass Moonlight Bay.

48.5 Turn left on Highway 57.

49.1 Pass through Baileys Harbor.

49.4 Take a right on Bluff Road.

50.5 Turn left on Red Cherry Road.

51.5 Take a right County Road E.

52.8 Turn left on Logerquist Road.

55.1 Pass Logerquist Nature Preserve.

56.3 Take a right on Highway 57.

57.8 Pass Jacksonport. (Note: The 43-mile option returns here.)

58.3 Turn left on Lake Shore Road.

59.2 Turn left on Cove Point Road.

61.5 Take a right on Clark Lake Road in Whitefish Dunes State Park.

64.7 Turn left on Bechtel Road.

65.7 Take a right on Whitefish Bay Road.

66.7 Turn left on Highway 57 in Valmy.

68.4 Take a right on County Road P in Institute.

69.8 Turn left on Mathey Road. (Note: The 25-mile option returns here.)

71.3 Cross Highway 57 and continue on Mathey Road.

72.8 Pass County Road T.

75.0 Take a right on Buffalo Ridge Trail.

76.0 Take a right on Canal Road. **Side-trip:** Turn left to ride 2 miles to the lighthouse.

76.5 Take a right on Cove Road.

76.8 Turn left on Utah Street.

77.1 Turn left on South 18th Place.

77.6 Take a right on Memorial Drive.

79.0 Return to park.

Local Information

Sturgeon Bay Visitor & Convention Bureau, 23 North Fifth Avenue, Sturgeon Bay; (800) 301-6695; www.sturgeonbay.org.

Door County Visitor & Convention Bureau, 1015 Green Bay Road, Sturgeon Bay; (920) 743-4456; www.doorcounty.com.

Local Events/Attractions

Door County Museum, Door County Historical Society, 18 North Fourth Avenue, Sturgeon Bay; (920) 743-5809.

Spring Blossom Tour; first week in June; (414) 964-5822; www.edenexcursions.com.

Door County Weekend Ride; third week in June; (847) 707-6888; www.pedalacross wisconsin.com.

Door County Spoke Out; last Sunday in September; Family Centers of Door County; (800) 856-1651; www.doorcountyfamilycenters.com.

Restaurants

Coffee Kick, 148 North Third Avenue, Sturgeon Bay; (920) 746-1122.

Cupola Cafe, 7836 Highway 42, Egg Harbor; (920) 868-2354.

Gibraltar Grill, 3993 Main Street, Fish Creek; (920) 868-4745.

Accommodations

Colonial Gardens Bed & Breakfast, 344 North Third Avenue, Sturgeon Bay; (920) 746-9192; www.colgardensbb.com.

Potawatomi State Park, 3740 County PD, Sturgeon Bay; (920) 746-2890; www.wiparks.net.

Bike Shops

DC Bikes & Latitude 45, 20 North Third Avenue, Sturgeon Bay; (920) 743-4434.

Edge of Park Rentals, Peninsula State Park, Highway 42, Fish Creek; (920) 868-3344.

Nor-Door Cyclery, 4007 Highway 42, Fish Creek; (920) 868-2275.

Restrooms

Start/finish: Martin Park.

6.0: Olde Stone Quarry County Park.

14.3 Horseshoe Bay Farm Park.

26.9: Peninsula State Park.

57.9: Jacksonport Park.

64.9: Whitefish Dunes State Park.

Maps

DeLorme: Wisconsin Atlas and Gazetteer: Page 69 B6.

Wisconsin State Bicycle Map (Northern Section).

Door County Back Road Bicycle Routes.

41 Three Rivers Classic

At the far northeast corner of the state, along the shoreline of Green Bay, enjoy a ride that takes you through a region influenced by three rivers. You leave from a community that shares its Indian heritage with the first river, while introducing you to the Copper Culture people that inhabited this area around 5600 BC. You then ride along the riverbank and visit a community named for a surveyor who connected the railroad to Military Road. After rolling into the next county, you will pass a few small villages on your way up to the second river, whose name means "snapping turtle." Follow the winding lane along the riverbank to a state park that makes a great place for a picnic. Now cruising east to a town on the bay named for a remarkable woman, ride along a third river named for a Indian tribe who greeted the French explorers when they first arrived. Circling to the south, down the shoreline of the bay, you will visit the second river again and a town with the same name. You then continue down the shoreline to the mouth of the first river and turn inland back to the park in Oconto.

Start: Sharp Park in Oconto.
Length: 80 miles with 33-mile and 44-mile options.
Terrain: Moderately rolling to flat.

Traffic and hazards: Use caution riding on Highway 22 out of Oconto, on County Road W in Marinette County, and on Highway 64, as traffic can be fast.

Getting there: From Highway 41 in Oconto, turn right on Chicago Street, then take a right on Main Street and follow it to Park/Collins Avenue. Turn right and head south to Seventh Street, where you turn right again to the park.

Before the Oconto River ends its 100-mile journey to Green Bay, it flows through the historic Bay Shore community with the same name, where this classic begins. Experts have documented that the area's first inhabitants were Copper Culture tribes who lived here around 5600 BC. In the 1600s the peace-loving Menominee tribe had a settlement here and called their village *O-kon-toe,* which is said to mean "black bass." Around 1630 missionaries came and built the first permanent settlement at the mouth of the river. For the next 150 years, the French and English jockeyed for position, influencing the area's landscape. In the early 1800s timber enticed several individuals to build sawmills here, and the large stands of timber were harvested. As the timber era ended settlers moved in, and the town's current location was surveyed in the early 1830s.

Oconto offers many options before and after your ride. The classic leaves from Sharp Park and takes you north across the river and through the downtown district before heading out to the southwest. After crossing the highway onto Mott Street, you pass Mill Street, which leads to Copper Culture Mounds State Park. As you continue west on North River Road, the route offers light rollers as it follows the river inland. At the junction of Funk Road, where the Little River flows into Octono, take a right on Stiles Road. After crossing Highway 141 heading west, follow County Road I into the village of Stiles.

This was the site of a Menominee Indian village named *Pak-wu-kiu,* meaning "pointed hill." When the town was established in 1856, it took the name Howard from an early settler, but was then renamed Stiles for the surveyor when it was platted. There is a park and tavern here if you need to stop. Now following the route north on Pioneer Park Road, take a right on Duame Road to Stiles Junction. This was the junction where the railroad line met with Military Road. After crossing Highway 141 back to the east, make your way up to the northeast on Military Road.

Military Road runs along the Little River until it turns east on County Road A. In about another 2 miles, turn left on Hogsback Road. Those who prefer the 33-mile option should continue east on County Road A. As the classic continues north, you will soon ride up North Range Line Road. In a couple miles you enter Marinette County, riding on County Road W. After 2.1 miles turn right on Church Road and ride east. When the road turns back to the north at the church, you are in May Corner, so-called by the locals because Sam May had a large farm here and the big redbrick house was once his residence.

As you approach County Road B from Mortinson Lane, the route continues north on Hartwig Road. Those who prefer the 44-mile option should turn east on County Road B to Peshtigo. The classic crosses County Road D, cruising north, and you enter Harmony. It is said that when the residents moved into the area in 1855, a good mix of craftsmen were available to make this village self-stainable, in what some believed to be a "harmonious" environment. When the railroad came through, the village was platted and took the name of this working environment. The small village survives today as a residential community.

At Highway 64 turn left and ride the paved shoulder for a short distance before resuming your trek north on Town Line Road. Jogging to the northeast again, you soon cross the Peshtigo River, the largest tributary that flows into Green Bay between the Menominee and Fox Rivers. You then turn east on Grasser Road, a half mile before Porterfield. In case you're curious, this town was named after John Porterfield, who owned a large farm here and had a business block in Marinette. There is only a gas station (with limited snacks) and a post office in town.

As the classic turns toward the southeast on Bagley Road, it follows the river. At about the 44-mile mark, you are at Peshtigo River State Forest Park, a great place to stop for a picnic or to stretch your legs and watch some wildlife. In a couple miles turn east on Highway 64 into Marinette.

Both the city and county are named in honor of a remarkable women who established a fur-trading post on the banks of the Menominee River. She was christened Marguerite Chevallier, but later through some quirk, came to be known by the then-popular nickname "Marinette." This was the diminutive for *Marie Antoinette,* Queen

41 Three Rivers Classic

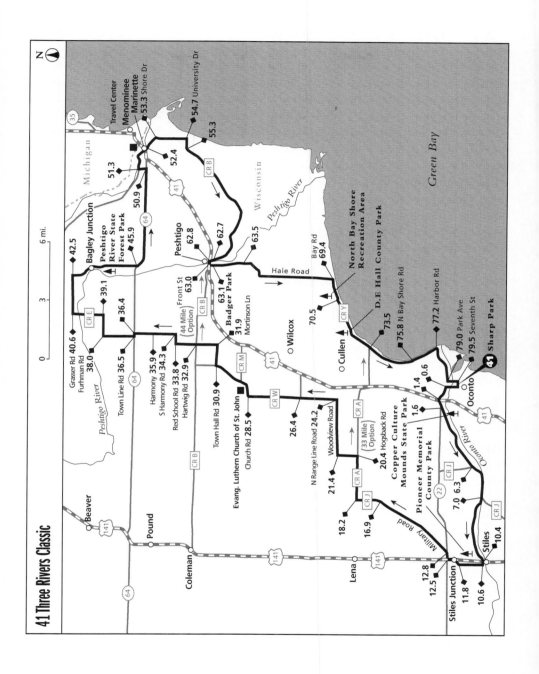

of France, whose tragic death at the time of the French Revolution caused much excitement among the French settlers in this territory. When pronouncing "Marie Antoinette," the French and the Indians on the river would shorten it to "Marinette." A trading post center for many years, in 1822 the town was platted and named in Marinette's honor.

This town at the river's mouth is a great place to stop for lunch. To avoid heavy traffic, the route jogs up to Riverside Avenue until crossing Highway 41 onto Main Street. After exploring the downtown district, head south on Shore Drive, which turns into County Road B at the city limits. For the next 4 miles enjoy the scenery riding down the Green Bay shoreline. Ride with ease, as traffic is restricted to a posted 40 mph limit. After passing the Little Red Schoolhouse, head back along the north bank of the Peshtigo River until reaching Highway 41. After crossing the river, you are in the town of Peshtigo.

Pe-shet-i-go is an Indian word meaning "snapping turtle." Settled in 1858 in Oconto County, the town was centered around a woodenware factory and was booming with more than 1,700 people by 1871. That fall, on the same night that Chicago burned, the city was wiped out of existence in the greatest forest fire disaster in American history. More than 800 lives and every building in the community were lost. After rebuilding, the two counties divided in 1879, and Peshtigo became a part of Marinette County.

Here the classic and 44-mile option merge and follow the river on Bay Road. You soon turn west away from the river and ride some small rollers as the route turns south again. At the 70.5-mile mark you pass North Bay Shore Park and Campground, if you need to stop.

As you ride along the shoreline of the bay, you again pass D. E. Hall County Park. In another mile you pass County Road A, where those who selected the 33-mile option return to the classic route. You soon turn on North Bay Shore Road, which offers another pass along the shoreline. Reaching the harbor where the Oconto River flows into the bay, you will pass Splinter Causeway Park and Marina. Now follow the river inland, back to the west. Turn on Park Avenue, cross the river, and return to the park in Oconto.

Miles and Directions

0.0 Turn left on Scherer Avenue from Sharp Park.

0.4 Cross the Oconto River.

0.6 Turn left on Main Street.

1.4 Cross Highway 41 onto Highway 22.

1.6 Turn left on Mott Street.

1.8 Pass Mill Street, which leads to Copper Culture Mounds State Park.

2.9 Mott Street turns into North River Road.

6.3 North River Road turns into County Road J as it merges from the north.

7.0   Take a right on Stiles Road when County Road J veers to the left.

7.6   Stiles Road turns left as Fun Road turns right. Stay on Stiles.

10.4   Cross Highway 141 onto County Road I in Stiles.

10.6   Take a right on Pioneer Park Road.

11.8   Turn right on Duame Road into Stiles Junction.

12.5   Take a right on Highway 22.

12.8   Turn left on Military Road.

16.9   Turn left on County Road J.

18.2   Take a right on County Road A.

20.4   Turn left on Hogsback Road. **Option:** Continue east on County Road A for the 33-mile option.

21.4   Take a right on Woodview Road.

24.2   Turn left on North Range Line Road.

26.4   Merge onto County Road W heading north.

28.5   Take a right on Church Road.

29.4   Pass May Corner.

30.9   Take a right on Town Hall Road.

31.9   Turn left on Mortinson Lane.

32.9   Cross County Road B and go north on Hartwig Road. **Option:** Turn right on County Road B for the 44-mile option.

33.8   Take a right on Red School Road.

34.3   Turn left on South Harmony Road.

35.9   Cross County Road D into Harmony.

36.4   Turn left on Highway 64.

36.5   Take a right on Town Line Road.

38.0   Take a right on Furhman Road.

39.1   Turn left on County Road E.

40.2   Cross the Peshtigo River.

40.6   Take a right on Grasser Road, just before Porterfield.

42.5   Take a right on Bagley Road.

43.9   Pass Peshtigo River State Forest Park.

45.9   Turn left on Highway 64.

50.9   Turn left on Van Cleeve Avenue in Marinette.

51.3   Take a right on Riverside Avenue.

52.4   Cross Highway 41 onto Main Street.

53.3   Take a right on Shore Drive.

54.7   Take a right on University Drive.

55.3   Turn left on County Road B.

62.7   Turn left on Highway 41.

62.8   Cross the river into Peshtigo. (Note: The 44-mile option returns here.)

63.0 Turn left on Front Street.

63.5 Cross the railroad tracks onto Hale Road.

69.4 Take a right on Bay Road.

70.5 Turn left on County Road Y at North Bay Shore Park and Campground.

72.3 Pass D. E. Hall County Park.

73.5 Pass County Road A. (Note: The 33-mile option returns here.)

75.8 Turn left on North Bay Shore Road.

77.2 Take a right on Harbor Road and pass Splinter Causeway Park and Marina.

79.0 Turn left on Collins/Park Avenue.

79.5 Take a right on Seventh Street.

80.0 Return to park.

Local Information

Oconto County Tourism, 1113 Main Street, Oconto; (888) 626-6862; www.oconto county.org.

Marinette County Tourism, 601 Marinette Avenue, Marinette; (800) 236-0230; www.marinettecounty.com.

Local Events/Attractions

Beyer Home Museum, Oconto County Historical Society, 917 Park Avenue, Oconto; (920) 834-6206.

Copper Culture State Park, west end of Mill Street, Oconto; (920) 834-7711; www.wiparks.net.

Peshtigo Fire Museum, 400 Oconto Avenue, Peshtigo; (715) 582-3244.

Menominee River Century Bicycle Ride; last Sunday in June; Bay Area Medical Center; (715) 735-4200, ext. 3116.

Restaurants

Wayne's Family Restaurant, 432 Highway 41 North, Oconto; (920) 834-4262.

Firehouse Grill, 1439 Main Street, Marinette; (715) 735-3415.

Accommodations

Ramada Limited, 600 Brazeau Avenue/Highway 41, Oconto; (920) 834-5559.

Holtwood Park, 1718 McDonald Street, Oconto; (920) 834-7732.

Bike Shops

Marinette Cycle Center, 1555 Pierce Avenue, Marinette; (715) 735-5442.

Restrooms

Start/finish: Sharp Park.

9.9: Pioneer Memorial County Park.

43.9: Peshtigo River State Forest Park.

52.2: Travel center next to boat landing.

63.1 Badger Park in Peshtigo.

70.5 North Bay Shore Park and Campground.

72.3 D. E. Hall County Park.

Maps

DeLorme: Wisconsin Atlas and Gazetteer: Page 68 A2.

Wisconsin State Bicycle Map (Northern and Eastern Sections).

Marinette County Bicycle Route Map.

Appendix

National Bicycling Organizations

Adventure Cycling Association
P.O. Box 8308
Missoula, MT 59807
(800) 755-2453
www.adv-cycling.org
A nonprofit recreational cycling organization that produces bicycle route maps and offers a variety of trips.

League of American Bicyclists
1612 K Street NW, Suite 401
Washington, DC 20006
(202) 822-1333
www.bikeleague.org
Works through advocacy and education for a bicycle-friendly America.

Rails to Trails Conservancy
1100 17th Street NW
Washington, DC 20036
(202) 331-9696
www.railtrails.org
Connects people and communities by creating a nationwide network of public trails, many from former rail lines.

Bicycling Resources

Bicycle Federation of Wisconsin
106 East Doty Street, Suite 400
P.O. Box 1224
Madison, WI 53701-1224
(608) 251-4456
www.bfw.org

Madison Bureau of Parks and Recreation
P.O. Box 7921
Madison, WI 53707
(608) 266-2181

Have Fun Biking E-Magazine
1321 East 66th Street #100
Richfield, MN 55423
www.havefunbiking.com

Wisconsin Department of Natural Resources
101 South Webster Street
Madison, WI 53703
(608) 266-2621
www.dnr.state.wi.us/org/land/parks/trails/tbike.html

Wisconsin Department of Transportation
Bicycle and Pedestrian Section
4802 Sheboygan Avenue, Room 901
Madison, WI 53707
(800) 657-3774
www.dot.state.wi.us/bike.html

Wisconsin Office of Tourism
201 West Washington Avenue
P.O. Box 8690
Madison, WI 53708-8690
(800) 432-8747
www.travelwisconsin.com

Wisconsin Bike Clubs

Bay City Bicycles, 412 West Main Street, Ashland; (715) 682-2091.
Bay View Bicycle Club Inc., Milwaukee; (414) 299-0317; www.bayviewbikeclub.org.
Bicycling Club of Trempealeau County; www.ridebctc.com.
Bombay Bicycle Club, Madison; www.bombaybicycle.org.
Brazen Dropouts Bike Racing Club; www.brazendropouts.org.
CAMBA; (715) 798-3599; www.cambatrails.org.
Capitol Velo Club; www.capitolveloclub.com.
Chippewa Valley Cycling Club; www.cvccbike.com.
Cream City Cycle Club, Milwaukee; (414) 299-9398; www.creamcitycycleclub.com.
Cycling Club at University of Wisconsin Madison; www.uwm.edu/studentrg/cycling.
Fat Kats, Sheboygan; (920) 208-8471; www.fatkats.org.
Flambeau Fatties Price Co.; (715) 339-4486; zumach@pctcnet.net.
Greater Milwaukee Recumbent Bike Club; jeffreym8472@sbcglobal.net.
Hayward Bicycle Club; (800) 754-8685; www.newmoonski.com.
Janesville Velo Club; www.veloclub.org.
KB Bike Club, Kenosha; www.krbikeclub.com.
Kenosha Velo Club; www.kvcc.homestead.com.
La Crosse Wheelman, P.O. Box 1601, La Crosse, WI 54602; (608) 785-2326.
Lakeshore Pedalers, Manitowoc; www.lakeshorepedalers.com.
Osceola Bike Club; Neil Soltis, Village Administrator; (715) 294-3498.
Ozaukee Bicycling Club, Cedarburg; www.ticon.net/teampaul/obc.

68th Street Silent Sports Club, Kenosha; ejpotente@sopl.com.
Southwest Chain Gang Bicycle Club, Dodgeville; (608) 935-RIDE;www.mad
    people.com/dmataya/chaingang/aboutus.htm.
Spokes & Folks Bicycle Club, Marinette; (715) 735-5961; www.spokesandfolks.com.
Sugar River Pedalers, New Glarus; http://personalpages.tds.net/~raven1/join.html.
Watertown Bicycle Club, Lake Mills; (920) 648-5116; http://my.execpc.com/~
    coolbike/page5.html.
Wausau Wheelers; www.wausauwheelers.org.
Westside Bike Club, Milwaukee; mbrady4718@sbcglobal.net.
White River Cycle Club; (262) 728.6533; www.whiterivercycleclub.com.
Whitewater Optimist Club; www.uww.edu/uwwoptimists.
Winnebago Riders, Fond du Lac; (920) 923-3211.

Minnesota Bike Clubs Riding in Wisconsin

Duluth Road Cycle Club; (218) 724-8525.
Hiawatha Bicycling Club, Minneapolis and St. Paul; www.hiawathabike.org.
Major Taylor Bicycling Club, Minneapolis and St. Paul; www.geocities.com/
    major_taylor_mn.
Twin Cities Bicycle Club, Minneapolis and St. Paul; www.biketcbc.org.

Ride Index

Beer Barrel Ramble, 190
Beetown Challenge, 128
Chocolate Lovers Ramble, 179
Commuters Cruise, 149
Cornucopia Challenge, 10
Coulee Country Challenge, 111
Covered Bridge Ramble, 195
Cranberry Cruise, 100
Devil's Head Challenge, 143
Door County Classic, 224
Firehouse Classic, 20
Five Arch Cruise, 158
Greg's Packer Ramble, 25
Hodag Cruise, 44
Hustler Ridge Challenge, 116
Lance's Wisconsin Challenge, 168
Leinenkugel Classic, 72
Manitowoc Challenge, 218
Mineral Challenge, 136
Moonshine Alley Cruise, 15
Mound Builders Challenge, 55
Musky Cruise, 38
Northern Kettle Challenge, 200
Pearl of Pecatonica Cruise, 132
Pepin County Challenge, 86
Pickerel Cruise, 184
Pleasant Place Cruise, 33
Red Cedar Challenge, 80
Rib Falls Challenge, 49
Round the River Cruise, 121
Round the Rock Cruise, 163
Southern Kettle Challenge, 174
Sparta/Elroy Classic, 105
Stardig's Co-Motion Cruise, 67
Step Back in Time Challenge, 60
Sugar River Ramble, 154
Three Rivers Classic, 231
Tranquil County Cruise, 29
Trempealeau County Classic, 92
Two Lakes Cruise, 212
Wanikamiu Cruise, 206

About the Author

An avid biker, Russ Lowthian has carved his way throughout most of the Midwest and has chronicled his adventures for numerous outlets. Starting his writing career for the corporate publication *Meetings and Events Magazine* in the early 1990s, he has had ample opportunity to explore the many areas of Wisconsin featured in this book. As a past president of the Midwest Sport/Ski Council and an editor of the *Midwest Sportster,* Russ has long followed year-round sports activities. His articles have also appeared in *Minnesota Cyclist, Slide and Glide Magazine,* and the e-zine of Travel-Wisconsin.com. Russ is currently working on books focused on birding and paddling in Wisconsin.